Would you like to be the man Xaviera comes home to? Would you like to be the man who escorts her to orgies, bails her out of jail and satisfies her after a long day's night she's spent satisfying other people?

LARRY "THE SILVER FOX" IS THAT MAN

"I've had three years of fun," he says, "of living twenty-four hours a day, of enjoying a relationship with a girl, experiencing moments when I wanted to eat her up and moments when I wanted to kill her. . . .

MY LIFE WITH XAVIERA
THE HAPPY HOOKER

is the intimate story no one but the Silver Fox can tell!

My Life with Xaviera "The Happy Hooker"

by Larry "THE SILVER FOX"

INTRODUCTION BY XAVIERA HERSELF!

**WARNER
PAPERBACK
LIBRARY**

A Warner Communications Company

AUTHOR'S NOTE: The events in this book have all actually happened. The people are real. Only the names have been changed, and we genuinely regret any inadvertent similarity between these fictitious names and the names of real persons.

WARNER PAPERBACK LIBRARY EDITION
First Printing: April, 1974

Warner Paperback Library is a division of Warner Books, Inc., 75 Rockefeller Plaza, New York, N.Y. 10019.

 A Warner Communications Company

Printed in the United States of America

Inscription on first edition of *The Happy Hooker:*

1/10/72.

To my dearest darling Larry
who stood with me all those
months, through heaven (?)
and hell (!).
If it wasn't for your help
and assistance I most
probably would never have
finished this book.
Even though you were
"pushy" at times, go on,
UP TO Bestseller NO. 2
Your Xaviera

Inscription on first edition of *Xaviera!*

TO LARRY.
Here it is, our second baby.
After all, it is in a way a
product of the two of us, though
I won't admit this to anyone.

As in LOVE, the second
time is always better than
the first. Keep coming
back for more.

Xaviera

INTRODUCTION

I feel it is certainly appropriate for me to introduce this book—and I am very pleased to do so—because much of what you will be reading here deals with the torrid, zany, merry, uneven, ecstatic, unpredictable, warm, tempestuous, compassionate, memorable, off-again-on-again, sex-filled upside-down, inside-out relationship between Larry "The Silver Fox" and yours truly. Was this the love affair of the century? Read his book and make your own judgment.

It was surely not like any love affair you've read about in novels or seen in films. At least not in any books I've read or films I've seen. But then, the only movie I've seen of late is *The Exorcist* and the only books I've read recently are *The Happy Hooker, Xaviera!,* and *Letters to The Happy Hooker*. Hated the movie. . . . Loved those books!

All joking aside, I do of course realize that if it were not for Larry's devotion, love, and thoughtfulness, I might never have written *The Happy Hooker*. Indeed, if not for Larry's steadfast concern for me, I might have ended up penniless and in very severe trouble. Every time the chips were down, Larry came through in winning fashion. When I got into trouble with the New York police, there was only one friend who stood by me, who was there to bail me out, who took me out to dinner to cheer me up and help me forget my problems. And while Larry was no admirer of the profession I was in, he helped me when I needed help and he prevented outside elements from "moving in on me." I may have courted serious trouble on more than one occasion, but he did his best to keep the number of those occasions to a minimum and I am most grateful for what he has gone through in the years we needed each other most.

I have to admit that there were a few times when I felt that Larry was more a kind of brother to me than my lover, but those were times when he was being typically unselfish and helping me out of some nasty business I'd gotten myself into—and perhaps these times *I* was merely being selfish in my feelings. It's no secret to anyone who has read any of my books that Larry has often been an easy target for my playful, naughty games, and subconsciously I may have been taking unfair advantage of his goodness by creating these situations or by teasing him and ordering him around. This was never done, however, out of viciousness or any desire to hurt him or damage his ego. There was also the matter of self-interest. If I went too far, he might have taken this as one provocation too many—and walked out of my life. Fun's fun, but there would have been nothing funny about that.

Much has been made of the few times I've cheated on Larry. Again, this was never done to cause Larry any pain or to make him jealous. If I cheated, it was because there was a man I was interested in, and I wasn't about to ask Larry's permission to pursue this interest. I am a wild lady, I know, by anybody's standards, and I must compliment Larry on how well he kept up with my around-the-clock swinging life-style. If he hadn't already been "The Silver Fox" when I met him, I daresay I'd have given cause for a few gray hairs.

I have never written a bad word about Larry, although we have had more than our share of fights—and I will confess that he was almost always right. He would argue for what was best for me. But there is one area of criticism where I am sure I was right: Larry has a fine frame for wearing Pierre Cardin suits and other expensive clothing. He buys bright-colored expensive shirts, and they look very well on him. So why does he insist on not wearing a tie, or else wearing it looped around his neck, but untied? And why does he wear a great-looking suit and a handsome dress shirt, open at the neck, with three or four chains dangling around his neck?

Why? Because he sometimes refuses to act his age, *that's* why! And whenever I would tell him that, he would become indignant and angry with me, particularly when I used the line, "You're acting like twelve and dressing like seventeen." This did not make a big hit with him.

Yet despite his peculiarities, Larry can be very easy to get along with and very comfortable to be with. Sometimes I think he was just *too* easygoing with me—he has a tendency to make the woman he loves into a princess and spoil her silly. I know he meant well with me, but he was dealing with someone who is predictably unpredictable in her actions. Let's face it—life with a Xaviera would be too much for the average man to handle, and the nicer Larry was to me, the more tempting it was, sometimes, to take advantage of him.

Some of these little adventures of mine turned Larry into an extremely violent man, and in retrospect I can't say I blame him—I am the kind of person who can easily make a man climb up the wall. So while I didn't always respect his tolerance for my behavior at the time, now it's easier to see that his kindness is a strength, not a weakness, in his character.

True, whenever he found out I was involved with a new man he would become intensely jealous and go to great lengths to destroy the relationship, which he usually managed to do. I forgive him for these actions because I know he simply cannot share my sense of freedom.

As you doubtless know, there have been many imitations and rip-offs of the *The Happy Hooker* since it was published in early 1972. Just as *The Sensuous Woman* started a trend, so did my book, and I can't say that I'm especially made happy or pacified by the old adage that imitation is the sincerest form of flattery. I would just as soon none of those other books had been published because none of them has been very good—which is reflected in the fact that not one has sold even one-fifth of what *The Happy Hooker* has sold. Certainly none of those books had my approval or cooperation—as does this book by my Larry.

Naturally it occurs to me that Larry is also riding on my

bra straps with this book—after all, I introduced him as "The Silver Fox" to the reading public in my first book—but I do not deny him the right to tell our story from *his* point of view. And don't be surprised if I have some comments to make on *this* book in my own new book, *Xaviera Goes Wild!*—scheduled to make its first appearance on your friendly neighborhood newsstand this July—but suffice to say that I truly wish him all success in his debut as an author.

Larry, good luck, good health, and a full happy life for you!

Xaviera Hollander
Toronto, Canada
February 10, 1974

FOREWORD

Friends have been asking me of late, "Hey, Larry, how come you're doing a book?"

It's a fair question.

I am writing a book not because my life has been so unusual, although parts of it—especially the years spent in India—have been a bit more exotic than the usual American male's experience. But more to the point, I have been asked to write a book because these past few years with Xaviera Hollander have been the experience of a lifetime.

No, more correct to say that these past few years have provided me with enough experiences to last several lifetimes.

I don't say it's always been a jolly experience being with Xaviera—anyone who's read either *The Happy Hooker* or *Xaviera!* can attest to that. But it's certainly been a unique experience—let no one deny that.

I'm also writing a book because there are stories Xaviera could not tell at the time, stories Xaviera would not tell at any time, and stories she simply doesn't know. What's more, there are stories which I think will intrigue male readers especially—because they're being told from a male point of view.

Another question I've been asked is: What's it like to be with Xaviera?

Well, it would take a book to answer that—which is another reason I'm writing *this* book.

Xaviera can be charming and excellent company. She mixes very easily with people. When we went places together we never felt ill at ease with each other. We never sat like two bored people on opposite sides of the table, chewing on our food and having nothing to talk about. With Xaviera, there are *always* things to talk about. . . .

Since Xaviera has become a celebrity we've been to a lot of places where she gets instant recognition, and I've been content to remain in the background, watching her enjoy this popularity. But I've always been proud to walk down the street or enter a room with her, to call her my girlfriend, to have her introduce me as her boyfriend. To be seen in public with her.

Of course there have been bad times, too—going to bail her out of the Tombs, Manhattan's horrible jail, is the exception to *all* the statements immediately above—and her promiscuity has caused me no little amount of grief. Still, whenever it was a smart time to walk away, something inside me told me to stay around. I couldn't leave my baby alone. She needed me.

Sure, there have been times when we fought like the proverbial cats and dogs, and times when I could have thrown her through a window, but somehow we managed to weather the storm. Because the good times far outnumbered the bad ones. . . .

Speaking of storms, for instance, brings to mind a flight Xaviera and I took from Los Angeles to Las Vegas. The weather was fine, but Xaviera's horniness, I soon found out, was worthy of a hurricane warning. And what ensued could have gotten us pushed out of that plane sometime before it landed. Without a parachute.

The plane was mostly full, although the aisle seat next to us wasn't occupied. Xaviera was sitting next to the window, looking out at the stars, and I was just sitting relaxed in my seat, which was in the "recline" position—that is, as far back as it can go. The lights had been dimmed and I thought I'd catch forty winks before we got to Vegas, when I felt Xaviera's hand traveling along my stomach in a southwardly direction headed for you-know-where.

"Xaviera," I said, half whispering, "cut it out—the plane's full of people."

12

She was now playing with my fly. "Shhhh," she said. My fly was now half opened.

"For godsakes, Xaviera," I said, "the stewardesses—they'll see us and tell the pilot or something."

"Who cares about the fucking stewardesses," she laughed. "Besides, on short flights like this they just sit in the back of the plane and take it easy."

I was feeling more ill at ease than horny myself, but Xaviera had one thing on her mind. She had taken a blanket and covered my lap with it, and that one thing was now free beneath that blanket.

"Xaviera, cut it out—you can't give me a blow-job beneath that blanket—the passengers will start a riot!"

By now the armrest between our seats was back and she was more on my seat than her own, and also partly under the blanket. "Fuck the passengers," she whispered into my ear, her tongue punctuating each syllable. "I want to fuck *you*. I . . . am . . . very . . . horny. No blow-jobs this time, just plain Dutch-American fucking."

What was I supposed to do? Ring for a stewardess and say, "Could you please help me out—there's a crazy lady in the seat next to me who wants to get laid . . . would you please ask her to leave the plane and let me alone?"

Besides, her horniness had become contagious. I may have been pleading disinterest, but part of me was fully interested —indeed, fully aroused—by what was going on beneath the blanket.

Working with the stealth and skill which only she possessed, Xaviera had by now managed to get my pants open at the belt level and to push my bikini shorts down around my thighs and out of the way. Then she turned her attentions away from me for a moment, which meant to me that her own bikini underwear was on its way into her pocketbook.

Now comes the shocker!

Off comes the blanket and on comes Xaviera. She pulled me toward her somewhat, and she is now on my lap hugging and kissing me as though we are two newlyweds who can't wait to get to the hotel. Since her dress has covered my groin area, and my pants are still on, we look as though

13

we're a couple of high-school kids necking on an airplane instead of in the back seat of a car.

But what is going on beneath her skirt—with that one swift move she has impaled herself on me, her head is on my shoulder, and her hips are slowly grinding out a subtle, but magnificent, fuck. It's slow and steady, and Pratt & Whitney couldn't have produced a more reliable number of revolutions per minute.

I'm sure the head of my cock is a ruddy red by now, but so is my face—and any second, I'm expecting a stewardess to tap me on the shoulder, saying, "Sorry, sir, but we will have to ask you to leave the plane. Please pick up your things and leave by the rear exit."

But no one bothered us and I was rapidly reaching the point where I couldn't care less. Xaviera and I were making beautiful love at twenty-five thousand feet, and I would even have welcomed a little air turbulence at that point. Anything to make what felt wonderful feel even better.

I heard Xaviera hissing into my ear, "Give it to me, *give it to me....!*" With some women, this is an invitation to get things started, but with Xaviera it means that she is past the point of wanting to hold back, and close to her orgasm, and wants everything to go full speed ahead.

She got no argument from me—she was coming, and so was I. If they wanted us to leave the plane at this point, they'd have gotten no argument from me—I felt so light-headed I could have floated back to earth.

Xaviera stayed on my lap for a full five minutes longer—she was spent and so was I, and even if I'd had the energy to push her off me, I didn't want to. It felt so great growing soft inside her.

Eventually, in another single graceful motion, she took herself off me without causing a ripple of attention, and slid back into her own seat. "Hah," she said, grinning her familiar grin at me, "we made it—now aren't you glad?"

I was—which is another reason I'm writing this book. However, I also had to go to the toilet in the rear of the plane because a combination of sweat and jism had made me feel kind of sticky around the middle and I wanted to clean up a bit.

As I walked down the aisle toward the rear of the plane, I

half expected the entire plane to rise and point a finger at me and shout, *"J'accuse!"* or clap. But nothing at all happened.

Except when I returned to my seat, Xaviera leaned over to me and whispered, "Guess what—the guy in the aisle seat across from us leaned over, as soon as you got up, and offered me 'one hundred dollars for a second act.'"

Which is another reason I'm writing this book. . . .

PART ONE

X HITS THE SPOT

CHAPTER 1.

In the beginning, there was Cookie.

At least that's the name Xaviera was using when I first met her at the El San Juan Hotel in Puerto Rico in the late winter of 1970. She had been there, I later learned, for a few months—having left New York to escape the weather and much harassment by the New York City Police Department. Cookie had better things to say about the New York Sanitation Department than she did about the men in blue and plainclothes.

I'd gone to Puerto Rico the day before Washington's Birthday not because I wanted to celebrate the birthdate of the father of our country but because I wanted to celebrate some sunshine for a change. The weather in New York had been rotten—not so much cold as just plain drab—and five days of San Juan sunshine seemed like a great way to recharge my juices. Little did I know my juices would be more restored by the fortune of meeting Cookie than by the warm weather.

My favorite hotel in San Juan is the El San Juan, but even though I'm a good friend of Tito, the hotel's casino manager, I couldn't get in because it was peak season and they were completely booked. But Tito kindly arranged for me to have a suite at the Caribe Hilton—which isn't exactly slumming, either. It's just that I have a lot of friends at the El San Juan and knew I'd be spending most of my time there. I was wrong about that—at least about the evenings.

The first night there—I had just left the gambling casino at the El San Juan—I came across a young-looking girl wearing a short green and red flowered dress and sandals. She had large green eyes, wore no makeup and looked as innocent as Little Bo Peep—for a moment I was reminded of Cinderella meeting the Big Bad Wolf, since I was certainly attracted to her. But she also confused me some—unless I was blind, her big green eyes were definitely flirting with me, but I wasn't sure if her interest was professional or just a natural response to my overwhelming charm, super-duper personality, and straight teeth.

Oh well, you can't win 'em all; after some pleasant conversation it became clear that the evening was mine—for a price. This sort of surprised me since she looked so unlike a lady of the night; in fact she gave me very positive vibrations (good vibes, as the kids say), and I guess I was mostly amused. However, I'd never paid for my pleasure so I politely declined. But I didn't want her to go, so I tried to keep the conversation good-natured and entertaining.

I explained that I was down with friends for a long week-end and that if she wanted to join us for some drinks I'd be only too happy for her company. She thanked me, but didn't seem too interested, so we said good night and went our separate ways.

About fifteen minutes later I felt a light pat on my shoulder while talking with an acquaintance at the hotel bar. It was Cookie, who had thought about my offer and, yes, she would like to join me and my friends. Her eyes were sparkling and she looked very pretty.

I finished my drink, said so long to my friend, and took Cookie into the hotel's Honka Monka discotheque, where I'd arranged to meet a bunch of people. They were there and I made the introductions, but it was pretty much impossible to carry on a conversation because the music from the "live" band made the place as noisy as Times Square on New Year's Eve. I asked Cookie what she wanted to drink, and she ordered—to my surprise—a 7-Up. She never drank hard liquor, she told me; which made her kind of a novelty in my crowd of fairly sophisticated people. When she was sixteen, she explained, her parents had made a deal with her: no smoking or drinking before the age of eighteen and they would buy her a motorscooter on her eighteenth birthday. Well, that scooter was so important to her that she didn't smoke or drink before the age of eighteen—or since then, for that matter. Not even a sip of wine.

Since it was ridiculous to attempt to talk in the din of that discotheque, we did what Man created discotheques for—we danced. When we weren't dancing we watched the other people dancing, which is fun, too. So all in all it was a good time and I was glad I'd invited Cookie along for the evening.

Later that night when I told her I'd be heading back to my hotel and would be happy to drop her off at the nearby little rooming house where she was staying, she suggested— to my delight and some surprise, too, I have to admit—that we spend the night together, for more fun—and for free. We'd go to her rooming house in a cab, she'd pick up a bikini for the next day, and then we'd head back to my hotel. "And no charge," she said in a kind of comical voice. From then on, regardless of how many times we went to bed together, we were friends—and friends don't charge you for sexual favors. I certainly agreed with that. . . .

So away to her room we went. She asked me to come in with her since some of her roommates might be home and would prevent her from coming out. I didn't quite understand what she meant, but I found out soon enough. We skipped, arm in arm, up to her place like a couple of fourteen-year-olds, and she threw open the door and announced our arrival like some herald in King Arthur's court—holding her fist up to her mouth, she made like a bugle: "Ta da ta dah ta da!" If anyone had been sleeping inside they'd surely have been awakened, but the place was empty of roommates, or much furniture, for that matter. There were six cots, and not much else. Cookie explained that her roomies were all guys, and she needed me along in case one or more of them were horny and required immediate attention. I thought she was kidding—now I know she wasn't.

Cookie went to a large fabric valise and took out one bikini bathing suit, one douche ball, one toothbrush—and that's all. Fifteen minutes later we arrived at the Caribe, which was to be her home for the remainder of my stay in Puerto Rico. I had a friend staying with me in the suite, but he moved out after that first night. I guess the noises Cookie

20

and I made throughout the night made him emotionally unstable, sexually discombobulated, and just plain horny. So we had the suite completely to ourselves, which was very nice since most of the time we were as close as Siamese twins. Not just sexually, which was certainly true, but as loving friends—we'd taken a great liking to each other in this short period of time.

I never did take Cookie back to the rooming house. Since she needed more than a bikini for clothing, we bought some dresses in one of the hotel's stores, plus a great-looking black pants suit for the evenings. I really enjoyed spending *this* kind of money on her, and we were very good together —it was a short, intense, deliciously happy experience which I still consider one of the fondest memories of my life.

But our fun in the sun (and in the dark) was going to have to end, so on our last day together, while sitting by the pool, we discussed her finances and future. She told me about the money she'd made while in San Juan and about the peculiar friends with whom she'd been sharing a room. She seemed to think of them as good friends, but they sounded more like bona fide bums to me. They lived off stolen credit cards and smoked grass all day and were—to use an old Jewish expression—a bunch of nogoodniks. And Cookie trusted them as though they were Boy Scouts—or worse yet. fat-cat bankers, since she was keeping her money in that same crummy room she shared with them. I told her she ought to put the money into a checking or savings account, and offered to arrange for someone to take her to the bank to accomplish this. She didn't say anything, but she was clearly thinking about it.

Later, when it was time to go to the airport—which is quite a distance from the Caribe Hilton—I hired a cab, intending to drop Cookie off on my way to the airport. When we got to her rooming house she said, "Wait a minute. I'll be right back." I was getting a little anxious about missing my plane but she returned about five minutes later, holding an envelope, a set of keys, and a piece of paper with a sketch on it.

"What's this all about?" I asked, since in the envelope was an impressive quantity of money.

"These are the keys to my apartment," Cookie explained.

21

"I've written my address and apartment number on this piece of paper, and here is a sketch of my closet. There's a small metal box in there—please take this three thousand dollars and put it in that box. I've thought about what you said about being robbed here, and I think you might be right." With that she gave me a hug, said good-bye, and I headed for the airport.

My second day back in New York, I went to Cookie's apartment on East Fifty-first Street and when I arrived at the address she'd given me, there were some porters taking a bed out of her apartment and moving in a new one. I asked them what they were doing and one of them informed me that Cookie had ordered a new queen-size bed for her apartment and they were moving it in. She had spoken to the super about this, asking him to switch the beds when the new one arrived. Well, that seemed logical enough, but it also gave me some cause for apprehension. What if I went up to her apartment, left the money in the closet as she'd asked me to do, and one of these workmen discovered it? I couldn't prove anything, and she might have even felt I'd taken the money myself.

On the other hand, I didn't want to keep coming back to her apartment, either. I decided the safest course of action was to write her a check for the amount of cash she'd given me, but not sign it. If anyone found the check, it would be useless to them—since it was made out to her, it had to be endorsed by her, and since it wasn't signed, no one could get it cashed. So when the workmen left I wrote the check and put it into the metal box, along with a note saying, "Please call when you get back."

As I was about to leave I noticed some photo albums on the bureau, and I felt I deserved a peek at them. Some of the photos were nudes of Cookie, and I was feeling fairly randy when I left her apartment. After all, she'd been quite a new experience for me.

I didn't hear from Cookie for some time, and since I was deeply involved in my business. really didn't think about her much. Then one day the phone rang and there she was, back in my life. After an exchange of pleasantries she asked,

22

"Larry, where's the money I gave you?" I replied that rather than explain over the phone, I'd come right over, and after clearing up some business matters that were pressing, I drove uptown to see her.

I don't recall if I'd anticipated any difficulties over the money, but there weren't any. I offered her the cash I had on me—it was too late to go to the bank when she'd called, but I did have a fair amount of cash on me—and said I'd bring the balance the next day.

"No," she said with a smile, "bring it all tomorrow night, and then let's go to dinner."

We went out to dinner that night and practically every night for the next two and a half years. My life with Xaviera wouldn't always be fun, but it'd surely be different from the life I'd been used to leading. Move over, Square Businessman, here comes "Larry the Silver Fox." . . .

CHAPTER 2.

When Cookie—the name 'Cookie' hadn't yet crumbled in favor of *Xaviera*—first returned from Puerto Rico, she had very few "business clients," and those she did have were either friends she'd met in Puerto Rico or friends of some of the girls she knew in the business. Sometimes a girl had two guys coming to visit, and she'd call Cookie to complete the foursome. Then there'd be an occasional summons to Georgette Harcourt's apartment—Georgette was a madam who used Cookie for rescue missions when there were more Johns than Janes on board. But compared to how things were when she was madam herself, Cookie's life was relatively uncomplicated. What business she did have usually took place between four and seven P.M.—the commuter's special, you might call it. It also helped that she tried to work Monday through Thursday and take long weekends—a practice she continued, as much as possible, when she became a madam. Sometimes there'd be a prearranged party on one of the weekend nights, but I doubt that this happened more than three weekends out of the year. Weekends aside, she kept her evenings free to be with me, and that was the most important thing.

To be perfectly honest though, these evenings weren't without their little complications. We often went out with my friends and Cookie was seldom less than generous with her business cards. She was a little devil. So finally I said, "Hey, please—no propositioning my friends and no card passing." She grinned mischievously and promised to cease and desist, but I still kept my eyes open.

On the other hand, I was starting to meet a lot of her friends—friends she still has today—and while I knew she had probably slept with most or all of them at one time or another, it was now friendship rather than sex which kept them in touch with one another. And she gave me no reason to feel uncomfortable with them; she remained true to me in this regard, never horsing around with them or causing any embarrassing situation. I guess that's called "thank God for small favors" department.

As a result, our relationship really prospered and we did a lot of traveling together—back to Puerto Rico, to Las Vegas, the Virgin Islands, Curacao, back to Puerto Rico, then back to Vegas, to Florida, wherever it was warm and beautiful. And wherever we went, our lovemaking was warm and beautiful too.

She and I really enjoyed each other's bodies. We'd go to bed and make love three or four times, always experimenting and always climaxing—together. This may seem remarkable, but we would wait for each other, and help each other to come—we'd found 69 to be our favorite position, and we'd lie quietly between each other's legs, our heads on pillows, and eat each other in a dreamy way. We'd stop when one of us was nearer to a climax than the other, and then, after

24

several near-climaxes, we'd know automatically that *this* was the right time and we would come all over the place. It was a very, very wonderful and fantastic experience. Sexually we belonged in Ripley's "Believe It or Not," we were so unbelievably attuned to each other's needs.

When the weather got warm in New York we began going out to Long Island—mostly the Hamptons—but there were two weekends when I had to do without her company. On one of these she went to the infamous bankers' convention in Miami which she now discusses openly on television, and "took on," as they used to say, enough bankers in one night to run several branches of Chase Manhattan. The total, according to her count, was an even thirty! She'd gone there with another girl, Rachel, who apparently didn't manage the same volume of male orgasms for the evening, and after the convention Cookie spent a day on the yacht of a gentleman who owns a very large hotel in Florida. My souvenir of this pleasure cruise was a packet of about twenty-five nude photos she brought back. I still have them as a kind of weird momento of that missing weekend.

Another gap in our relationship—another missing weekend—took place on a yacht tied up at the Seventy-ninth Street Boat Basin on Manhattan's west side. The passenger list must have included a lot of Washington, D.C., names of some prominence, because later the newspapers asked me to identify people aboard. I refused.

There was also another gap in our relationship— the gap between Cookie's promise not to hand out her business cards all over the American landscape, and the number of cards she was handing out wherever we went and whenever I wasn't watching. Her plans for the fall were becoming obvious, and there was nothing I could do about it. A New York legend was about to begin. . . .

This was also about the time when we were discussing a more sophisticated name for her rather than Cookie. We were driving out to visit someone, and were tossing names back and forth to help pass the time, when she decided to use her real first name, Xaviera—her Dutch nickname is Vera, which she dislikes—and match it with Hollander—which is a play on words—and by the time we arrived at our

25

destination, my companion was the now-well-known Xaviera Hollander. But whenever I got angry at her, I called her Vera.

In retrospect, three particular events from that eventful summer stand out. The first was Xaviera's birthday party. Her birthday falls on June fifteenth, but we decided to throw the party on the seventeenth because it was a Wednesday, and the middle of the week rather than the beginning. We borrowed an apartment from a friend of hers who lived on East Seventh Street and Xaviera made up her guest list, deciding what friends she wanted to have at her party—there were only about two *hundred* of them, plus a few Johns she particularly liked as people. And only about five hundred people showed up.

One good thing, though: I'd bought a lot of club soda and other mixes for the party, several tons of ice, plus a couple of cases of liquor—frankly, I didn't expect a lot of help in that department even though Xaviera had asked the male guests to bring bottles. But enough of them responded so that there was the equivalent of five cases of liquor left when the party finally broke up late the next morning—or early the next day, if you care to look at it that way. The only shortage we suffered was in ice, and at one stage in the party, when it was really at its height, I had "runners" going down to the bar on the corner every ten minutes or so. There was a powerful lot of boozing going on that night.

Plus a lot of sex. The apartment had two very large rooms, plus a large photographic studio, and people kept slipping into this dimly lit room to shed some of their clothing and all of their inhibitions. There was some wild dancing to the music being piped in from the living room, and I saw Xaviera going in there with a few people, but all I know for sure is that a lot of guys got blown or jerked off in the darkroom of this studio. I don't know about the double exposures—there surely must have been some.

None of this was my business, so long as I didn't confront Xaviera with someone, but when the party was just about over I discovered Xaviera in a situation I hadn't anticipated. She'd flipped for a girl named Jeannette—a friend she hadn't seen in some time—and when Jeannette passed out on the large master bed in the bedroom of the apartment, Xaviera tiptoed in while the rest of us were cleaning up, took off all of Jeannette's clothing, and started to make love to her.

Missing our birthday girl, I went looking for her—and then went berserk. I guess I was just naive about such things in those days, despite my years of sexual experience, and I thought I had lost my girlfriend to a goddamn little sleeping beauty. I screamed at Xaviera, I screamed at Jeannette—which if nothing else woke her up from a drunken sleep—and Jeannette quickly got up and dressed. For her part, Xaviera screamed at me: What was I trying to do—make a fool of her in front of her friends! Her friends didn't see anything wrong with what she was doing! And truthfully she was right—it seemed that I was the only person there, regardless of sex, creed or religion, who took offense at Xaviera balling Jeannette. Later on I met Jeannette again and we became good friends. Time heals all wounds, they say—including those of sexual ignorance.

Anyhow, it was some birthday party. I'm not sure *I* had a good time, but people called for weeks afterward thanking us for the terrific time *they*'d had.

About a month later I went to my first nudist colony with Xaviera. Since I didn't enjoy her total lack of inhibitions, I was genuinely worried about what would happen when I had to take off my clothes in front of men and women and—quite literally—let it all hang out. If a pretty lady—and very naked—passed by, wouldn't I get a hard-on? Much as I was always happy—and occasionally even grateful—for the appearance of a hard-on, I didn't want to be the dumb schmuck who can't keep his cool just because beautiful naked bodies are passing before his gaze.

As it turned out, I (almost) had nothing to worry about. My penis behaved itself—in every instance, thank God. We arrived at the gate to the grounds of an old mansion in New Jersey and before paying an entrance fee, we were asked for references—namely, who had sent us. We were issued a membership card and then drove about a half mile—the place was that big!—to a parking lot. And then we stripped . . . we got out of the car, I opened the trunk, we took off our clothes, neatly fold them, and put them into the

27

trunk. I felt somewhere between very silly and very, very silly.

Absolutely stark bare-assed nude-naked except for our footwear, we found our way to the pool area. A friend who frequented this place had instructed us to go to a cabin in which everyone kept their beach chairs, and once we found his chairs and were able to sit down by the pool, I felt much less conspicuous. I just kept talking to my penis, asking it to stay right where it was and not embarrass me by looking around. Later on I found out that it was considered no disgrace to get an erection, but that good manners called for the man to jump immediately into the pool. In other words, if you couldn't be cool, cooling it off was recommended.

While I was worried about part of me saying a big "hello" to everyone around the pool by pointing itself toward the heavens, Xaviera, who loves to swim, had gone into the pool and seemed to be having a grand time in the water—and in the buff. Finally I got up—no pun intended!—enough nerve to join Xaviera in the pool, and I found out the fun I was missing was indeed all wet. Each time we talked with some prospective swingers, part of the talk was with our hands, and beneath the surface. I put my fingers in quite a few cunts that way. Yep, it *was* fun to play games in the pool. But just a kind of tease. . . .

But later in the day, when Xaviera led me and another couple for a walk in the woods, I suffered—enjoyed?—my first absolute turn-on of the day. We had gone down a side road and followed a little creek to a natural pool. When we got there, as if by signal this other couple—both attractive people, probably in their late twenties—began to touch and fondle us. And it just happened. I was soon kissing the other girl, and someone—knowing Xaviera, it would have to be her since she knew how to arouse me so well—was placing a finger up my behind and I was getting as tall and hard as Bear Mountain.

As though on cue, the girl I was kissing dropped down on her knees and started to lick my cock and run her hand between my thighs and under my balls. While this was going on, Xaviera leaned over and began kissing me on the mouth and the other fellow came up behind his companion and began to screw her, doggie-style. There was no place to lie

28

down because there were pebbles and rocks alongside the pool, so we were like four statues in motion and I had my first orgasm in a nudist colony. It sure wasn't bad, but I must confess that I felt silly about five seconds later. Among other things, I'd been sucked off for only about a minute and here I'd already popped my load, filling this young woman's throat with my come.

When everyone had been satisfied, one way or another, we returned to the pool, where our friends who owned the beach chairs were seated taking in the sun. They were the ones whose idea it was to come here in the first place, and now, it seemed, they had some other ideas. Yes sir, it was going to be a busy day.

After some small talk they suggested we visit a couple they knew who had a large cabin on the estate. The purpose of this visit? Well, to get to know that couple, and some other couples, a lot better—and I use the word *know* in the biblical sense. And, to use a famous proverb—a little knowledge goes a long way: that afternoon I made love to three women and Xaviera made love to three guys, in addition to eating four of the women. (Incidentally, Xaviera goes wild for redheads, and two of these gals were naturally that way.) Toward the end of the swing I was getting more than a little aggravated by Xaviera's insatiable appetite for sex—particularly pussy—but I certainly can't deny I had a good time. Maybe I was being a little selfish and didn't want her to have as good a time as I was having . . . yeah, lots of luck on that score. Trying to compete with her in sexual gymnastics is like trying to outrace an Olympic sprinter.

We went back to that nudist colony for more sex and sun, usually in that order, and one Saturday instead of heading back to the city in late afternoon, we went to a nearby party being given by a couple in the film business. They'd asked us to come by for cocktails before, but our usual preference was to get back to the city in time to have dinner and a nice evening there. This particular evening, however, we decided to see how these people spent their Saturday nights and I can tell you this—if you remember the old hit song, "Saturday Night Is the Loneliest Night in the Week," it certainly wouldn't be the theme song for *these* folks.

When we arrived, around nine o'clock, there were already

about forty people there in all sorts of dress and undress—including one guy with only a tie on and several gents sporting erections—and it soon became evident that this was a full-scale swap party. You could either change partners or else go off with anyone who attracted you, and one female in particular, a lovely brunette who looked just great walking around wearing just a Pucci top, certainly attracted me. But I wouldn't do anything as long as Xaviera was by my side—which wasn't long, folks. Before you could say "Peter Piper picked a peck of purple pickled penises," she had spotted a nice-looking young guy and had eased herself out of my immediate vicinity. They chatted for a few minutes, then went off into another room. To my surprise, I wasn't at all jealous, and I wasted little time introducing myself to the pretty Pucci lady.

Her name was Phyllis, and I asked her if she was busy.

"No," she said, smiled, took my hand and led me to one of the bedrooms—this house was really just one big bedroom anyway—where who should be waiting for us but her husband! She introduced us, and before I could say "Carla Cowlick caught a covey of cute cuddly cunts," he was asking me if I'd mind if he stayed and watched us. Just one surprise after another in this crowd. I wasn't sure whether or not I wanted this spectator around, but before I could produce a polite answer declining his company, Phyllis was down on her knees, had my penis out, and was merrily nibbling away on it. It felt too good to make a fuss about her husband, and when I felt I was about to come I pulled her up on the bed with me, caressed her while I cooled down a bit, and then joined her in a magnificent fuck. I happened to glance at her husband—he was sitting in a chair in the corner of the room, watching me ball his wife, and whacking off with pleasure at the sight. Since it's a democracy I can't complain about how he got his jollies, but I don't care to be on the sidelines myself. Anyhow, given his accuracy of stroke, I think we both came at the same time. . . .

After resting a while I left this couple—I suspected the whole thing had turned him on enough so he could make it with her now—and went looking for my friend, Miss Hollander. She was talking to someone over by the bar, but when she saw me she hurried over and asked me where I'd been.

"I was looking for you," I said, keeping a straight face. "Where were you? I didn't see you in any of the rooms I explored."

"I was out on the back porch," she said. "Did you look there?" "No," I said, grinning, "I didn't think of looking there—was it nice out there? Good view?"

"Oh yes," she replied, "very nice view," and we both knew the only view she'd had in the past twenty minutes was that guy's penis staring her in the face. But since she didn't hassle me, I wasn't going to question her activities. Anyhow, she was soon dragging me over to meet a couple she'd met at a Pennsylvania nudist camp, and before you could say "Bashful Bertha brought a big bunch of beautiful boobs," the four of us were off in a room making it.

Now this should have been a whole lot of relaxed fun, but Xaviera warned me I'd better not come inside anyone but her, which made me a little uptight. In other words, it was perfectly all right to have this girl suck my cock, play with my ass, tongue my anus, and stick my flaming hard-on inside her, but it wasn't all right for me to have an orgasm. When I couldn't stand it any longer I yelled, "Xaviera—quick!" and we switched partners. And just in time—the bed almost received my load instead of Miss Hollander. Xaviera could be terribly jealous at times, and this was obviously one of them—if I *had* come inside that girl, Xaviera warned me after we'd both climaxed together, she would have cut off my penis when I fell asleep that night. Oh well, you know, those things are always good to know. . . .

After the party we gave an executive of the National Basketball Association a lift back to the city, and though I was not at all horny after this Saturday of sex, it didn't feel bad when Xaviera, sitting between us in the front seat, started to play with me. Then, since she had another hand she wasn't using, she began playing with him too. Nothing she does shocks me now, but it was the first and only time I saw her masturbate another guy. Anyhow, it was important that I concentrated on my driving, but since his feelings were being concentrated in the head of his penis, he came off just as we passed Exit 16 on the New Jersey Turnpike.

When the guy had his orgasm I handed Xaviera a handkerchief from the glove compartment to clean up the mess.

31

In return she gave me a dirty look. Hell, I'd be damned if I was going to clean up after him!

Despite the look, she turned her full attention—and both hands—to me, but since it'd been a long, hard, dazed night, I was good for almost two more miles. . . . But I don't recommend this kind of thing for safe, sane driving.

It had been a sex-filled summer, and when fall arrived I was kind of looking forward to staying in New York on weekends and enjoying the city with Xaviera—just the two of us, for a change. Well, they don't call me a cockeyed optimist for nothing. September was only ten days old when I got a frantic call in the middle of the afternoon from Xaviera, asking me to please come to her apartment. What was wrong? Her old boyfriend, Carl, that strange bird (remember him from *The Happy Hooker*?) she lived with and thought she was engaged to—was back in town for a few days and wanted to see her. He had called as though nothing had ever happened, as though he hadn't treated her like a swine, hadn't left her and gone off to Caracas, Venezuela—and what should she do? I had some strong opinions on the subject, and I knew that if I insisted on her not seeing him, she wouldn't, but that wouldn't really solve anything if she really was carrying a torch for him. So I said I'd be over as soon as I could manage it, and left work early to see her.

To tell the truth, I'd been dreading this moment since I first met Xaviera because she'd told me how deep had been her feelings for Carl, and there were always things reminding her of their years together—certain music, a restaurant they liked, even an old movie on television they'd watched in bed together. But now that the real thing—and I *do* mean "thing"—was here, I felt pretty calm about it. Either the relationship Xaviera and I had built really meant something to her, or it didn't, and if one call from Carl could upset that relationship, better that I should know now rather than later.

When I got to Xaviera's apartment we sat down and talked very calmly. She seemed pretty upset and I was kind of proud of myself for feeling sorry for her rather than being angry at her, and finally decided she *should* see him. I figured you don't get rid of a cancer by pretending it doesn't exist, so let her spend the weekend with him—this was a

Thursday—and ei
system. We had tic
but I gave them awa
to a party on Saturda
able to be there. I did
myself and tried to ha
really in it. . . .

I stayed completely out
time I saw her in her apart
day when, knowing that Ca
went over to the apartment
Xaviera's first reaction to me   ay was
astonishment that I hadn't calle   g this three-
day period—not even in the day   en Carl was out of
the apartment, visiting his family or whatever—but it was
her second reaction that truly mattered. She threw her arms
around me, kissed me all over my face, and then led me to
the bedroom. Let me tell you, it was worth the long, miserable weekend's wait for an answer.

Xaviera slowly undressed me, sock by sock, button by button, until I lay on the bed completely nude—also completely erect. Then she brought over her daily desk calendar and let me read the notations she'd made earlier that day, Sunday the thirteenth of September. As I recall them, they read as follows: Carl back to Caracas, no loving feeling; Carl still stingy; happy to have Larry; I love Larry. When I got done, Xaviera took the desk calendar away and returned to take care of my three days of sexual abstinence. If I were a more religious man I'd have thanked the Lord for those three days of abstinence. . . .

Xaviera started at my toes and licked every part of my body. I was so aroused from her lovemaking that she would constantly get up, run into the kitchen, bring me back a cold drink, take an ice cube and rub it all over my body, especially around my groin area, put the ice cube in her mouth, and then put her mouth around my penis. Finally we got down to serious business—about two solid hours of lovemaking, and each time that I felt I couldn't hold off any longer, somehow I held off. And the same thing happened with her. We

CHAPTER 3.

When I look back at those early days with Xaviera I re-member most of that period with fondness, if not nostalgia, because of how well I got to know her. For instance, through her books and public speaking and media appearances she has projected an image of the worldly, terribly sophisticated woman who probably would have made a fortune at what-ever career she had chosen. Bob Abel, her editor, says she might have been the "Mary Wells of Holland" if she had stayed in that country. On the other hand, if Carl hadn't turned out to be such a rat, she would have married him and they'd be living in suburbia somewhere, happy, bored or whatever. And the Happy Hooker would never have existed.

But there's another side to Xaviera which only a very few people very close to her know about. She has little quirks of character which are slightly amazing. For example, she has a truly remarkable talent for taking at face value what other people would recognize as pure unadulterated bullshit or at least something slightly suspicious. On a Richter scale for gullibility, she would score 9.9.

To illustrate the point, here's just one story that shows how naive this really sophisticated lady can be. This happened when Xaviera was still living in her studio apartment in the low East Fifties—the place I'd first visited to put her money away for safekeeping. At the time Xaviera was having her usual problems with her immigration status, and some friends, meaning well for her, suggested a marriage of convenience—perhaps with a gay lad who wanted to be married for his own reasons of convenience. The important thing was that such a marriage might help her to become an American citizen.

There were also discussions between Xaviera and myself about getting married, but I'm afraid our ideas of matrimony were pretty far apart. Xaviera wanted to be a weekend wife, and play her little games the rest of the time. For my part, despite the crazy sexual adventures we'd sometimes share with other people—which, for all the fun I had, I willingly would have done without—I'm very old-fashioned when it comes to the idea of marriage. Being married to Xaviera would have been a full-time commitment on my part, not a weekend sensation, and there was no way I was going to buy *her* idea of the ideal marriage.

A candidate did come along, however; a guy who was represented to Xaviera as a rich, very eligible Jewish bachelor who wanted to get married to please his parents—which meant, to get his mother off his back. So Xaviera met him without any illusions as to his own motives for wanting to get married, and soon understood that what he really wanted was to pursue his bachelor life, and so the marriage would be a good thing for both of them. He'd make his mother happy, and it would help Xaviera to stay in America, which she had come to love.

His mother, he told Xaviera, was visiting New York and was staying at the Waldorf Astoria, and he wanted Xaviera to come meet her and they'd announce the marriage. Xaviera agreed, and to cement the deal he asked her for a blow-job. She agreed, and then wished she hadn't—by her estimate, he hadn't bathed in a week or so. But she kept her word and gave him—pun intended, I'm sorry to say—a stinking blow-job. She figured it would be the first and only sexual contact she'd ever have with him.

As they were leaving her apartment to go to the Waldorf,

35

he said, "Wait a minute—I just thought of something. You know we're Jewish, and in the old Jewish tradition a bride always has a dowry for the marriage. So if you have some money lying around the place, it'd help to impress my mother."

Xaviera, without thinking twice about it, agreed that it was a good idea.

"Listen," the prospective bridegroom said, "take a thousand or fifteen hundred dollars, put it in an envelope, and bring it along. We'll meet my mother, you'll show her you have plenty of *gelt,* and she'll be happy . . . you'll be happy . . . I'll be happy, and we'll 'live happily ever after.' " Knowing something about Jewish mothers, she agreed that it was a clever scheme to get ma on their side.

When they were downstairs, Mr. Prospective Bridegroom moved from the sublime to the outrageous. "Look," he said, "I don't feel safe with you keeping that money in your pocketbook. There are too many sneak thieves around. Let me carry it in my inside breast pocket, where no pickpocket can get at it." She agreed that this made sense, and handed over the fifteen hundred dollars.

Yes, *I* know *you* know this sounds like a naked con game, but remember—this guy came recommended by a friend and everything he said made sense. Asking for a blow-job made sense, suggesting a dowry made sense, protecting the money made sense.

When they got to the Waldorf he went over to the house phones to call his mother, and when he came back told Xaviera, "Ma wants to make herself pretty, so we should wait fifteen minutes before going up to see her." They chatted for a few minutes, then he excused himself to go to the men's room. "Look," he said to her, "go over to the coffee shop, have a cup of coffee, and I'll meet you there. Okay?"

It was okay with her Xaviera, although she mentioned she'd have orange juice instead of coffee. "Fine," he said. "Please don't be long," she said.

Well, *you*'re not expecting him to come back, are you? Well, *you*'re right—but that's not all. After about ten minutes had passed she began to wonder about him and, while not alarmed, asked one of the hotel's porters to check the men's room for her. She thought perhaps he was worried about meeting his mother and had taken ill and needed some help. No, what he'd taken was *off*—the men's room was empty, the porter told her. She immediately realized that her intended dowry had been turned into an unintended present, but what was almost worse, at the moment she had no other money on her and couldn't pay for the orange juice.

Recognizing that Xaviera's embarrassment was real, the waitress was as trusting as Xaviera had been, and Xaviera sent over the money for the bill, plus a big tip. And just to show you how embarrassed she was, it was a week before Xaviera told me the story.

On another occasion, it was her large appetite for money which got her taken by a smoothie, but this time she had company—yours truly. A friend of hers had introduced Xaviera to a well-known jockey—whom we'll call Gary Fischorn, which is a fairly appropriate name for someone on a fishing expedition—who starting using a lot of girls for other jockeys, trainers, and even some owners. After a few visits by this guy and his racetrack entourage, Xaviera's friend suggested that she ought to cultivate the friendship of this guy because he really was a top jockey. Xaviera didn't understand her friend's reasoning at first, but he explained to her that many races are fixed, and this guy would surely know about some of them, given his racetrack connections. And it wasn't beyond the realm of possibility that on occasion he controlled the performance of the horses he rode.

Almost immediately Xaviera had dollar signs whirling inside her head. Step One in Operation Racetrack would be to win the confidence of the guy, and she did this by inviting him to spend the night. Her invitation was accepted and he got to share an orange juice with her in the morning. (If Xaviera had to choose between sex and orange juice, I don't know which would win.) When she felt he'd become a real friend, she called me—I had neither met the guy nor heard of him—and informed me that there was a very interesting "business proposition" in the works, and that Mr. Fischorn and I should meet each other.

"What for?" I wanted to know.

"I think all of us can make a great deal of money," she

37

answered. "He wants to meet you tonight, at the Drake hotel. We'll have dinner there and talk it over."

That night I picked up Xaviera at her apartment and because it was a nice night and the hotel wasn't too far away, we decided to walk. On the way, Xaviera filled me in on her scheme for a mutual parlay, and since I do like to gamble, I wasn't uninterested.

When we got to the Drake we headed for the dining room and asked for Mr. Fischorn. The maitre d' obviously knew who Mr. Fischorn was, and suggested we have a drink at the bar while waiting for him. "As soon as he arrives," he told us, "I'll let you know. I know him well," he added with a smile.

Xaviera and I sat down at the bar—she had a Coke instead of her usual orange juice—and waited for the arrival of Gary Fischorn, patron of the noble art of racing and of the Drake hotel. After about fifteen minutes at the bar the maitre d' came over and announced that Mr. Fischorn had indeed arrived, and would we join him at his table? Yes, we would. With Mr. Fischorn was his manager, who was carrying two dozen flowers for Xaviera. My first thought was of the garland of roses a horse gets for winning the Kentucky Derby, but I kept that thought to myself. Flowers are always nice and, anyway, it was going to be a swell-smelling dinner, if nothing else.

Gary Fischorn introduced his manager, and we all sat down. Dinner passed smoothly enough, and along with dessert came the nitty-gritty: Gary would be riding tomorrow —in a jump race—and he would win. Not only win, but win big, since he was riding a 25–1 longshot.

We would be happy to bet his horse, we said, but he didn't seem too enthused by the idea.

"No good," he said. "You have to be out at the track since something can always go wrong."

"I have to be at business during the day," I said.

"Well, if you want, you can give me whatever you want to bet . . . if the fix is on, I'll bet it for you. Otherwise I'll hold on to it."

"Never mind," I said, changing my mind. "I'll see you out at the paddock tomorrow and you can tell me then whether or not I should bet. If it goes okay, and we win, I'll remember to show you my appreciation. Okay?"

"Okay," he said without much expression.

Xaviera, however, was all turned on. How much should she bet? Should she keep betting after the fifth race? And on and on and on. Finally I was getting a little weary of all this racing around the table and suggested we leave; I would have to get to the office early in order to get away to the track, so I'd drop them both off. I figured I was dropping them at their respective apartments. but Xaviera had other ideas. She was inviting Gary to stay over and teach her more about racing—I had no doubt about what she'd be teaching him—and they'd both meet me out at the track the next day. From my facial expression Xaviera could tell I wasn't too delighted with this arrangement, but as Xaviera said good night to me she whispered in my ear, "Don't be angry —he's going to make us a lot of money, isn't he?"

Good old Xaviera. She'd go to bed with Smokey the Bear if he was going to make her a lot of money. . . .

The next day, around ten in the morning. I got a call from Xaviera, saying that Gary had already gone to the track without her. What had happened? I asked her. Hadn't they gotten along?

"We got along fine," she said a little huffily. "He must have left while I was taking a bath."

"Didn't he say good-bye?" I asked, trying to hold down the sarcasm in my voice.

"He probably talked to me, through the bathroom door, while the water was running and I didn't hear him. . . ."

"Did you give him money to bet for you?"

"Well. not exactly."

"What does *that* mean?"

"He took the money from my metal box—there was twenty-five hundred dollars in there."

"Did he tell you he was going to do that?" I asked, kind of vexed with her.

"Well, he probably yelled it to me through the bathroom door."

Not able to resist the joke, I said, "Hmmm, that may be twenty-five hundred dollars down the drain."

Xaviera was silent for a minute. Then she said, "Larry, you *are* going out to the track with me, aren't you?"

"Well, I don't know—I really do have a lot of work to do. . . ." If nothing else, I was going to tease her a bit.

"Oh, Larry, please—we can both make a lot of money."

"We could both lose a lot of money—have you thought of that?"

"Please, Larry, I want to go out to the track."

As you may have noticed, I was never very good at saying no to her, so half an hour later there I was at her apartment, and out to Belmont racetrack we went. Since Gary was running in the fifth race we felt we had plenty of time to look for him and get the word on how to bet.

It would have been about as easy to find Martin Bormann. We went to the training area and Xaviera asked for him, but we were told he wasn't around, and we looked all over the track for him, but no luck. I finally convinced her it would be best to look for him near the paddock, before the start of his race, and that's exactly what we did. About ten minutes before the fifth race we went over to where all the jockeys were walking around, waiting to mount their horses, and Xaviera asked a guard, "Where is Mr. Gary Fischorn?"

Without a moment's hesitation, the guard responded, "Oh, there he is—the jockey standing by that horse over there." Xaviera and I both looked in the direction he'd indicated, and neither of us saw anyone we knew or recognized. We walked over to the jockey the guard had indicated and Xaviera asked, "Is your name Gary Fischorn?"

"Yes, it is," he said. "Who are you?"

She didn't know what to say, so I offered an "excuse us" and led her away. We left the racetrack knowing that Xaviera's twenty-five hundred dollars had gone somewhere, if not down the drain. I'm sure that Drake hotel jockey is someone connected with racing—he had the strong hands and ruddy complexion jockeys have—but even though I invested quite a bit of time and money trying to run him down, I never managed to find him. Whoever and wherever he is, I hope he loses his next 2,001 races. . . .

But that was, unfortunately, typical of Xaviera. She was always telling me she'd been out with the president of *this* concern, or the owner of *this* corporation, or the executive vice-president of *this* organization, or the brother of so-and-so, who owns one of the biggest whatevers in the world . . . and most of the times that I've checked out these guys, they've proved to be big phonies, and that's about all. There were a few who turned out to be exactly who they said they were, but Xaviera, for all her business savvy, got taken by more than a few ersatz celebrities or jetsetters who promised they could do all sorts of things for her. She liked to think of them as conquests, but they were really con men, whether they represented themselves as the owner of the Krupp Works in Germany (I kind of admire this guy's sense of grandeur), a first cousin of the Prime Minister of England, or Frank Sinatra's brother. In this last instance, I said to Xaviera, "Look, this gentleman *cannot* be the brother of Frank Sinatra because Mr. Sinatra does not have a brother." She wouldn't believe me, but after a few phone calls had convinced her that Mr. Sinatra has no brother, she looked at me, disappointed, and said, "Larry, why do you always have to be right?"

Xaviera gets taken sometimes because she can be a good-natured schnook who gives away her favors for false promises, but her good nature often demonstrates itself in another way, in the genuine-hearted generosity she has displayed toward friends. Yet when she wants to pinch a penny, there is no bigger miser in the world. She sometimes tips cab-drivers and waiters as if tipping were some disease she didn't want to catch, and her favorite way to use money is to make money.

For example, no one else I know can go to the Caribbean with four hundred dollars and return with nine hundred. I remember one evening when we were at Paradise Island and Xaviera got a call from the assistant manager of the hotel at which we were staying. It seems that a very prominent Canadian gentleman, a former finance minister, had taken a fancy to Xaviera and wanted her to have dinner with him. This was impossible since I was there, but I suggested we get a dinner date for him. I had in mind a pretty gal named Helene who worked in the casino, and when Xaviera called her, she said she could switch her work hours with another girl and get the night off.

Helene, Xaviera, and I got together for dinner, but our Canadian friend was conspicuous only by his absence. At least that's what we thought; he showed up, drunk as a skunk, just about the time we'd finished dinner. For some reason, the girls both treated him as a long-lost friend, and since he showed no interest in food, we decided to head for the casino. On the way over he acted like a complete jerk, but both girls continued to baby him. I would have babied him with a good swift kick in the butt, but he wasn't *my* date.

When we got to the casino I gave Xaviera a hundred dollars to play with—it was lost money because whether she won or lost, she wouldn't return my stake. The former cabinet minister was too smashed to play, and Helene couldn't because she worked at the casino, so we all watched Xaviera play and lose. Would I stake her again? I would not. So she went over to our Canadian friend and asked for a loan to gamble some more. As it happened, Mr. High Finance only had seventy dollars in his wallet, but Xaviera took his wallet from him, extracted the money, and returned the wallet. Looking slightly dazed, he wandered off and Xaviera headed for the crap table and began rollin' them.

Her luck had taken a sudden turn and in no time at all she'd built the seventy dollars to twelve hundred. While Helene and I were intent on watching the table, I felt something go into my coat's right pocket. I was afraid to look. Ten minutes later Xaviera cashed in her chips, which, she said, totaled six hundred dollars. She gave three hundred to Helene—her share of the winnings. And, having dated this creep, she also deserved something for making the tipsy Bank of Canada available to Xaviera for a loan.

Then Xaviera said to me, "Larry, better cash in your chips from yesterday since we might not be back tomorrow." That was interesting since I hadn't done any gambling yesterday, but now I knew what was in my pocket. The other six hundred dollars! Xaviera had been generous to Helene, but not *that* generous. . . .

As we got ready to leave Mr. High Finance asked for his seventy dollars back because he'd heard that Xaviera had won. Xaviera looked at him, then at me, and said, "Larry, give him ten dollars for a taxi," and we walked out. So much for instant high finance, Xaviera-style.

If there are times when I think Xaviera must still have the first dollar she ever made as a madam, I know it isn't true because she has enough clothes to fill up a small department store.

In New York City there are still three closets filled with her clothing—each a folding-door closet about six feet long. In Holland, at her mother's home, there are two tremendous closets jammed with her clothing. And in Canada she has a wardrobe large enough to last any well-dressed woman a lifetime. Well, maybe only half a lifetime—styles do change.

Whenever we were traveling and it became time to fly back, we would have to worry about overweight penalties because of the amount of new clothing Xaviera had bought, or I'd bought for her. Now, lots of people play this game, but we became quite expert at carrying on board as much luggage as possible. It's all perfectly legal, but we had some truly inspired schemes for managing the most you can fit under an airline seat.

There's no question that Xaviera likes fine clothes, but I sometimes get the impression that she never wears anything more than once or twice. In fact I wonder if she really knows what she owns in the way of clothing—she wears her Leonardos, which cost between two hundred and four hundred dollars, to formal parties or to smart restaurants, but hanging around her hotel suite she is just as likely to be found wearing a man's shirt—and not too much else.

Last year I bought her a black pants suit for a hundred eighty dollars and I'm not aware she ever wore it or even misses it. I took it back to New York with me at her request —she often does that because she can't physically carry all her luggage and she *absolutely* hates to pay overweight charges. When she came from Holland to Canada, she was charged a hundred sixty dollars in overweight fees. She moaned and groaned for days, so finally, to keep her quiet, I reimbursed her.

If there is anything really unusual about Xaviera's wardrobe—apart from the size of it—it's her collection of footwear. She can't wear high-heeled shoes. We were in Paris once and Xaviera wanted to buy a pair of boots with high heels and high insteps.

"Don't buy them, Xaviera," I advised her. "You're just not going to be able to walk in them."

"No, Larry, they'll be fine. They make me three inches taller, and I'd like to try them. Besides, I'll ask the saleslady to score the bottoms of the heels so they'll be easier to walk in."

"Okay, they're your feet—you do what you want with them." I knew I wasn't going to win that argument because Xaviera liked the idea of the extra height—and she bought the boots and wore them out of the store. With head held high and chin extended, she proudly walked in her new boots, enjoying them for the length of a single block. We had to go back to the store and exchange the boots, at half price, for a pair of flat-heeled shoes.

There is a Japanese place in New York on East Forty-fifth or Forty-sixth Street where I buy Xaviera four-dollar slippers. So you might see her, at some gala, wearing a two-hundred-sixty-dollar dress and her four-dollar slippers. This could keep her from making the Ten Best-Dressed Women's list, but if you don't tell anyone I won't either.

CHAPTER 4.

During the weeks and months between the time I met Xaviera and became so intrigued by her and that sad day she had to leave the country, there were many exotic adventures and crazy times, many of them involving a cast of characters so ridiculous that if I read about them in a novel I wouldn't believe a word of it. I mean, some of the people were just plain k-i-n-k-y. Yet one of the wildest sex-go-rounds in which I participated involved a nice little virgin from Philadelphia. I received a phone call from a friend, a woman named Lorene who had been raised in Philadelphia and still had close ties there. Friends of her parents had asked them to ask Lorene to help their daughter find an apartment in Manhattan. Lorene had called me because I do have regular dealings with real-estate offices in the city and might know of a suitable apartment.

The girl's name was Judy, Lorene told me, and she'd just graduated college and was hoping for some interesting job in New York. This always amuses me—Philadelphia is a perfectly civilized place to live, with lots of fine old town houses and a practically rebuilt downtown area, but I know a number of people who commute from there to work in Manhattan and I've met a number of young people who feel the Big Apple, despite all the bad-mouthing New York gets in the national press, is the only place to test their talents. Apparently Judy was one of these. . . .

Judy was coming in on a Saturday morning, when I'd be staying at Xaviera's Fifty-first Street place, and I told Lorene to have Judy call me there. Judy sounded very cute over the phone and, without thinking twice about it, I told her to come over. In retrospect that may have been a mistake, but the invitation was spontaneous and sincere—I was going to help her find an apartment. But I keep forgetting that my friend, Miss Hollander, can turn a meeting of the Plymouth Rock Gideon Bible Society into a daisy chain.

When Judy arrived she looked just like she sounded over the phone. Long black hair, large saucer eyes, a pert nose, and the kind of figure I guess they call petite. In other words, there wasn't too much of her; and she looked as innocent as Heidi of Sunnybrook Farm, or whoever that was.

But still waters really do run deep, because something in Judy was wise beyond her years. She and Xaviera took one look at each other and you could have cut the vibrations in the room with a knife. I felt like some kind of jerk keeping up the conversation for all of us while those two were spending most of their time staring into each other's eyes. Judy may have read some books about sex, or else she took the right courses in college, or else she just *knew*, because her intuition about what was going on was correct. Xaviera took her hand, led her to the couch, and the two of them finally began talking—as though they'd been bosom buddies for years. Xaviera does this to men sometimes—makes them feel one hundred percent redundant—but somehow I was too intrigued with what was going on to resent it.

I had an errand to do, and no one seemed to mind my leaving, so I left Judy and Xaviera together, wondering what kind of intimate advances Xaviera would be leading up to by the time I got back. Intimate advances, hell—when I returned Xaviera had Judy nude on the bed and was giving her a tongue bath from stem to stern. Knowing that Xaviera is a nut on cleanliness—she ought to be listed in the *Guinness Book of Records* for "Most Baths Taken in One Day"—I was sure she'd made Judy take a shower, and now she was following up with a very special bath. Judy seemed to be loving every wet caress, and when Xaviera's mouth even came close to her vagina, Judy'd give out little yelps and screams of joy.

I didn't know about those two kids but *I* was now very horny, and I decided that three wouldn't be a crowd in this instance. Judy wasn't much in the bosom department, but she had a great little ass, and thighs which were beautifully tapered, like a dancer's.

Since no one was paying any attention to me—I could have been the Loch Ness monster for all they cared—I quietly undressed and took the world's quickest shower; since I'd already missed the early innings of the ball-game in the other room, I wanted to be there in time for the seventh-inning stretch.

I returned naked to the living room with a hard-on approximately six feet long—which instead of turning Judy on, immediately turned her off.

"Don't think I'm square," she said in a tiny scared voice. "I know about a lot of things, but I never made love— well, fucked—with a man before . . . in fact I've never made love—ah, *fucked*—with a woman before. I don't want to be a virgin, but I'm afraid that's just what I am. . . ."

46

So much for the sexual revolution on one Philadelphia campus.

Xaviera was very patient with Judy, and gently coaxed her into making love to me. She may have been a virgin, but here she was licking my legs and thighs and balls and stomach and nipples, and partly because she was so pretty and innocent-looking, it was a delicious sexual experience. Somehow I held off coming for almost half an hour as Xaviera instructed Judy on things to do to please a man, and finally, when Judy seemed to be getting very horny playing with my cock, Xaviera eased her aside and plunked herself down on my literally throbbing erection, and in about fourteen seconds we both were coming.

In some circles this would have been the event of the day, but apparently Xaviera was just getting warmed up. After relaxing for a few minutes, caressing Judy all the while, she got up and called her friend Gisela and invited her over. Gisela was a big German girl with enormous breasts, and if I describe her as being wall-to-wall sex, I am not exaggerating.

Gisela had made some advances toward me on other occasions, and for reasons I didn't quite understand, I'd never been interested. When she arrived this night I rolled over on my stomach and pretended I wasn't as naked as the day I was born. Rots of ruck!, as they say in bad Chinese jokes. Gisela had quickly shed her clothing and there she was, blond hair everywhere a lady has hair, gigantic jutting breasts, and thighs like a truck driver's. With little or no effort she rolled me over and began to work over my penis as though she were King Kong doing the Empire State Building. I suddenly found that I'd vastly underestimated her sweet disposition, genteel manners, and ability to give a great blow-job, but just as I was about to let her blow me to her heart's content, Xaviera pulled her away and gave her a pep talk about Judy.

After huddling with the coach, Gisela took Judy and arranged her on the bed: she placed her body over Judy's, one leg bent, the other held stiff, but completely cunt-to-cunt, and without actually moving very much was doing something to Judy's vagina with her vagina that was making Judy very aroused. Her young face made it clear that she was very, very

47

excited, and because of her obvious excitement I got aroused and without really realizing just what the hell I was doing, I had put my cock into Judy's mouth and she was sucking on it as though lollipops had gone out of style.

Imagine my amazement when Xaviera pulled me away, whispering into my ear, "Don't distract her—I want her to enjoy this." Well, Judy did enjoy herself; when she came she gave out a wail of pleasure which must have been heard in Philadelphia.

Xaviera was just getting warmed up. No sooner had Judy come, *con mucho gusto,* as we used to say at the Met, than Xaviera was on the phone again, calling a French couple we both knew who, though young, were veteran swingers. And while Xaviera was on the phone, Gisela, just getting warmed up, came over to me, eyeing my still-erect penis, and proceeded to put it deep inside her. I hadn't planned on this, but as she began to work on me it became pretty interesting, and everything was going pretty nicely until she bounced once too often on top of me and broke wind at the same time. Perhaps it shouldn't have bothered me, but I gently pushed her off me. In sex, I believe, anything goes so long as both parties want it, but just please don't fart on my parade!

The French couple, Nicole and Claude, arrived fifteen minutes later. It's amazing—Xaviera gets on the phone and people drop whatever they're doing and come right over. Even if they're "doing" each other, they rush right over; Xaviera has a reputation for being a "fun" hostess, I guess.

I knew Nicole and her husband from some previous get-togethers; both had light blue eyes, blondish hair, and pale features. In fact they looked very much like brother and sister, each being on the slim side, but you couldn't deny they were very attractive people, particularly Nicole. On the other hand I may have been prejudiced in her favor since I knew she liked me.

When Nicole and Claude arrived they exchanged pleasantries with Xaviera and then presented her with a bottle of perfume. She introduced them to everyone and they promptly began shedding their clothes. Nicole and Claude were all ready to begin the swing, not having counted on Xaivera's belief that the French are unsanitary people.

"The French—they are the worst," Xaviera explained to all of us as she hustled Claude and Nicole off to the shower. They returned a few minutes later, still wet behind the ears, and Claude looked slightly annoyed at having been dragged into the shower. For all Xaviera knew Claude could have already taken six showers that day, but they wouldn't count since she hadn't personally supervised turning on the water.

However, now it was swing-time and Xaviera assumed the role she liked best—play-group director—with everyone doing something to someone. Nicole lost no time in burying my cock in her cunt, and we were having a good time until I remembered Xaviera's warning not to come inside anyone else, so I gently pushed Nicole toward someone else and went over to where Judy was sitting, looking kind of dazed by what was going on. I held her in my arms and began hugging and kissing her to relax and comfort her. She'd come over to Xaviera's apartment to get some help in finding an apartment and here she was getting an instant sexual education. Judy snuggled close to me, her long black hair sometimes getting into our mouths, and we were having a very tender time together when I felt someone playing with my prick and balls. It certainly felt good and the next thing I knew my legs were up on her shoulders and my rectum was being explored by tongue and finger. This felt just fine too, and I continued kissing Judy. My kissing friend below now returned her attention to my balls and I knew I was about to explode so I bent around Judy to call a halt to the activity down below. Jesus, the doll below was Claude, and he looked up at me with loving eyes. Not at all reluctantly, I pushed him away, but laughing at my absolute certainty that it had been a female providing my groin with all those wonderful sensations.

If nothing else, the French are a versatile race. Claude immediately wanted to fuck Judy, but I warded him off, making him settle for Gisela's rear end, which was the only accessible area of her since she was being kissed by Xaviera at one end and by Nicole at the other. Claude lubricated the head of his penis with some saliva and entered Gisela without any trouble. She was so excited and agitated from Xaviera's loving ministrations to her front that her ass kept squirming and moving around and Claude looked like he

49

was having a grand time. All he had to do was let her ass do all the work. Like the Greyhound commercial: "Leave the driving to us."

Seated on the couch, I had cradled Judy's head in my lap and was stroking her shoulders and back to relax her, and she seemed to be responding. Her eyes were closed and I almost thought she might be going to sleep, but her mouth sure wasn't asleep because she was now licking my balls and the underside of my penis. I realized Xaviera was now watching us closely and she left Gisela—who was having plenty of fun with Nicole at one end and Claude at the other end, in a matter of speaking—and joined us on the couch. To my surprise, she put her mouth right where Judy's was, kissing her mouth and my penis at the same time, and I have to admit I was in seventh heaven. Two women's mouths on my penis was a new experience for me. Then someone began to fool with my ass again and I couldn't hold off any longer, shooting my load right into Xaviera's mouth. Evidentally she hadn't expected this; she got up and ran into the bathroom, and I heard her gargling in there. Judy curled up on the couch and this time she did fall asleep. Claude, having had his share of fun with Gisela's behind, was now getting dressed. I asked him why he was going and he answered, "I have to take ze showair and I do not get to fuck ze Judy and ze Xaviera, she hees too busy for me, zo I am going."

If I were Gisela I would have been insulted because *she* certainly had made herself available to him, but she didn't seem to mind.

P. S. He took the perfume with him.

I expected Nicole to chase after her husband, but she wasn't tired of the party and she and Gisela and Xaviera fooled around for another twenty minutes before everyone admitted they were tired of sex and needed a breather. The two other women got up, dressed and left together, while Xaviera and I sacked out on the bed. Hours later we woke up and sent out for some Chinese food, only waking Judy when the food had arrived. "Gee," Judy said when she was fully awake, "some first day in New York."

Later we all took a shower together but the only real sex

was the soapy hand-job Xaviera let Judy perform on me. I had to see someone early the next morning so I left Judy and Xaviera, watching television together on the couch, and I wouldn't want to bet more than a dime that there wouldn't be any more postgraduate education for Judy this evening. After all, Xaviera hates to waste a shower. . . .

I didn't see Judy for some time. Xaviera had gotten her a job in a doctor's office and Xaviera's friend Mary Lou had offered to take Judy in because the kid was interested in the theater and Mary Lou had a lot of friends in the arts. But the job didn't work out very well—Judy found working as a doctor's receptionist pretty boring—and Mary Lou's hospitality had to be measured against the fact that she asked Judy to go down on her boyfriend whenever he visited. Some boyfriend—he was more interested in balling Judy than his own girlfriend, who is a pretty voluptuous gal herself, but at least Mary Lou helped keep Judy a technical virgin.

I found all this out later, and when Xaviera found Judy another apartment—this time with some Lesbian friends in Brooklyn—I began to suspect that Xaviera was keeping Judy away from men, and myself in particular, because she wanted to maintain her own influence over the pretty young woman. I quietly mentioned this to Xaviera and she responded by suggesting that we call Judy in Brooklyn and all spend the day at the beach.

"Fine," I said, "we can pick Judy up and go out to the Rockaways. How long will it take you to get ready?"

"How long does it ever take me to get ready?" she retorted.

"About the length of a shower," I answered.

"That's all I need," she said, laughing.

We spent a nice day at the beach and decided to return to the city without changing. Xaviera sat between Judy and me and of course she wouldn't be content just to let it be a nice, pleasant drive back home. No, she began fiddling with Judy's bikini top and my bikini briefs, then took off my suit for me because there was only about three inches of space inside my trunks and I took up more than that. Then she removed Judy's bikini bottoms and got on her knees on the

51

thick carpeting in front of the seat, and began alternating between the two of us, first sucking on me and then eating Judy's neat little pussy. It's lucky my car has a large front seat so Xaviera had enough space to work in. It's also lucky no police cars went by when Xaviera was doing her thing. It's even lucky that Xaviera didn't bring me to orgasm. Otherwise we might never have made it back to Manhattan. I'm a good driver, but not *that* good.

Too bad cars don't have automatic pilots.

I didn't mind, though, because I was envisioning a friendly li'l orgy when we all got back to Xaviera's apartment.

When we got back to the apartment the first thing I knew was that Xaviera had locked Judy and herself in the bathroom. I heard the shower go on, and then I heard the shower stop, but no one was coming out of the bathroom. Then I heard Judy's moans and groans of pleasure and I knew Xaviera was keeping Judy for herself. Disgusted, I decided to leave. All I'd gotten for my day's efforts were a slight case of sunburn and a large case of blue balls.

Judy left New York not long thereafter and, so far as I know, she was still technically a virgin. I hope she's used what she learned here to advantage and has met some decent guy who will be good to her—which includes depriving her of her technical limitations. It only takes once, Judy, and if all goes smoothly, life can be a bowl of Philadelphia brand cream cheese.

With nuts.

CHAPTER 5.

Thinking back on the time Xaviera and I spent together in America, I think the thing I never really got used to was her habit of taking at least four baths a day. Even the bluenoses who think she used her body to lead a life of filth would have to admit what an absolutely clean body it was.

Before Xaviera makes love to anyone, whether she is in her own apartment or their place, she takes a bath. If she has to defecate, she takes a bath afterward. She bathes as soon as she comes home during the day and again before she goes out in the evening. I may be exaggerating—I'm not sure--but I'd just hate for Xaviera to be in a place where there's a water shortage.

Moreover, not only does Xaviera take a lot of baths, she's very particular about the kind of baths she takes. One large cake of Aramis soap—usually a male soap—lasts a week in her bathroom. And no bath is complete with a mere squeeze of Vitabath; Xaviera takes a very special kind of bath. First she squeezes some Vitabath into the tub, when she gets in, and *then* she turns on the water and sits in the tub while it fills up. That's a Xaviera Bath, friends, and nothing else will do. If I filled the tub for myself and for some reason couldn't immediately take the bath, I'd offer the tub to her. And she simply would not use it. She'd let out all the water and start over again.

Whenever we would come home at night Xaviera would shed her clothes and do her bath routine. In the morning, whether we'd screwed like a couple of billygoats or slept like pure little lambs, she'd get the bath going. But—and here's what confused me—we could be at an orgy and after I'd been inside four women, Xaviera would think nothing of eating me. Or arriving at an orgy filled with sweaty, nearly fucked-out people, and balling seven of the men and going down on four of the women. And not complaining for a second that anyone was less than kissing sweet, much less smelling sweet.

Yet she can be terribly fastidious about such things. Once, in Nassau, we got into a little scene with a guy named David and his lovely wife, Liz, who happened to be rather pregnant—which is something that really turns Xaviera on. The four of us had been horsing around and Xaviera began to eat Liz as though cunnilingus were going out of style, and really drove Liz out of her mind. I thought Xaviera had had a wonderful time with Liz, but when we got back to our hotel room she immediately complained: "You know something, Larry, I asked Liz to go to the bathroom and freshen up . . . and I didn't know she hadn't done it."

"Well, you seemed to be enjoying yourself tremendously."

"I know—but she didn't smell or taste good to me."

"What'd she taste like?" I asked, not really anxious to hear the answer.

"I'd rather not say—it wasn't so very pleasant, I can tell you that."

"Well then, maybe you should say something to her."

And Xaviera did. A day or so later when Liz, Xaviera, and I were chatting, Xaviera turned to Liz and said, rather nonchalantly, "Listen, Liz, in the future, if you're going to have a swing with someone, you really ought to go to the bathroom and wash up."

Liz looked hurt. After all, she *was* pregnant, and hadn't planned on the swing. "Why?" she said to Xaviera, "did I offend you?"

"Yes, you tasted like shit," Xaviera said.

Liz looked really hurt and Xaviera quickly corrected herself. "I didn't mean that literally," she explained. "I only meant that you tasted like . . . well, like piss." I didn't know if Xaviera was being funny or very literal, but her remark immediately eased the tension, and we all laughed.

Later Xaviera said to me, "Larry, she really did taste like piss."

Another peculiarity of Xaviera's is her kind of double standard when it comes to people's pain. If we are driving along in my car and she sees an accident, she'll insist on stopping to see if we can be of any help or else offer some comfort to the unfortunate people. Yet she is the same person whose eyes gleam with pleasure at a wrestling match when one of the guys is getting the crap beaten out of him. And she loves getting physical—she told a story in *Xaviera!* about our having a fight in which she was bouncing my head off the floor and we ended up black and blue for days. Well, my head was bobbing up and down because I was hysterical with laughter, which drove her crazy, and we had our own wrestling match, which ended up with my making violent love to her on the tile floor. Black and blue for days? Try doing some spirited screwing on a tile floor—try it, you won't like it . . . if you bruise easily.

I really believe that Xaviera has a strange sado-masochistic streak; she loved provoking me into physical fights, and the more physical they got, the more excited she became, and the more her eyes blazed, and these fights would end with our fucking up a storm. Yet at the same time Xaviera liked inflicting pain—at least I believe this to be the case. I think Xaviera really enjoyed doing freaky things to men for money —humiliating them both physically and psychologically. This may have started during the year spent with Carl, who liked to be tied down and beaten—and became thoroughly aroused this way—but whatever the origins of her knowledge in this area of behavior, she certainly developed a specialty in it.

On one occasion I was sitting in the living room of the large Sixty-fifth Street apartment Xaviera had moved into with some friends when some guy came out of the bedroom on all fours, naked, a doggie leash around his neck, and Xaviera alongside him, holding the leash in one hand and a paddle in the other. Presumably he was enjoying himself because he had an enormous erection. Every few feet she would give him a whack on the behind, and this seemed to make his hard-on get harder. Later I asked Xaviera what

55

pleasure he got out of being in that doggie bag of his, and she said he came without anyone even getting near his penis. Other freaks of this type, I learned, were content to get hard that way and satisfy themselves by masturbating. I guess that's what they mean by "different strokes for different folks."

Xaviera had one "slave" client—a very well-known celebrity whom she'd visit in his apartment early in the evening. She'd force him to strip and dress himself in women's clothing and then tie him down to his bed in such a manner that he would have to have been Houdini—or Superman—to get loose. Then she'd turn out the lights, all the while telling him about the cruel and vicious acts she was going to perform on him when she returned. Then she'd leave the apartment and either meet me at the restaurant we had planned to dine at, or else go home. A few hours later she'd return to his apartment—sneaking in as quietly as possible—find her way to the kitchen, light a candle there and then move spookily through the darkened apartment.

When she entered the bedroom, her face would look positively movie-ghoulish above the flickering candle, and she would see from how rumbled the bed was just how desperately he had tried to free himself. This would "outrage" her and she would scold him, slap his face, and—on some occasions—drip a little wax on his penis, which would be hard as a rock for the occasion. The more "cruel and horrible" she acted, the more frightened he became, and the sooner he came. To add variety to the spice of his life, she sometimes used handcuffs and leg irons on him, and the more secure she made his bondage, the more guaranteed his kinky kicks. He needed what Xaviera did for him so badly that he visited her in Europe, but she kept turning him down. Finally, in southern France, she made him happily miserable for one evening—for *auld lang syne* or something. Knowing Xaviera, I bet "something" included a nice little token of his appreciation. And I guess you'd have to say it was something of a compliment—that he couldn't find anyone who made him as scared shitless and sexually aroused out of his gourd as she did. You think maybe they should give Academy Awards for "best sado-masochistic performance by an actress"?

56

I don't pass moral judgments on other people, but I would have preferred that Xaviera didn't get into these S-M scenes, but she felt that she was answering a need and it certainly didn't bother her. I'm glad I can't say the same—I've attended one "slave party" and that was one too many. It took place in the same Fifty-seventh Street building Xaviera was living in, in the posh duplex apartment of a madam who may have been the country's leading "slavemaster" a century after the end of the Civil War. The apartment was gorgeous—a circular staircase leading to the upper floor being the really dramatic feature—but the scene was kind of sickening: all these guys in confinement of some kind, looking slightly dazed by what was going on, but there of their own accord—and paying handsomely for it. I don't feel superior to these guys—at least I hope I don't—but I sure don't relate to what gets them off. I'm just sentimental, I guess, for good old-fashioned fucking 'n' sucking.

This particular evening I witnessed enough bondage to last me several lifetimes. In one room was a guy tied up into a ball. The madam pulled him out of the room by his hair, which certainly had no deleterious effect on what must be called a very healthy hard-on. Pushing him forward so that his backside was totally accessible, she opened a drawer, took out a dildo, and pushed it up his behind as casually as some people make chicken soup. I say *casually,* but I don't say *gently*—she shoved that dildo up him so unceremoniously that it almost hurt me to watch. But he didn't seem to mind, and she grabbed his penis and started to play with it—and just a few seconds later he came all over her hand. So I guess she had his *number*—69, to the fifth power, divided by 2,345.87. Or whatever the formula is. . . .

In another room was a couple in the famous "missionary" position—male on top, his penis inside the female—who were bound to each other. From the welts on both their behinds you could see that they'd been given a steady workover, and from the expressions on their faces you could see that they loved it. Later on I learned that they also got the dildo treatment—one for each rear entrance. "Double your pleasure . . . double your fun. . . ."

Xaviera and I strolled into the kitchen, and there was a distinguished-looking guy busily doing the dishes. The butler, right? Or a hired servant? No, this guy got his jollies by coming to these "slave parties" and shining the silver, polishing the furniture, doing the dishes, vacuuming up afterward—and paying for the privilege of playing domestic servant. I don't know where he took his sexual pleasure from all this--maybe he was on intimate terms with the vacuum cleaner—but I'd sure like to have him around for *my* parties. . . .

Back in the living room there was a tall, well-built guy walking around in shirt, tie, apron, and hard-on. No pants or shorts. He asked us if we wanted drinks, and we said yes and thanked him, and while he was making our drinks—the usual soft drink for Xaviera—a young woman came over to him and taking his cock in her hand, squeezed it as hard as she could. His face registered pain, but it also displayed pleasure, and she kept squeezing it and he kept talking to us and smiling his tight smile. Then she started actually slapping his poor hard-on around—while I started wincing —and at one point looked at me and asked, "Care to give him a tap?" I declined and suggested, somewhat sternly, that perhaps she'd had enough fun with him for the present, and she seemed to agree. As he turned to leave us she smacked him on the backside as hard as she could with her open hand. He looked back at us, smiled, and said to her, "Thanks." Do you think that could be the basis for the after-shave TV commercial where the guy says, "Thanks . . . I *needed* that"?

Xaviera had watched all these goings-on with detachment, and some amusement, while I was both offended and amazed. But if I'm going to be honest, over the course of the evening I had also become rather aroused by all this Krafft-Fbing carrying-on, and while—unlike a lot of the paying guests at the party—I wasn't burdened with a hard-on, I was horny as hell. I wanted to get fucked, and I wanted to get fucked real bad. I suggested to Xaviera that we leave this Fun City party and go down to her apartment, and she certainly seemed agreeable, and as soon as we closed the door to her apartment I had her in my arms, kissing the hell out of her.

I won't say she exactly responded. but three minutes later we were lying down on her couch without a stitch on. In another three minutes she was as horny as I was, and if Xaviera were anyone but Xaviera, three minutes later we'd have been in bed, maybe even assuming the missionary position.

But no, Miss Clean Thoughts of 1971 prevailed and we ended up in the bathtub together. But I'm not exactly complaining, mind you, as this had to be one of the sexiest baths since Cleopatra offered Marc Anthony's cock a milkshake. Xaviera kept working up a lather around my cock, rinsing it off, then giving it some mouth-to-mouth resuscitation, at the same time playing with my rear end with the bar of soap and several agile fingers. For my part, I soaped her breasts into a bust of bubbles and returned the compliment to her backside. How I managed not to come during all this, I can only attribute to clean living.

Finally, with two of the best-scrubbed balls in town, I got Xaviera and myself out of the bathtub and we dried off each other—by now the bathroom floor was a lot wetter than we were. I went into the bedroom and lay down on my stomach, somehow—probably without realizing it—wanting this night to be a bit different, and when she joined me she immediately understood this. Soon I could feel her hands moving my legs apart, and her mouth caressing the insides of my calves and thighs.

Then she rolled me over—thank God, my poor horny penis was suffocating beneath me—and while her hand still toyed with my asshole, she gave my body a mouth-and-tongue loving that it will never forget—even if *I* do. Again, my not coming is all a tribute to clean living and Xaviera's brilliant ability to know when to stop doing one thing and start another. But most of the time I felt I was on the brink of orgasm, and so it was an extraordinary experience— Xaviera's mouth on the head of my penis, her tongue on my balls, her soft hands and mouth on my stomach—any of these should have produced a climax which would have registered on the nearest seismograph, but somehow, with her knowing participation, I kept holding out.

We finally moved into our favorite 69 position, and I was eating her clit with grateful, loving feelings for all the pleasure she'd given me thus far, and now it was she who was trying not to come. We were both kissing and sucking each

59

other in a most indecent manner—as they used to say in Victorian novels—when suddenly she said something to me she'd never said before.

"Spank me!" she more or less ordered.

I was a bit startled since all the blood which normally resides in my brain was now reposed in the head of my penis, but I gave her a few taps on the fanny, as ordered.

If a mother used my spanking technique to punish a child, she would guaranteed herself a lot of grief—and an unrepentent child—because Xaviera looked up at me and said, "No, no, spank me *hard!* Make noise!"

To my complete surprise, I responded by whacking her on the fanny with a lot of force, and I anxiously awaited tears on her face. And a retaliatory slap on my face. But no, Xaviera wanted more—in fact she moved her ass closer to me so I could really whack it. I slapped her ass maybe twenty times, until it was definitely reddish in hue, and I was beginning to disbelieve that there was any way the evening could end in a fine old-fashioned fuck. I don't ask much out of life pure 'n' simple, but a fuck was very much in order. . . .

Almost to my surprise, Xaviera maneuvered herself above me and put me inside her, and again, to my continued surprise, I continued to slap at her backside as she pumped up and down on me, and within a few moments we both came with such unbelievable force that we had to cling to each other just to stay on the bed. I don't recommend it, unless you want to revisit your childhood, but it was surely a night to remember.

On the other hand, so was the sinking of the *Titanic*.

I am not now, nor was I ever, nor will I ever be, someone who has been or even *wants* to be spanked as part of a sexual experience. I am told by European friends—and particularly my English friends—that spanking is very big abroad. Particularly with men; guys will beg to be spanked.

I know I'm naive, but I like to blame it all on the heating shortage in England.

CHAPTER 6.

Upon consultation with my priest, rabbi, guru, accountant, attorney, physical therapist, tobacco dealer, Chinese laundryman, psychiatrist, favorite waiter, old-time friend the bartender at the Hotel Doral, favorite massage-parlor girl, plus the local fruit dealer I help keep in business, I have decided not to try and recreate the days when Xaviera was the hottest madam in town. Xaviera's first book made Polly Adler's famous book, *A House Is Not a Home,* seem like the memoirs of a genteel little old lady, and my part in Xaviera's life has been laid out in great detail by her. Had certain things not happened, Xaviera could have avoided a great deal of legal problems, and might well still be living in America. For that matter, if she had not gotten involved with certain gentlemen creeps—particularly Teddy Ratnoff —*I* wouldn't have had the legal problems I did, but that's another issue and I will go into it at some length elsewhere in this book. I can only say that I always wanted Xaviera out of the sex-for-sale profession—and out of trouble—but trying to persuade her to give up such a lucrative profession was like telling an elephant in heat to go to the movies. In any case, rehashing those events won't shed much light— a little heat maybe—on her brief but meteoric career first as a prostitute and then as a madam. There were some wild times and some laughs, but bailing her out of jail was no fun, and I had to do it more than once, if you recall.

So I was glad as hell when Xaviera was out of business

and working on her book. No more surprising a John in the apartment and having to throw him out bodily. So now my only problem was Takis, the good-looking Greek boy who had worked as a bartender for Xaviera when her business was going full blast. Xaviera had warm feelings for Takis, and so did I—once I really got to know him. He was a very good-natured guy and it was easy to like him, and he and I would often go to an after-hours gambling club to play a Greek dice game called *barbotte*. Two sets of dice are used, and the players roll against each other—it's similar to the card game of baccarat—and we had a helluva lot of fun together.

Takis spent a lot of time at Xaviera's place, but he was having an affair with one of Xaviera's roommates, a Canadian girl named Josee—or so I believed—and Xaviera swore there was nothing between Takis and herself. So one weekend, when we were going out to East Hampton and Xaviera asked if we could take Takis along because his girlfriend was back in Canada visiting her folks, I readily agreed. I saw no reason not to invite him along—in fact, since he was a lot of fun, I was glad to have him with us. But what followed was pretty much like what would have happened had Charlie Chaplin turned his comic talents to making a blue movie.

When we got there Xaviera asked me to run out and get some food because the refrigerator was bare. When I came back in about twenty minutes, Takis had an embarrassed grin on his face and that made me a little suspicious, especially knowing what Xaviera can accomplish in the span of twenty minutes. But I didn't say anything because I had no proof. But that night I got all the proof I needed about those two sneaks—Xaviera and I had gone to bed fairly early, and around five or six in the morning I woke to find Xaviera slipping out of bed and tiptoeing to the door. She went out of the room and a few minutes later I could hear the springs banging away in Takis's room. At that moment I could have killed them both, but I controlled myself and decided to go back to the city instead. Somehow Xaviera managed to calm me down by promising to behave and why should I spoil what could still be a nice weekend, and so on. If you've read *Xaxiera!* you may recall that there's a scene in it where Takis and I do Xaviera up brown—and I'm not speaking of giving her a suntan—on the beach, but what she doesn't tell you is that the next day, when we returned to New York, I threw Takis out of her apartment.

That should have been it, but nothing is ever simple with Xaviera. For the next two weeks she paid his hotel bills and I'm sure he had visitation privileges when I wasn't there. Then one night she announced he was moving back in and for reasons of my own I didn't oppose it. For one thing, I'd learned from Xaviera's various flings that threatening her won't make her see the sense, or lack of it, in what she's doing. She has to learn the bad news for herself. And Takis would turn out to be bad news to Xaviera—I was certain of that.

As I mentioned earlier, Takis loved to gamble, and it bugged Xaviera that he went out so many evenings to gamble—sometimes with her money, too—and only returned when he'd lost everything. But in another area Takis was becoming quite independent of Xaviera. He'd gotten a job as a bartender in a posh bar and he was meeting a lot of girls through his job, and this didn't sit well with Xaviera. Since Takis had the morals of a coyote and the sexual appetite of a rabbit, he wanted to go out with some of the women he was meeting, but Xaviera would not hear of it.

Finally Takis got another job: he was in charge of hiring all the cocktail waitresses at a supper club, and one gal in particular, a former Israeli belly dancer whom Takis had dated some years earlier, became quite close to him. When he insisted on seeing her Xaviera became furious—no single standard for this lady—and that really marked the end of their little love affair. What she told friends, however, was that she had caught Takis making love to someone in the apartment. Which was also true. Or at least partially true. What really happened was that a Dutch girl living in New Jersey had come over to the apartment to ask Xaviera for some help in getting settled in New York. Her name was Heidi and she was the proverbial pretty, but so dumb, blond. And while Xaviera was on the phone trying to help her, Takis calmly took Heidi into the bedroom and fucked her. Xaviera didn't know about this because she was so busy on the phone, but Takis, actually feeling a little guilty, later that evening told her what he'd done. This led to some physical violence—he hit Xaviera a few times—and Takis took back the money he'd been giving her in recent months to help pay the rent. He also took off with a good suitcase and silk dressing gown that belonged to me. Which, so far as I was concerned, was a small price to pay for finally getting him out of Xaviera's life. It was many months before Xaviera would even set foot in the supper club when Takis was working, and when she did stop by to say hello, they didn't have much to say to each other. But I've been to that club many times.

You see, the irony is that Takis and I have maintained a pretty good friendship to this day.

He cared for Xaviera, Takis has told me, but it was never anything meant to be lasting. She had been warm and friendly to him She was good in bed and she'd taught him things. She'd also bought him things. It was very nice--for Takis—while it lasted. My own view of the matter is that Takis can never love anybody but himself . . . fully.

It's a complicated world, folks.

Once Takis had moved out, things were relatively tranquil. No more worrying about Takis and Xaviera making it out of sheer boredom. She was spending a lot of time at the district attorney's office—which wasn't any fun—and working on her book, and so it was a busy time.

However, I could sense Xaviera becoming very moody. In part I attributed this to her sessions with the D. A., but it was also probably the change in her life from those "exciting" days when she'd been a madam and the money had poured in. Well, she had no money problems and I could do without that kind of "excitement," but I did understand that she needed a lot of things going on in her life. So I was pleased to receive a call from her one day saying that she'd been asked to deliver a series of lectures to a singles club, and she had to see me that night in her apartment. She sounded very enthused, and I was glad for her. I was also glad that she'd be making some money in a manner which was one hundred percent legal.

That night, when I arrived at Xaviera's apartment, she gave me all the details. She'd been approached by a guy who managed a singles club, Richard Collins, and he was coming over that evening to work out the financial arrangements. That's why it was important for me to be there.

"What do you know about this guy?" I asked her.

"Oh, he's been recommended to me by a mutual friend."

"Okay," I said, "go on."

"Well, he wants me to give the lectures here—"

"Wait a minute," I interrupted her. "Why here? That sounds crazy. Aren't lectures always given in some kind of hall?"

"I don't know," she said. "He stressed using my apartment. . . . Anyhow, what's wrong with that?"

"For one thing, how many people can you fit into your living room compared to a large lecture hall?"

We were discussing this issue when the doorbell rang and it was Richard Collins, an attractive guy in his late twenties or early thirties. He seemed nice and friendly, insisting we call him Dick instead of Mr. Collins, and set out to explain what he had in mind. He represented a large organization of swingers, he said—not just singles, but couples as well—and he believed he could get his member to pay twenty-five dollars apiece to hear Xaviera give a lecture. She would discuss prostitution, of course, but her main topic would be "as broad as life itself"—in other words, s-e-x.

"Can you be more specific?" I asked him.

"Well, I'd like Xaviera—who's an expert—to explain the various ways of turning on both men and women. . . . I figure the lecture itself, plus the question-and-answer period, will take about three hours, and I can guarantee you a fee of at least four hundred dollars."

At twenty-five dollars per member, only sixteen members had to show up to cover Xaviera's fee, so Dick wasn't being too terribly generous, but Xaxiera only heard the "at least" part, and she obviously wanted to do the lecture.

"Okay," I said, "we're agreed that the fee will be *at least* four hundred dollars, but why do you want to have it here in Xaviera's apartment?"

If the question fazed him he certainly didn't show it. "It's important to have the lecture here," he explained calmly, "because it is going to be an illustrated lecture."

"What do you plan to do," I quipped, "show a pornographic film?"

"No, no," he laughed. "I want Xaviera to get me a couple of girls to demonstrate the techniques she's talking about."

"Forget it," I said, "she's not in that kind of business anymore."

The frown on my face should have told Xaviera the answer had to be no, but she popped up and said, "That will cost you an additional six hundred dollars. That's the 'champagne' rate—one hundred dollars per girl per hour."

This time Dick *was* fazed. "Oh, I don't think we can afford that," he said, clearly troubled over the high cost of "champagne."

"Well," Xaviera responded, once more the tough businesswoman, "that's what the girls will want." Sure, that was what the girls would *want*, but you could bet your bottom dollar that that wouldn't be what they'd *get*; Xaviera would surely take a service charge for herself.

I was adamant about Xaviera not hiring any girls for this "live" sex show, and Dick kept insisting that the price was too high, and Xaviera had adopted a "take it or leave it" attitude, but we finally worked out a compromise: No paid teachers apart from Xaviera, and if live bodies were needed for demonstration purposes, they would be volunteers—of both sexes—from the audience. With the ground rules worked out, we agreed that the first lecture would take place in two weeks.

Dick seemed very pleased with the whole arrangement, and so did Xaviera. What he couldn't have realized was that she intended to invite some friends to catch her debut as a lecturer—at fifty dollars per couple. Xaviera was always one to make both ends meet. . . .

The night of the lecture arrived, and so did a lot of people. Dick had stressed that there be no liquor available —only soft drinks—and this pleased me. However, it certainly didn't please Xaviera's old friends, who were used to standing around "the biggest bar in town." I say *biggest* beacuse Xaviera's bar had mostly been stocked with half-gallon bottles which we bought in Connecticut (now you can get them in New York), and the lineup of all those half-gallon jugs was quite an impressive sight. But tonight the bar held ice, club soda, Coke, and nothing else.

The lecture was scheduled for 7:30 and I arrived at around six o'clock to make sure that everything was ready for the big event—plenty of ice and soda for the swingers to sip while they learned what sex is all about. I was very relaxed about the evening—it was Dick's baby, and I would just sit back and learn what sex is all about. It's never too late, I told myself, for a man to go back to school and get some higher education.

When Dick arrived he set up a table near the door, and as people came in they paid their twenty-five-dollar lecture fee and were told where to put their coats. Those who wanted soft drinks could stop by the bar, otherwise they were to make themselves comfortable in the living room. Before too long there were about fifty club members sitting in the living room—mostly on the carpeted floor since there were only enough couches and chairs for ten or twelve people—plus maybe ten of Xaviera's friends. Since everyone paid the twenty-five dollars to get in, I realized that Dick had grossed around fifteen hundred, and decided to share this information with Xaviera, who was getting dressed in the bedroom.

Xaviera, as you have probably predicted, was ready to call a teacher's strike.

"I'm not going to let him pocket eleven hundred dollars while I get only only four hundred!" she said in a huff. This tough Dutch Jewish broad was not going to be taken in by any Dick, Tom—or Harry.

"You're right," I said.

"He certainly has no right to the money my friends paid to get in."

"You're right."

"He isn't paying anything for the apartment. He's only paying for me. It isn't right!"

"You're right," I agreed. This was rapidly becoming a comedy monologue.

"Call Dick in here—either we renegotiate or there'll be no lecture tonight. Or any other time, for that matter!"

I went out and got Dick, and when he came into the bedroom the expression on Xaviera's face must have in-

67

stantly convinced him to renegotiate, and in good faith. We worked out a quick compromise whereby Xaviera received nine hundred dollars and Dick six hundred, and now that the time for talking shop was over, it was time for Xaviera to . . . well, talk shop.

When I went out in the living room to be part of the audience one thing struck me that I hadn't noticed before. Almost everyone there was male—there were just a few girls in the audience. And another surprise: the few girls who were there were all fairly pretty. Not at all what I expected.

Dick introduced Xaviera to the audience and she began talking about the benefits to society of prostitution—using arguments and theories she has since made familiar through her books, talks, and media appearances all over the United States and Canada—and then began discussing sexual techniques and the various forms of pleasure to be derived from sex. I must say it was a pretty entertaining lecture—Xaviera talking about all her "penetrating research" in the field—especially when you consider that it was her first time speaking to a group of people. (On the other hand, she did have a kind of internship as a lecturer when she was a madam and her apartment was filled with guys and girls.) After talking nonstop for almost three-quarters of an hour, Xaviera called for questions from the audience.

There were a few silly questions to which Xaviera provided funny answers, and then one guy got up and asked, "Is there a proper way to give a man a blow-job?" Xaviera immediately motioned to a girl—a petite blond sitting on the floor directly in front of the couch on which Xaviera was seated—and without any hesitation the girl got up and went over to Xaviera's side. Then Xaviera asked for a male volunteer, and about tens hands shot up. She asked all ten men to come up to her, and then she examined their hands—if you've read *The Happy Hooker* you know her theory about the relationship between large hands and a large penis. There is nothing scientific about this theory, but Xaviera swears by it, and of course she picked a guy with very large, powerful hands. She then requested him to take off his clothing, and with no reluctance he stripped and—following Xaviera's instructions—stretched out on the couch

68

on which she'd been sitting. All the others on the couch had been waved off, so the couch was free to be used as Xaviera's li'l red-light schoolhouse.

When the guy was naked and decked out on the couch, Xaviera asked the petite blond to "go blow his as you normally would a man," and she went over and took the guy's penis—if Xaviera's hand-job on these guys had been designed to come up with something spectacular, it hadn't worked out that way—and began kissing and sucking it. The girl was still fully clothed, and the guy was really responding, and the two of them were behaving as though they were alone in the room. He was thrusting himself as far into her mouth as she could manage, and she was all over his cock with her lips, and I have to admit I found the scene very erotic indeed, but "teach" did not approve of the way the Fellatio I class was proceeding, and she went over to them and began explaining, very patiently, what the girl was doing wrong. Forget it. The little blond just kept blowing that guy as though she were trying out for *A Star is Born*, and I must say he didn't seem to be finding anything wrong with her technique. His face was lit up with pleasure as he held her head between his hands and moved her mouth back and forth, back and forth, on his penis. She had one hand on his ass, and the other was holding his balls, and was certainly all wrapped up in her homework.

Now Xaviera got really vexed—teacher knows best, you know!—and literally pulled the girl off the guy's penis, and took over. With one zip! of her gown, she was standing there naked, and almost gobbled up the guy's cock in her haste to demonstrate her mastery of Proper Fellatio I.

Well, expertise is where it's at—Xaviera had been working on him for less than half a minute and suddenly the guy was flailing around and coming all over the couch. In my mind I could hear Xaviera, surprised that the guy had come so quickly, saying to herself, "Okay, schmuck, in addition to your entrance fee, you get a nice dry-cleaning bill," but she remained gracious, saying to the crowd, "Ah, sorry, folks, the lesson was quicker than I'd intended—that's what always happens when 'The Fastest Tongue in the West' goes to work!" Everyone laughed, including the guy himself, who looked so content I figured he wouldn't need any more sex

69

for a week. However, if *he* was content, Xaviera *wasn't*. Somewhere in her makeup there lies a kind of puritan—or at least someone who insists on doing things right—and she wasn't about to give an illustrated lecture with poor illustrations.

Ignoring the guy standing there with a dripping penis and a grin on his face, Xaviera led the tiny blond over to the crushed black velvet loveseat next to the couch and just started undressing her as though she were a rag doll. The girl didn't seem to quite understand what was happening to her and when Xaviera whispered something in her ear, she just looked bewildered. So Xaviera eased her down on the loveseat and arranged her body there, more or less upside down. Her head was cushioned at the front of the pillow, and her shoulders were where her backside would normally be, and her belly and thighs were drapped over the back—which meant her vagina was nearly at the top of the piece of furniture. Xaviera took hold of the girl's vagina and, spreading the hair back—a natural blond, folks! —started to explain about the outer and inner lips, the clitoris, and the rest of the female anatomy.

I don't know who in the crowd found this very educational or even a turn-on, but I thought the whole thing was pretty hilarious—here was this poor little girl drapped over the loveseat, the blood rushing to her head, having her private parts the objects of a gynecological inspection by about ten people. When it got a little too crowded around her crotch, Xaviera shooed the people away so everyone would be able to see the next part of the lesson. And if I'd taken notes on the instruction here, they'd read something like this:

1. Xaviera goes down on the girl, pausing periodically to make a point or explain proper technique. A dedicated instructor.

2. Girl becomes terribly aroused. Only natural.

3. Xaviera, feeling that two's company but three's more fun, asks a male member of the audience to join the lecture circuit. He takes out his penis and jams it into the girl's mouth. *He's* not shy. . . .

4. The girl almost gags, then begins blowing the guy in earnest. She likes blowing guys.

70

5. Xaviera begins eating the girl in earnest. She likes eating girls.

6. The girl is very, very aroused. Good for her.

7. The guy is very, very aroused. Only natural. So am I. . . .

8. The girl is breathing very heavily and still blowing the guy.

9. Xaviera explains to the men in the audience that this is how they should excite their women.

10. The guy, as excited as can be, comes. His jism drips from her mouth onto the carpet. Is jism good for a carpet?

11. The audience is so entranced by Xaviera's lecture that no one replaces the guy.

12. The girl, as everyone can plainly see, has had a fine orgasm.

13. Xaviera, as everyone can plainly see, is in a classroom by herself. . . .

At this point I had to leave the room to make an important and fairly lengthy phone call and when I returned to the living room, there was Xaviera with four men around her. Someone in the audience had asked her how many men she could satisfy at one time, and so there she was—getting ready to blow one guy, be balled from the rear by another, and playing with two other guys! The odds were four to one, but I can tell you who was running this show, and I started looking around the room for something to throw at this cozy little group. Xaviera was supposed to deliver a lecture, not star at an orgy, and I was going to break up that fucking little fivesome if it got me into a pier-six brawl doing it, but fortunately she saw me and how angry I was, and broke it up herself. Good thing, too, because I was about ready to break some lamps over people's heads.

The lecture was now officially over, and people began milling around, talking excitedly, and then something bizarre happened. One of the women who had attended the lecture had come, or so I thought, with a tall, handsome black guy, but now she was sort of fooling around with everyone around her. The next thing I knew she had taken off her sweater and stood there, bare to the waist, her sensational large boobs staring everyone in the face, and then she began rubbing against some of the men, feeling their cocks and putting their hands on her breasts. Then she found one guy whose cock she must've really liked by the way it felt through his pants, because she went down on her knees, unzipped his pants and took him into her mouth.

Everyone backed off, as though watching some expert couple do the tango, and about a minute later this guy was trying to hold her bobbing head still while he shot his load into her mouth. She paused for breath, licking her lips as though she'd just experienced some fantastic taste treat— Beluga caviar or 1947 Dom Pérignon champagne or the newest Baskin Robbins ice-cream flavor—and then moved on her knees to the nearest guy and began giving him the same treatment.

Sensing that this thing could turn into a group daisy chain, and could result in a visit from the law, I made Xaviera go into her bedroom while I tried to empty the apartment. By the time I got back every one of the girls in the room had cocks in their mouths, and men crowded around them, and I asked Dick to help me clear everyone out before there was trouble. I really don't know how much help he was because every time I threw some guy and girl out, the girl managed to sneak back and begin making it with another guy, and at one point, really to my surprise because I didn't know any of these people, two girls had me backed into a corner and were copping feels off *me*. In another situation I might have been flattered and delighted, not to speak of horny, but not this night—I just wanted the lecture to end in peace and quiet and in *no* legal visits. I took one gal's hand off my hardened joint, unwrapped myself from the other's arm, and ushered them out of the apartment. And though it took another fifteen minutes or so, I finally cleared the apartment. If Dick was supposed to be helping me, he was nowhere in sight, so I managed it myself and when there was no one left in the living room I felt greatly relieved.

For at least two minutes. . . .

When I entered the bedroom in which I'd put Xaviera, there she was—not exactly resisting good old Richard, who was busily yanking off his pants, obviously intent upon completing the lessons of the night. I rushed over to the bed and yanked him off of it and onto the floor.

"For chrissakes," he yelled, "Xaviera made nine hundred

dollars tonight—the least she can do is give me a freebie!"

"Get your rotten ass out of here!" I yelled.

"But—"

I picked up the trousers belonging to Richard the swinging manager and then grabbed Richard the swinging manager himself and escorted both him and his loose trousers out of the bedroom.

Throwing his trousers on the living-room floor, I said, "You have about thirty-seven seconds to get the hell out of here."

"Fuck you!" he said as he bent over to get his pants, and I couldn't resist the opportunity to give him a boot in the ass that sent him flying across the living room. By my measure, it was at least a ten-foot field goal. . . .

Richard was now clearly aroused in an area different from before, and he picked himself up and headed toward me, wanting to teach me some lesson or other, but I guess the sight of me waiting for him, a bottle of club soda held in my right hand like some battle club, slightly discouraged him. I'm glad for that, in retrospect, because I was really ready to crease his skull as a reminder of the evening's activities.

"Get out of here for good," I ordered him, "or I'll break your goddamn neck!"

"Oh, fuck you," he said, getting into his pants.

"You have about a minute to escape being an eunuch," I replied, brandishing the bottle of club soda. As I said it I wanted to laugh, because I am really a pretty gentle man and wouldn't hurt anyone except in great anger. And by now I was semi cooled off.

"Fuck you, Larry," he said. "I don't have to take orders from you."

"No, but you'll look very funny walking around Manhattan with a bottle of club soda up your ass," I said.

He left. Rapidly.

When I went back into the bedroom I asked Xaviera why she'd let him get to the point of taking off his pants.

"Oh, I don't know . . ." she replied. "I thought the lecture had gone so well that maybe he deserved a freebie . . . maybe he *was* entitled."

Fortunately for her, I was no longer carrying the bottle of club soda in my hand.

73

Some months later, after Xaviera had left for Holland, I received a call from Richard, suggesting a new deal.

"Listen, Larry, no hard feelings from this end. You had every reason to be pissed off. The whole thing got out of hand."

"Dick, what do you have in mind?" I responded, trying to be cool.

"Well, if we picked one of Xaviera's best gals from the old days," he said, "we could repeat that 'lecture scene' every other week."

"Oh . . . ?"

"Yeah, just so long as we use Xaviera's apartment, it'll work—I'm sure of that."

"Richard, in case you haven't fucked anyone recently, why don't you just kindly go fuck yourself!"

"Hey, listen, Larry—"

"Richard—maybe you're known to your friends as Dick, but to me it ought to be *Prick*—now just hang up and go away. Go swing somewhere else. You're not welcome any-place I happen to be—that's the message of *my* lecture to *you*." I wasn't really angry, but he didn't have to know that.

"Well, uh, gee, Larry, if you feel that way. . . ."

I felt that way.

Little did I dream that Xaviera would later make herself famous *just* by giving lectures. And with none of Dick's little "illustrations."

CHAPTER 7.

On more than one occasion Xaviera has called me a "square businessman," and from her point of view, she's right. I certainly wasn't into her kind of life-style when we met—for that matter, I never wanted to be, or needed to become, that kind of "swinger." And I'm glad she's right— her idea of "square" is pretty oblong compared to most people's ideas of "square."

In any case, thinking back upon the lecture for swinging nincompoops, I am reminded of how often she has gotten into trouble because she does things on impulse without thinking of the consequences. Just as she was determined to do that lecture, she will jump into a business deal without consulting her lawyers or, if she asks my advice, do the precise opposite of what I advise her.

This also happens on a social level: she will accept invitations from men she hardly knows, and later learn that the guy was merely being horny, not hospitable. When she visited Italy she was taken by some friends to a party at the house of a very well-known painter. That night, I learned, she was raped four times by her host and not once did she scream or try to stop him. When I asked her why she hadn't yelled for help or at least fought back, she told me that she'd been afraid people would think badly of her if she created a scene. She hurt for over a week and her body was black and blue, but she had preferred to suffer this guy's attacks on her rather than suffer the embarrassment of making a scene.

75

Similarly, we went to Nassau one time and I had to return to New York after the weekend, while Xaviera stayed there. I was joining her the following weekend, this time for a longer vacation, and during the week we kept in touch by phone. Everything was "wonderful," she said whenever I called.

When I got to Nassau I found Xaviera on the beach with a couple we knew from New York—Jim and Mary—and everything seemed just great. But as soon as we got back to the hotel we started getting a series of obscene phone calls. After the first one, Xaviera wanted me to answer the phone. Well, I did, and each time it was a native's voice saying pretty much the same thing: "We want to fuck your girl." Now that wouldn't have bothered me so much, but each time it was a different native, and after several calls it began to sound as though Xaviera had some large fan club out there.

"That's quite a native following you've built up," I said after hanging up on yet another obscene caller. "What's it all about?"

"I don't know why they should be bothering me," she said. "I've been with Jim and Mary most of the time."

That afternoon, sitting on the beach with Mary while Xaviera was running around in the surf with Jim, I told her about our friends on the phone, and she responded by telling me about a "horrible rape" which had taken place on the beach a few days earlier.

"A young couple were walking on the beach," she said, "fairly late at night, when three native men landed their boat on the sand fairly near them. The couple thought nothing of it, assuming that the men had been out fishing or something like that, but as soon as they'd secured the boat, the three men grabbed the couple and brutally beat the guy, leaving him badly hurt on the beach."

"Jesus," I said, "do I want to hear what happened to the girl? And what's this got to do with the phone calls?"

"I'll get to that," she replied, continuing her story. "The girl was raped repeatedly and then, instead of leaving her alone, they took her with them on the boat, raped her even more times, and then broke both her arms and threw her overboard."

76

"That's awful," I said. "That poor girl. . . ."

"Well, somehow she made it to the shore and she'll be okay. But she'll never forget that experience."

"Who could blame her? But what's that got to do with Xaviera?"

"Nothing that I know about, really, but while you've been away she's been going out a lot, I gather, and for all I know she's become the sex symbol of the entire island and a lot of natives are lusting after her."

Later on, when I'd gone back to the hotel to take a shower—Xaviera was still down at the beach, sun-worshiper that she is—the phone rang and it was another horny-handed guy at the other end.

"I want to fuck your girl," he said, without any heavy breathing—no class, these callers; they should take some instruction from a New York City obscene phone caller.

"Listen," I said, bluffing like crazy, "I know exactly who you guys are and you'd better knock it off if you don't want to end up in the police station." This time the click was on the other end—he'd hung up before I could.

When Xaviera returned from the beach I told her about the latest call and asked her again what it was all about. She denied she knew and I didn't press the issue. I could guess, but whatever had inspired the calls made me much more fearful for her safety than anything else.

So for safety's sake I kept Xaviera away from the beach in the late afternoons and we certainly avoided dark streets at night. Instead of strictly relaxing and having a good time, I felt like some kind of bodyguard, and when I flew back to Manhattan I made sure Xaviera was on the plane beside me.

Part of Xaviera's problems in these matters is that she's such a crazy exhibitionist. She'll think nothing of walking out on a hotel balcony nude or sitting on the upper deck of a boat, nude to the waist, waving at everyone passing by. Give her a party and a few people urging her to do a strip-tease, and away go the clothes. But her daredevil exhibitionism isn't always to her advantage—not everyone admires her for letting it all hang out whenever she feels like it.

Just one instance of same: Xaviera was in Acapulco and I was in New York. I was planning on spending time there with her, but business matters were keeping me in Manhattan for a while, and in my absence she'd gotten herself a temporary escort, a good-looking—naturally—young guy named Marty, from Canada. Marty's a nice enough kid—I later got to know him—but he had about as much control over Xaviera as does a keeper of trained fleas over a herd of water buffalo. So I don't blame him for what happened that night—in fact I learned some of the facts in this story from him. Other details came from Xaviera, still others from people I met in Acapulco.

It was Xaviera's second night in Acapulco, and she'd heard there was a wild sex show at a place called Rebecca's Whorehouse. With Marty's help she recruited a party of nine or ten people to go to Rebecca's that night, and she and Marty went over to Rebecca's to arrange things. The place had a big bar with lots of sailors and tourists, and about fifty million prostitutes milling around. There were five bedrooms upstairs, and Xaviera was curious as to where the shows were held. She was taken by Rebecca—a fat old dyed blonde—to a small room which held a round bed with decorator sheets, a large wall mirror, two wooden benches, a floormat, and stool. There was a small bathroom to the side. That was the "sex theater."

The show would cost ten dollars per person, and I'll bet Xaviera was annoyed when Marty didn't offer to pay for her. The star of the sex show, Marty learned, was one of the waiters, JoJo, and there was a rumor going around that, although he was only twenty-two, he wouldn't be able to get it up because he'd been experiencing difficulty in precisely that area over the past few days. Poor JoJo—would he be able to get it up? Would he perform—did he, or didn't he, believe in that great show-biz tradition, "The show must go on"?

Xaviera and her party showed up at midnight for the great show, and took their seats, with Xaviera sitting on the front bench. Most of the other people in the party were married couples, tourists from the hotel and basically nice, respectable people. Rebecca told Xaviera's party that they could select the girls to perform with JoJo, and Xaviera picked a pert, sexy-looking girl, and someone else—one of the men—picked a girl who was, to use Marty's familiar expression, "built like a brick shithouse." Her dress was so tight, Marty recalled, that they either had poured or sewed her into it. In either or both cases, Marty thought she "looked great!"

The two appointees to the sex show excused themselves and went into the powder room to tidy up, and before very long it was time for "Lights! Action! More Action! Still More Action!" Both girls started to make amorous overtures to JoJo, stripping him of his clothes, fondling him, caressing his ass and thighs and groin, but mostly trying to get him hard. But JoJo's joint wasn't responding and the girls, Xaviera felt, weren't really trying. They weren't at all horny and so they were faking it, and that's why JoJo wasn't getting his penis up to where it had to be if the show were even to get started, much less go on.

Now I'd have expected Xaviera and the others to want their money back, but before anyone could realize what had happened—*Carramba!* Super Sex Symbol to the rescue! —Xaviera had shed her skirt and panties and was up there, on the bed trying to warm up the girls and make them sincerely want to get into the act. First she went to work on the girl she'd selected and was—to hear Xaviera describe it —"giving her head like no one had ever given her." And then on to the other one, the voluptuous one—Xaviera chomped on her with enthusiasm, but nothing seemed to get these girls going.

Evidently they were so hardened or had become so inured against sex that not even Xaviera's expert lovemaking could turn them on—which is a pretty sad commentary on their lives as prostitutes. But JoJo was becoming interested and he came over and began kissing Xaviera with a lot of enthusiasm. Unfortunately this wasn't being translated into some state of rigidity down below, so a few minutes later there was Xaviera, sucking his cock in a valiant effort to get it erect, if only for a little while. Goddamnit, JoJo, the show must go on—or at least come off . . . !

The two girls, sitting on the side of the bed, were intently watching the whole thing—probably more out of curiosity than any sense of passion—but since they hadn't paid anything to be there, *they* at least were getting their money's worth. Despite Xaviera's loving mouth working on him, JoJo still couldn't get it up—and Xaviera looked, I'm told, as though she couldn't believe what was happening (or *wasn't* happening) before her eyes.

Now she changed tactics, leaving his prick to kiss his ears, neck, eyes, moving her mouth over his chest, teasing his nipples with her lips, moving ever south of the border. Finally she could feel his cock growing in her hands. All the women in the audience were leaning forward to get a closer look, Xaviera told me, and when JoJo was really hard he pulled Xaviera over his face and they went into a "delicious 69." She sucked his cock and played with his ass and balls, and he ate her and fingered her and they began to put on a great show. Xaviera said JoJo was a fantastic lover, and she couldn't understand why the two working girls hadn't been able to get themselves worked up over him.

For the next twenty minutes, Xaviera said, they made love as though there were no tomorrow—getting into every kind of sex act and one position after another, and finally JoJo exploded inside her as she lay beneath him, her legs over his shoulders. (Funny, I'd never known her to enjoy that position. . . .) Her date, Marty, and another young Canadian were goggle-eyed, Xaviera said, at what they'd seen, and one of the older men was standing there, his penis exposed, masturbating. The women all seemed to be holding themselves at their crotches, obviously having been very excited by the scene.

As everyone filed out, including her date, Xaviera and JoJo remained cuddled on the bed while the girls got dressed. "I realized then that Madam X was still pretty good," she later told me, "and this was confirmed when I got up, dressed, and walked out the door. Those two girls actually clapped—they'd never seen anything like that!"

Well, that's one version of the story. Marty doesn't recall—maybe he doesn't *want* to recall, I don't know—anyone getting up and masturbating. He also told me that Xaviera had said to him, "I'm sure that if Larry had been there, this never could have happened."

Right.

Marty didn't know me then, but if I had been there it *wouldn't* have happened. Even if I'd had to throw her through the door of Rebecca's Whorehouse, it wouldn't have happened.

When Xaviera told me what had gone on that night, I could only say, "Xaviera, how could you?"

"Everyone loved it," she answered. "You have *no* idea. They went crazy. They all told me I had done what each and every woman there wanted to do."

A few days later, by coincidence, I was introduced to one of the women who'd been at Rebecca's that night. While Xaviera was talking to someone else at the bar, I went over to this woman and asked her in a soft voice, "Tell me truthfully—I'm sure you'll never see Xaviera again after this vacation and probably you couldn't care less—so please tell me . . . what did you really think of that exhibition she put on?"

She looked at me, seemed to hesitate a bit, then said in a cool, measured tone, "Perhaps I'm a prude—at the time I was more shocked than anything else—but in retrospect I think it was probably the most disgusting thing I ever, in my entire life, have seen." Then she added, after a brief pause, "Or probably will ever see."

I thanked her for her candor, adding, "You know something—you're probably right. . . .". What she'd said really depressed me, because Xaviera was acting out some kind of extravagant role she inherited by writing *The Happy Hooker,* as I think she was, then it may be too bad that book ever happened.

Especially when I recall that Xaviera's whole celebrityhood—or notoriety, if that's the way you look at it—came about in an entirely unplanned way.

CHAPTER 8.

There is a famous expression—"For lack of a boot nail, the war was lost."

In Xaviera's case—because of a stickup, her fame, fortune, and personal empire were born.

During her days as a madam, she did some business with a guy named Frank who at that time was a professional limousine driver. At night he hung out at an East Forty-fourth Street cocktail lounge and bistro which was a very swinging place—a kind of hostel for single people, more than a few B-girls and, at this time, some street girls who wouldn't win any merit badges for good looks.

Now, strangely enough, a lot of the guys who went there looking for some action wouldn't want to have anything sexually to do with the girls hustling drinks or the hookers frequenting the place. They'd dance with these girls, buy them drinks, but despite being horny and, more often than not, at least a little smashed after an evening of drinking, they didn't choose to sleep with these girls. My guess is that they were afraid of getting mugged or else a case of V.D. And that's when Frank would move it—offering sympathy as they staggered out ("Sure are a bunch of dogs here, right?") and mentioning his connection with Xaviera. If they were interested, he'd go to the phone and call Xaviera, and hustle a few guys over to her place.

I never approved of this arrangement because Frank would stay downstairs in his limousine, sometimes double-parked, waiting for the guys—which to me was a perfect tipoff to the police. And Xaviera sure didn't need any more interest in her activities from that department. And I must say that Xaviera's girls didn't exactly cheer for these kind of guests since for every hundred-dollar client he brought over, Frank got twenty dollars—ten from Xaviera's half and ten from the girl's half. Sometimes some especially tough-minded girls insisted on their full fifty dollars, in which case Xaviera got thirty dollars—which, as you might just suspect, really made her a little sad. Still and all, there were nights when things were slow, and Xaviera was grateful for the Johns Frank brought over. After all, the name of the game is "Business is Business." Thirty percent of nothing is bad business.

One night when I wasn't there, it was the day after Christmas, Frank showed up with a guy—a pleasant-looking, well-dressed man—and no sooner had he come through the door with this guy than he dropped to the floor, acting very frightened, and yelled, "Hey, it's a stickup. This guy has a gun. Everyone get on the floor!"

Well, no one was about to argue with him, especially since the only people there were Xaviera and a couple of her girls, and the girls lay down on the floor as the bandit proceeded through the living room and into the bedroom, went right to her bureau and pulled open the second drawer from the bottom. This was the drawer in which she kept a lot of Pucci lingerie and her favorite square—next to me!—in the world, the metal box in which she kept money and valuables. As it turned out, there were eighteen-hundred dollars in there that night, plus two gold wristwatches which belonged to Xaviera and were there for safekeeping. The robber didn't bother to rifle the box—he just took it along with him, waving his gun at the people on the floor and saying, "Don't anybody try to come after me!"

Well, under these particular circumstances it's not exactly the kind of thing you can report to the police, and when the guy had left and everyone felt it was safe to get up off the floor, all the questions were directed at Frank. As Xaviera reported it to me, the poor guy was crestfallen. It had been a quiet night at the East Forty-fourth Street place and the guy seemed nice and Frank had talked to him and everything seemed just fine. Then Frank had driven him over and just before they'd gotten to the door of Xaviera's apartment, the guy had pulled a gun. Frank was very shaken up about it, he said, and certainly seemed genuinely upset. After all, why would he risk a good deal just to con Xaviera one time?

For my part, when I heard the story the next day—and no matter how distressed Frank had seemed—I knew it had to be a put-up job. After all, how did the thief know exactly where to go for the metal box? Slowly the dawn rose for the second time that day for Xaviera, and she realized she'd been taken.

Well, a couple of things seemed obvious to me: the money and watches could be gotten back if we could find Mr. Burglar, and the way to find Mr. Burglar was to find Frank. And Mr. Burglar had to be someone whom Frank knew well enough to take this kind of chance with. And since I was not about to take chances with guys who use guns, I called on an old friend of mine, a police sergeant named Dave, to accompany us when Xaviera and I went looking for Frank and his friend with the gun and Xaviera's metal box. Now Dave is a strictly honest cop—in case you haven't noticed, they don't exactly grow on trees these days—but he can be physically tough, as well as being tough-minded, when it comes to crooks. And since this club we were going to visit in search of Frank was not exactly the local Boy Scout headquarters—it's since gone out of business—I felt it advisable for Xaviera and me to have some genuine protection when we went there. I didn't know who owned the club, but it wasn't beyond the realm of possibility that Xaviera and I could have made a one-way visit to this club. In other words, we'd go in, and not come out. At least not through the front door. I've lived in New York long enough to know that the Mob, among other things, is in the entertainment business. So Dave, in a manner of speaking, was going to be our guaranteed exit visa to safety this evening.

I picked up Dave first, then Xaviera, and we drove to the place where we expected to find Frank, and as we were walking through the door—I literally wasn't in the place yet —Xaviera began yelling, "That's him—that's *him*!"

"Where?" snapped Dave.

"There he is—standing by the hat-check concession!" Xaviera said.

I was still in the doorway to the damn place so I asked the doorman who the guy Xaviera had pointed out was. He didn't seem to know what to say for a second or two, then he offered the astounding revelation that the guy in question was the owner of the place.

"You've got to be kidding," I said to him.

"No, I'm not," he replied. "I guess I should know who my boss is, all right. . . ."

At the same time this sparkling dialogue was going on outside, Dave—the old pro—had gone over to the gentleman in question, showed him his badge, and asked him if he wouldn't care to join us for a little fresh air. Since Dave had a strong hold on the guy's upper arm, and since Dave is clearly no guy to mess with, we all four got into a private little huddle outside the place—but far enough away to be out of the doorman's hearing.

"Hey, what the hell is going on!" said the owner in a voice that sounded more outraged than convincing.

"Yes, you do," said Dave in a very firm voice. "You certainly know what's going on. Now what are you going to do about it?"

"You're crazy," said the owner. "I don't know any of you people."

Xaviera called him some kind of crumb-bum monster in Dutch, then said in English, "You are as big a liar as you are a thief. But you are going to return what you took from me."

"Look, friend," said Dave, looking this guy right in the face, "I think it would be better off for all concerned if you returned Miss Hollander's money and jewelry immediately, don't you?"

The guy said nothing. If he was frightened, he didn't look it, but he didn't look very happy, either.

"Well . . .?" said Dave. "Do we have your cooperation? Those things don't belong to you and should be returned."

"I don't know what you're talking about," the guy said, still "toughing it out."

"Look," said Dave, sounding very calm and reasonable, "I can understand why you might not care to visit Miss

Hollander's apartment again—especially given the peculiar circumstances of your last visit there—so why don't you just take one of this gentleman's business cards"—here he was referring to me—"and get in touch with him tomorrow about returning the metal box and its contents."

I handed the owner one of my cards and he grunted and took it, putting it in his side coat pocket. We all stared at him for a minute or so longer, but it didn't look as though anything more could be accomplished by having a staring contest with him, so we left.

I invited Dave to have dinner with Xaviera and me—he'd done this on a few occasions, but this was the entire extent of his social contact with Xaviera or any of her friends, apart from me—and he readily accepted. Xaviera and I felt it had been like something out of a crime movie—and a lot of fun—and we were in a good mood over dinner. Xaviera even offered to send Dave a girl, but he refused, saying a good dinner was thanks enough.

"Do you think he'll return everything?" I asked him at one point during the meal.

"I'm pretty sure he'll give back the money," Dave replied, "but I'm not convinced you'll get the watches back. He may have dumped them already."

"Those were very fine watches," Xaviera protested.

"I'm sure they were," Dave said, "but then you should have kept them in a safer place."

Then he added, as a kind of afterthought: "You can be pretty sure that creep isn't going to reimburse you for the value of the watches. If he does, I'll expect the millenium has arrived."

We all laughed, and I agreed with Dave that at least all the money would be returned.

How wrong I was.

A few hours later, having had a really delicious meal and then having dropped Dave off at his apartment, Xaviera and I arrived back at her place. As we walked down the hall to her doorway, there was this big, beefy-looking plain-clothes cop cruising by her door. He didn't introduce himself, and we sure as hell didn't ask him in, but we soon enough learned who he was—a vice cop from the Nineteenth

Precinct who was the most feared person in town by girls in the trade—his prostitution-arrests record would stretch from his station house on the east side to the Brooklyn bridge. And probably back again.

Now while I didn't know who he was at the time, there wasn't any doubt in my mind that he was a cop—he had the kind of face that *only* the mother of an Irish cop could love—and that it wasn't any coincidence that he was in the hall when we got back. There was always the possibility that there'd been a complaint about Xaviera, but later, when I consulted with people I knew in the district attorney's office, they said that if he'd been interested in making an arrest, he certainly wouldn't have been standing there, out in the open, when we got back to Xaviera's apartment. No, it's my belief that the owner of the restaurant had called him up and asked him for a favor—to go fight fire with fire, in other words. There's no way I can ever prove this, but if that was coincidence, I'm a monkey's great uncle.

When Xaviera learned who the cop was, she became instantly worried—for one thing, she was afraid of being framed. A girlfriend of hers, a hooker from Queens, had left her apartment to put the garbage down the incinerator, and upon returning to her door was stopped by a cop. As she tried to reenter her apartment, he placed her under arrest. As simple as that.

During this period, Xaviera was speaking almost daily to Robin Moore—who was to be one of her co-authors on *The Happy Hooker*—and she relayed her fears to him. She told him about the whole stickup caper, the sudden, well-timed appearance of the cop in the hall, and her fears about being framed. Robin said he had a couple of friends connected with the Knapp Commission, then investigating police corruption in New York, and he would ask them to stop by and talk to her.

Xaviera began suffering fairly constant police harassment, and in a week or so she *was* arrested. She thought she'd been framed and told Robin so, and a few days later two men showed up at her apartment, identifying themselves as investigators for the Knapp Commission. Xaviera immediately assumed that they were Robin's friends, and let them in. This time, however, it was a case of coincidence—we subsequently found out that Knapp Commission investigators, as a matter of routine procedure, studied the lists of arrested prostitutes and would sometimes decide to question one in the hope of getting leads on dishonest cops. This was done on a volunteer basis, their rationale being that arrested girls might be willing to talk more freely in their own homes, in a relaxed setting—and away from police stations or other places where they'd be required to give sworn testimony. It's a logical enough theory—after being arrested, these girls weren't going to have any affection for cops—and it works.

Xaviera told these two men from the Knapp Commission essentially the same things she'd told Robin, and casually mentioned that there was "only one nice cop" she'd ever known, and used Dave's name. Now Dave was truly an old and good friend of mine, but technically he should never have associated with me when I was with Xaviera. Not even for dinner, I guess. And when these two investigators heard his name, their "red alert" system went into operation; before Dave could realize what was happening, he'd been subpoenaed to appear downtown at 52 Chambers Street before the Knapp Commission.

Well, everyone—including myself—felt that Dave was in a lot of trouble because of what you might call guilt by association, and how helpless I felt watching a very close friend's career about to go down the drain because he'd done me a single favor involving Xaviera. Any evidence against him was at best completely circumstantial, but you have to remember how anxious the Knapp Commission was to find crooked cops and how anyone even being questioned by the commission was automatically in trouble—at least in terms of reputation.

Enter Teddy Ratnoff, whom I'd met through Robin Moore. Now Teddy was nobody I felt especially friendly toward, but he could see that I was deeply troubled by Dave's plight, and I told him what had happened. In fact, I put down on tape for him the entire story, assuring him that Dave had actually done nothing improper, and Teddy said he'd look into the matter and see what he could do to help clear Dave's name.

To this day I don't know where Teddy went, or to whom

he spoke, but he called me a few days later and said that for two thousand dollars he could absolutely guarantee that Dave would never be called as a witness and that he would never be prosecuted for any illegal or improper activities.

"How can you do that?" I asked, hoping he'd have some convincing explanations for me. Teddy, as I should have known, wasn't about to share anything with me beyond asking for money, so I told him I'd get back to him as soon as possible. I immediately called up Dave and he said the whole thing sounded impossible. Dave's lawyer agreed. But lo and behold, as they say in the fairy tales of yore, each time Dave was supposed to be subpoenaed to appear before the actual commission, the appearance was postponed. And it kept getting postponed right up to the week the Knapp Commission was dissolved.

It was because of Teddy's help with Dave and because of the legal "magic" he seemed to have—he told Xaviera and me about all sorts of wonderful things he had done to help convict dishonest judges, congressmen, and state legislators—that I was persuaded to get involved with him to help trap a certain New York State Supreme Court judge. I will have a lot to say about my unhappy relationship with Teddy Ratnoff—and other unsavory people—later in this book, but suffice to say here that if Teddy hadn't helped Dave, neither Xaviera nor I would have gotten so entangled with him and several things wouldn't have happened.

Xaviera would never have gone before the grand jury in connection with Ted Ratnoff's illegal bugging of her apartment.

She would never have been identified by name, during the open sessions of the Knapp Commission, as the madam from whom Phillips took money. Her initials, not her name, were supposed to have been used, but Phillips, being angry, used Xaviera's name as well as Ratnoff's. This was unfortunate, but in another sense it helped make her fortune because the publicity attendant to her Knapp Commission appearances helped her gain a six-figure advance from the publisher of *The Happy Hooker,* her first book. And the book was "crashed"—rushed out—to take advantage of all that extraordinary publicity. And her name and picture were used on it.

And remember, the original plan was to identify Xaviera as "Madam X"—and if not for the events to which I've just referred, the name Xaviera Hollander would not have become a household name in many countries. All because of a pretty dumb robbery.

I'm not saying *The Happy Hooker* wouldn't have been a publishing success, but not *such* a success—nearly seven million copies in print!—and "Madam X" wouldn't have gone on television, radio, and publicity tours.

Of course my life has also changed as a result of my knowing Teddy Ratnoff—and I do plan to have a lot to say about that in this book—but not as much as Xaviera's life has changed.

Oh, yeah. The owner of that East Forty-fourth Street place never returned the watches. Or the money.

Big surprise.

PART TWO

SO X HITS THE SPOT . . .
BUT WHEN DID YOU FIRST
PASS "GO"?

CHAPTER 9.

What's a nice Jewish businessman doing in situations like this?

This is a question I've asked myself on several thousand occasions—as perhaps you've done on at least one point in this book—and I guess there's no rational explanation for the strange routes the affairs of the heart take.

In any case, I was born a Gemini on June second. I had a pretty happy childhood, although it saddened me that my older brother—since his birthday was January twenty-eighth for six months of the year he was four years older than me and for the other six, he was five years older—was sickly, suffering from the condition then known as St. Vitus dance and, later on, tuberculosis, poor kid!

My editor and I have argued about how extensive this section should be—he's Bob Abel, the same editor who's midwifed Xaviera's three books into existence—but we've finally agreed that I should share with you just some passing memories and impressions, and not bore you with too much biographical material—and that's how we'll do it.

As I've implied, my parents were truly kind and loving to me, and I've certainly no complaints in that department. Color my childhood in Manhattan's Inwood section yellow —a bright color for happy—and you've pretty much shared how I feel about it.

There was just one event to mar my youth. My parents, being good Jewish parents, decided I should study music, and I began my career as a concert pianist at age four. And, if I do say so myself, I had "pretty good chops," as they say in jazz circles. But an Arthur Rubinstein I wasn't.

In any case my career as a budding Dave Brubeck or José Iturbi was nipped in the bud, quite literally, when I lost most of the small finger—the "pinky" finger, as we called it in those days—on my right hand. I was eight years old, and was climbing a picket fence at school to pick up a penny pencil sharpener I'd seen on the other side. Don't ask me why I climbed that fence for a lousy little pencil sharpener—when you're an eight-year-old boy, you do such things, and unfortunately I suffered the consequences.

I got over the fence and down the other side successfully, and had gotten back, with the pencil sharpener in my pocket, when I decided to jump down to the playground, but a ring on my pinky finger—probably something I'd gotten from sending away cereal-box tops, and which only fit my smallest finger—somehow got caught on the top picket. I fell to the ground and part of my hand stayed on the fence. Again, remember what boy kids can be like—I climbed back up the fence and retrieved the part of my finger I'd accidentally left behind, and then trotted off to see the school doctor. Like a good little martyr, I politely waited my turn until the school nurse saw what had happened to me, and then, reacting to *her* reaction, I almost fainted.

The doctors decided to amputate most of the finger because of their fear of gangrene—they didn't have the steps to prevent gangrene from developing that they do today—and so I lost most of that finger. Naturally self-conscious because of my right hand, I refused to play the piano any longer, and to tell the truth, I'm self-conscious about it to this day.

When I was around ten years old I developed a big white streak in my jet-black hair. A lot of the kids in the neighborhood teased me about it, kidding me that it was "a streak of yellowness coming out." However, since there was nothing I could do about it, I decided to like it. I thought it was cute. So did the girls. For the first time, about women, I'd guessed right. . . .

As a kid I went to summer camp for six or seven years in the Catskills. I loved it and had real good times there. I received a lot of awards for sports activities, and if nothing else, playing sports helped me grow up in one way—toward the sky. When I was nine or ten I was five feet six inches tall, but in one summer I grew to be six feet tall. But the only way I grew *was* up—I was the skinniest kid in camp, year in and year out. People used to ask me if my father was a glazier because, they quipped, they could see through me and count my ribs. I also heard, more times than I care to remember, that whenever I turned sideways, they couldn't see me. And it was almost true. At eighteen or nineteen, I still only weighed one hundred twenty-two pounds, and even after the army, two years later, I weighed about the same.

Camp was such good fun that I later went back there as a waiter, and I came to develop some tolerance for the kind of brat *I'd* been when I was a kid there. My specialty was catching snakes and putting them into the other kids' beds. Later on I was to catch a few snakes in other people's beds. The two-legged variety.

Looking back upon it, I think I prefer the garden variety I knew about in those youthful days.

At thirteen I started to think about girls. At that time we lived on West End Avenue and Ninety-seventh Street, and the big thing on the west side, for kids in their early teens, was the weekend party—chaperoned, of course. Some kids managed to kiss and pet, but that was the extent of our sex lives. A few kids who were more advanced than the rest of us—or else just more lucky—claimed to have "gotten bare tit" or to have finger-fucked someone, but for most of us it was a big event when we even got to squeeze some girl's breasts. There were a few occasions when a lot of kissing and touching led to some "dry-fucking," or "dry-humping," as others have known it, where you and the girl got your legs intertwined and sort of banged away at each other. Any girl who'd do that was considered really hot stuff.

I'm not sorry I missed the so-called Sexual Revolution,

but there was certainly something I missed from those days. Oh, well, I had lots of company.

Because the life we led was fairly sheltered during our early teens, it was a very, very sexy occasion when one of the neighborhood doormen—remember that my old neighborhood was composed of brownstones on the cross streets, except for the major ones—West Ninety-sixth, Eighty-sixth, Seventy-ninth, and Seventy-second Streets, and large apartment buildings on the major boulevards close to the Hudson river—Broadway, West End Avenue, and Riverside Drive—informed our gang that he'd gotten some new 8 mm stag films, and for fifty cents a head we would be able to watch them.

For a kid this age, in those days, that was a hefty admission price, but somehow we all managed to afford it— this may be where the expression "beg, borrow or steal" had its start. We'd plan a week in advance to allow every guy a chance to get the money, and to be able to be out for a while that evening, and then we'd tell the doorman to set up the screening.

The theater was whatever vacant apartment existed in that building, and the screen was the wall. As for the projection equipment, it was a rare theater party where the projector didn't break down every other reel. As for the audience, it was a rare viewer who didn't have some kind of spot on the front of his trousers when the films were done. For most of us, it was our first introduction to sex real or reel.

The rule was, you just didn't look at the other guy's pants when the films were over.

When I finally started to date, on a one-to-one basis—no party situations where you arrived with all your pals—I also started to stutter. The only way I could be sure of getting the words out was to plot ahead of time what I wanted to say and then let the words spill out a mile a minute, as they used to say. Otherwise I would be the quietest date in town.

Some of my so-called friends used to mimic my stuttering, but girls didn't seem to mind—I was tall and lanky and fairly good-looking. And, for better or worse, there were more silver threads among the otherwise black hair on my young head.

Anyhow, who had much time for girls! Afternoons in the fall we'd go down to Riverside Drive and play football. Then there was roller skating and punch ball, which is strictly a city game. You hit the ball with your fist at home plate —usually the round metal lid of a sewer—and then run around the bases set up in the street. And stoop ball, where you hit the ball against the front steps or the side of a building. If the ball was caught on the fly or the first bounce off the wall across the street, you were out. Otherwise, it counted —one bounce was a single, two bounces ranged as a successful double, and so on. We had terrific fielders, and a triple or home run were sure hard to come by. When you don't have regular playing fields for baseball, you invent games that work—and are great fun—within the confines of your block, and I know city kids still play these games. Anyhow, with football and curb ball and stoop ball, who had time for girls?

If our maturing minds were occupied with sports, sometimes our maturing bodies became a mite preoccupied with sex. I must have been fourteen when my virginity was finally taken. I didn't give it up willingly, you understand—it was *taken*.

I'd been playing stick ball in the gutter—still another city game—in front of my building when one of my buddies came over to me and whispered something to me that meant my Great Moment had at last arrived.

"Hey, Larry," he confided, "there's a girl downstairs who's playing with all the guys."

"Oh, yeah . . ." I said, ever the sophisticate. I really wondered what he meant by *playing*. I mean, here I was playing stick ball . . . did he mean that she was playing stick ball, too?

"You gonna go down there?" he asked.

"Oh, sure," I said, wondering if there was any way to get out of this one. I could always plead a sudden case of appendicitis, or yellow fever, or something like that, but I sort of trailed him as he led me through a side door into the basement and then over to a room where, I knew, brooms and other kinds of cleaning equipment were stored.

"She's in there," he said, and left me. As a matter of fact, he left me fairly quickly, running out of the basement. I wanted to follow him but I was too ashamed of what my friends out on the street would think, so I finally opened the door. I honestly expected the whole thing to be a gag of some sort, but no, there was a girl there who looked to be in her late teens or maybe even her early twenties. She had black hair and to me she looked like Venus de Milo. She was sitting on a pile of newspapers and she motioned for me to shut the door behind me and join the club.

I slowly went over to her and she started to fumble with my pants. By the time she got them down there was a big stiff penis staring her in the face, and she certainly seemed pleased by my response to her.

When I got out with the guys in the street I raved about how terrific it'd been—"Boy, we fucked like crazy!"—and how much she'd liked me, but the truth of the matter is that the second she touched my penis I came all over her dress.

She wasn't amused. In fact she looked as though she would've strangled me if I weren't a lot taller than she was. I hope she was able to get that spot out of her dress.

For the next couple of years, since I was now so experienced and expert about sex, I somehow managed to do without it. Not that I was antisocial. No, I dated a lot, but I suspect that my early stuttering on dates and that one abortive sexual encounter made me be something of a loner.

While most of my chums went out on double dates and triple dates and so on, I preferred to date by myself, and I did enjoy these evenings. I rarely went to the movies with a girl or to dance halls, like other guys did, but I did take them to places where we could dance—restaurants and hotels—and get a good meal. The meal part was important because, as I figured it, for every dollar I spent on the date, hadn't I spent fifty cents of it on myself?

These, of course, were weekend nights when I went out,

97

and even if I wasn't making any great progress as a lover, I was having fun. I saved my money during the week, spent it on the weekend on someone I liked, and even if my reward was only a goodnight kiss at the door, it didn't bother me. If nothing else, I was gaining more confidence with people, and girls in particular. My penis had spoken for me much too quickly that one time, but at least I didn't stutter with girls any more. In fact I used to go out with the prettiest girls in the neighborhood. Other guys were afraid to ask them out for fear of being turned down.

Anyhow, could I help it if my penis wasn't as articulate as I now was with girls . . . ?

As I moved into my first years of high school, I was really having a fine old time with my friends. Sometimes we'd just meet as a gang in front of various Broadway stores—our favorite was Ellman's at the corner of Broadway and Ninetieth Street— or gather at some ice-cream parlor for an ice-cream-cone orgy. But our really special interests were indoor sports, and I don't mean what you think I mean.

On every major cross street there were ping-pong parlors and pool halls—or billiard parlors, as some were called—and heaven to me in those days was a Ninety-sixth Street hangout for us kids that included facilities for ping-pong, pool, and bowling. I won't say I developed into the best ping-pong player on the upper west side, but I *was* about fifteenth in a group which included some of the nation's finest players. Our crowd included players like Dick Miles, Eddie Pinner, Saul Schiff, and Lou Pagliero, all of whom came to enjoy national ranking in the sport. As for billiards and pool, I seldom play anymore but I can still pick up a cue and run a rack. You see, early childhood training *is* important. . . .

We used to meet at the pool hall before we went out on dates. Then, after we took our dates home, we'd reconvene at the pool hall to recreate the evening's activities. At that point in the evening by far the most popular indoor sport was lying, and each and every one of us accepted that probably each and every one of us was lying about how well he'd made out that evening. Hell, if any of us had really had a chance to stay with a girl that evening, he wouldn't be at the pool hall telling us about it.

Still, looking back at this time, it was really kind of sweet. Since it was kind of accepted that no one was really sexually involved with anyone else, it was easy to form a large group of friends, male and female, who would want to be together each weekend. My close pal Buddy and I had two females friends we liked to see, and the four of us soon enough grew into a group of some thirty or forty young people. We were fortunate in that I'd met a girl named Chesna, whose parents had a giant penthouse apartment in a Central Park West building called The Century, that we were often allowed to use for parties. Buddy also knew some girls whose parents let them use their large west side apartments for parties, so there was a constant menu of parties on weekends, and we were all close and together a lot of the time. Some of us formed a club called *the Whippets* and even got blue club jackets proclaiming how "with-it" we were.

In retrospect, some of the nicest times were on Sunday evenings when a bunch of us would gather at Ellman's (the owner of this restaurant had formerly been in the garage business, and while the Broadway Ellman's is no longer in business, the Ellmans are now the biggest restaurateurs in Manhattan with their Cattleman and other chains of eateries) or the Tiptoe Inn at Broadway and Eighty-sixth Street—a really cavernous place which had a main dining room stretching from Eighty-sixth to Eighty-seventh Streets —to have dinner. I can't imagine kids doing this today—at any given time there were fifty or sixty of us sitting at the tables. We were allowed to go in and just keep filling the tables until there was no more space left for us. It was a sight the waiters were used to, and so were the regular patrons of these places, but today it would make some people wonder if the Revolution were starting. . . .

CHAPTER 10.

On occasion Xaviera has accused me of not acting my age. And friends have sometimes said, "Larry, do you plan to ever grow up—why do you kid around so much?"

Well, I think I kid around because it's fun to do so— if you absorb all the bad news that's available in the papers and on television and radio in any one given day, you could easily become a hermit—and because I'm too busy enjoying life to become an austere, so-called "dignified" person.

As a kid at the movies I would sometimes borrow my date's lipstick, rub some on my fingers, then put an arm around one of my friends and give the side of his face a little lipstick job. He'd know what I was doing, of course, but not before it looked as though he'd been smooching up a storm. It was silly, harmless fun.

Sometimes, as teenagers, we'd go to a Chinese restaurant as a group and if someone admired the teapot, I'd call the waiter over and ask if we couldn't have a box for some food to go, and then I'd pick up the teapot, put it into the box, and walk out with it.

Today, if I see a couple of salt shakers I like I'll manage to slip them into a friend's pocket. When they're discovered, a bit later on, I'll say, "Okay, I'm sorry I made you an accomplice to the crime—give them back to me and I'll take all responsibility when the feds close in on us." This is fun for me, a kind of moving away from the cares and troubles of the day. I don't think I hurt that Chinese restaurant when I took the teapot and I don't think the salt shakers were meant to remain indefinitely on the table.

Looking back upon those teenager days, the only really mean thing we did was to make a lot of dates for my brother. Two friends, Betty and Bernie, were over at the house and we found my brother's address book and decided to improve our social lives. Under Betty's direction, we went through the book from A to Z, calling every appropriate girl (Betty decided who was appropriate). Bernie and I took turns, each time saying that we were a good friend of Donald's, and making dates with most of the girls we reached. The funny thing was that Bernie ended up marrying Florence—one of the girls he called from the address book.

Bernie and Buddy were probably my two best male friends, but Buddy was my oldest and closest friend. We specialized in getting into trouble together. Buddy's parents owned a drugstore on Broadway between Ninety-ninth and One hundredth Streets, and he was able to get plenty of doctor's prescription slips which we used to "play sick" on any day we wanted to play hooky. Buddy and I both attended DeWitt Clinton High School, and many days my phone rang at seven A.M.—the signal for cutting class that day. We'd go to the old Paramount Theater in downtown Manhattan to catch Benny Goodman or Artie Shaw. The first few times the truant officer caught us because we were standing in line with our books, but then we got wise —a friend worked at a nearby Nedick's and we'd leave our books there when catching the show.

This "sickness" routine was great fun, but it's a wonder I got through high school, having accumulated so many sick days. In fact at first they wouldn't let me take my regents exams because the rules say you're ineligible to take the tests, whatever your grades, if you've missed too many days of school.

As we got old enough to drive, we of course wanted to get behind the wheel of a car as often as possible. Buddy's parents had no car, and when Bernie wanted to borrow his father's car we always had a problem. Bernie's father was a wholesale meat supplier, so he worked long hours, and when he relaxed he liked to play pinochle at home or at a friend's house—so some nights he'd go to sleep early and some nights pretty late. If we wanted to borrow the car—and I do mean borrow—we had to make sure that in the morning it was back in the same parking spot from which we'd removed it the night before. So we'd take enough garbage cans from the side of the building and roll them into the gutter so no respectable guy would be tempted to put his car in that spot. When we returned from our evening's activities, we removed the garbage cans and parked. It always worked.

Bernie had to deliver kosher meat for his father on Thursday so that the butchers would have it first thing Friday morning and sell it by sundown. He had the key to every butcher shop on his route. On this particular Thursday night, it was Christmas Eve and we were waiting in the poolroom for Bernie to come back so we could all go out and do something, he returned with a bottle of rye he'd swiped from a butcher shop while making his deliveries. There were five of us there and we passed the bottle around, just like real he-men in a western movie. Since our usual drinking was limited to one sloe gin fizz consumed over the course of an evening's date, we all got rapidly loaded and were convinced we were having a helluva good time.

When we killed the bottle Bernie said, "Come on down to my father's place—he's got a bottle in his desk drawer." We all piled out of the poolroom and as pie-eyed as we were, were a bit surprised to see that our mode of transportation would be Bernie's father's truck. Only two of us could sit in the front, with the rest of us holding on to meat hooks. For dear life, I might add.

Bernie was really loaded and his idea of good clean fun just then was to drive thirty or forty miles per hour and then hit the brakes. We could all have been impaled, and I seem to remember that I arrived home with a hole in my collar.

When we got to Bernie's father's store and parked the truck, we went inside, busted into his father's desk drawer, and proceeded to get the drunkest we'd ever been before.

102

Bernie had to leave the truck there and somehow we all got home on the subway. Bernie passed out so I got him home, got the key out of his pants, and brought him into the house. His parents never knew a thing—until the morning.

"When I finally woke up I was tucked in my bed, my clothes off," Bernie told me later. "My mother must have found me on top of the bed and taken care of me. . . . That was *some* night!"

Yeah, some night. After I got Buddy home and left his apartment building, *I* passed out. Some neighbors found me out cold on the sidewalk, leaning against Buddy's building, and managed to drag me around the corner to my parent's home. They put me to bed, too.

I flatter myself that I'm a very good driver, and a careful driver, but in those days, I must say, I was more than a little lucky that I was never involved in an accident. My father, who was in the construction business and knew very well about accidents, was nonetheless very liberal about letting his seventeen-year-old son borrow the car whenever I wanted it. In those days Buddy and I liked to drive up to Westchester on the Boston Post Road and hit places like the Post Lodge and Bill Reaver's, and I would get sleepy from drinking sometimes, though never getting drunk or ill. Since Buddy was a great driver on the highway, I'd drive the car to the highway and he'd take over from there. And on the way back, we had an agreement: if I'd fallen asleep and we were coming to a toll booth, Buddy would pull over to the side of the road, wake me up, and I'd drive through the toll booth.

He was afraid that the space was too narrow for him to drive through.

As I say, it's fortunate that our luck was wider than those toll booths, or neither Buddy nor I might be around now to laugh at those days.

Of course I used my father's car for something more than a vehicle to get me and my chums from one watering hole to another. No more necking in hallways when you could hug and neck in the front seat of your father's car

103

(if you made it to the back seat, you'd truly made it) and wish that collapsible steering wheels had already been invented.

For about six months before I went into the army I had been dating a girl named Marilyn Rabi, a very pretty, dark-haired girl with dimples and a voluptuous body, who lived in that fantastic twin-towered Beresford apartment building on Eighty-first Street and Central Park West. It may be an exaggeration to say that Marilyn taught me more about sex than all the other girls I'd dated, but then I *was* pretty naive and she certainly did give me my first "head start" introduction to the facts of life. And I was a slow learner.

I recall one night in particular when we were necking in the car, with not much in the way of clothing on, and I was caressing Marilyn's wonderful breasts with their large nipples, kind of amazed that they still pointed up even when she was laying on her back. I was so damned pleased to have these wonderful boobs in my hands and mouth that at first I didn't hear her whispering to me. Finally she put her lips to my ear and whispered, "Larry."

I wasn't quite sure about what she wanted me to do, but I wasn't going to let *her* know that, and I started to massage her down there. After four or five minutes, she almost screamed with frustration.

"Larry, that's my pubic hair. Rub down below. . . ."

I did what I was told, or thought I did, but after a minute or so she took one of my fingers and guided it between the lips of her vagina, moving my finger around in little circles and back and forth.

"There . ." she said, "*that's* more like it."

She certainly seemed to be having a good time, which pleased me, and now she had that finger higher up, moving against something which wiggled around against my finger, and that really set her off.

"Oh, Larry, that's really soooo good."

I still didn't know exactly what it was I was doing that was "soooo good," and I was certainly getting hot and bothered, but I didn't have the nerve to ask her to do anything for me. But my penis was thrusting against my jockey

104

shorts and when her hand brushed against it, she got the idea. Mental telepathy couldn't have done it more efficiently.

As I moved my finger—now two fingers—around inside Marilyn's pussy, she was squeezing and rubbing my still-virgin penis, and in about a minute my father's seat covers needed some dry cleaning.

For her part, Marilyn had been making all sorts of happy crazy noises and when we finally quieted down and just hugged each other, she said, "Larry, I love it when you rub my clitoris—it feels wonderful."

Hmmmmm, so that's what I was doing. Now I had to find out what a clitoris was.

Marilyn and I saw each other constantly before I went into the army, but we never became more intimate than we were that night, and my father's seat covers continued to take a beating. Just before the time for my induction—my buddy, Buddy, was also going in at the same time—there was a giant party for us at Chesna's apartment with about a hundred friends to say good-bye—"so long," hopefully, since the war was on—and I guess it was more or less assumed that Marilyn was my steady girl and we were more or less informally engaged. As for Marilyn and myself, we'd agreed to keep in touch while I was in the service, but I didn't ask her to wait for me, or not to date, or anything like that. She'd been my girlfriend, but I didn't expect her to become a nun on my account.

However, she did come along with my father when I went downtown to be inducted, but the moment I remember most fondly about that day was when my father took me aside, mumbled a few things about V.D. and the like, and then said, "Son, I can't be with you the rest of your life, standing behind you to looking over your shoulder. You may be traveling all over the world now, and you're going to meet an awful lot of people. I never insisted that you went to temple or read the religious books, but I would like you to have the same philosophy I have. If you follow this, it's all the religion you'll ever need."

"What's that, dad?" I asked, deeply touched by what he was trying to say to me. We'd never talked this way before.

"Well, I don't know—it may sound, maybe corny, to you, but I've really tried to live by the golden rule, and so the only thing I would like you to try to do, if you possibly can, is don't hurt anybody. Live by that rule, son, and I don't think you'll have too many problems in this world. . . ." With that he slapped me on the back, I kissed Marilyn "so long," and boarded the bus to take me to Fort Dix.

I'd like to say that ever since that day I've tried to live this way, and I've added one sentence to it: Do whatever you want to do, as long as your actions don't hurt anybody. I'm an easygoing guy who will help anyone if he can, but I've got to admit that there've been many, many times when I've had my help thrown back in my face. But, no matter—I guess there are some of us who'll keep throwing the proverbial petals upon the water in the hope we'll get some of them returned to us. . . .

PART THREE

FINALLY GROWING UP:
OH, CALCUTTA!

CHAPTER 11.

A lot of guys had horrible times in the service, but for a lot of us it was a time to grow up. And you could grow up without having been in actual combat. I know I did.

After basic training at Fort Dix, where I first learned the meaning of the expression "You'll freeze your ass off," I went to Augusta, Georgia, where my unit, the 809th Ordinance Company, was stationed at the Augusta arsenal. The duty itself was pretty soft since we worked at the arsenal itself and were off at four P.M. till nine A.M. the next day, and weekend passes were fairly easy to come by. And there were three thousand reasons to want an overnight or weekend pass: the civilian women who worked at the arsenal along with our unit of a hundred eighty men.

It was during this time that I finally lost my virginity, and I still remember with relish some of those sultry Southern voices murmuring nifty notions into my grateful young Yankee ears, but more meaningfully, it was living away from home and being with guys from various parts of the country that made these months the beginning of my growing-up process. After years of not getting laid, that suddenly wasn't a problem anymore, but getting along with a lot of guys I had to share quarters with, whether I liked it or not—that was a maturing experience. Maybe without realizing it, I'd been getting ready for this experience via those giant "chow" sessions we used to have at the Tiptoe Inn, but those were all kids from the same neighborhood and the same ethnic backgrounds, and this was surely different. And therefore very valuable, especially since our unit stayed together throughout the war.

So far we'd been in the States, but I learned we were soon to ship out—and without the furlough we'd all been solemnly promised we'd have before leaving the country. I called home to say I wouldn't be coming home this war (at least before it was ended), which must have sent my parents into a frenzy of political action. I don't know if it was fair—after all, we *had* all been promised we'd see our parents at least once before we left the country—but my parents had the gumption to buck the armed forces and called upon a close friend of the family, a senior member of Congress, to see that furloughs were granted as promised. And they were.

Our company commander somehow found out that I had been at least partially responsible for the order from Way On High permitting furloughs, and he called me in to explain that he wasn't thrilled that I had created this situation, and that I would live to regret it. I wasn't exactly thrilled myself to learn he'd singled me out, but I now recognized that he was just probably afraid that I somehow possessed political clout which could hurt him if I ever decided to use it.

There's no question in my mind that he was legitimately angry then, but the truth is that I never had any problems with him. If I was some threat to his authority, of course he should resent it—on the other hand, don't *promise* GIs they'll see their loved ones before going overseas if this a promise easily broken at the convenience of the military. Men fighting for their country are fighting for their loved ones—and that's what it's all about, isn't it? Your government should lie to you.

I got home, had a glorious leave, saw a lot of Marilyn, and *still* didn't sleep with her! I later learned that while I'd only written her about once a month, she regarded the bind between us as something fairly serious, and during the long months I was overseas, she spent a lot of time in my parents' house having dinner with them, sharing with them the letters I wrote to her, and wanting to hear about the letters I wrote them. I mean it in all sincerity when I say that I was very pleased with the attention she was paying my parents—and me, by reflection—but I couldn't imagine that she was being celibate on my behalf, nor should she be. I was thousands of miles away, and she was a very healthy young woman.

To be perfectly honest, the letters I was getting from her were frightening the shit out of me. They were often mostly about the sexual goodies we were going to share when I got back, and what she was going to do to me when she got me alone in her apartment. Instead of treating these letters as the evidence of a loving young woman's affection, I wondered if she'd become some kind of nymphomaniac.

That's how naive I still was about people's feelings. All she was saying to me was how much she wanted to be with me physically, like any loving couple, but I'd never shared that kind of intimacy with a woman before, and couldn't understand her very normal feelings when I encountered them in writing. I never wrote her anything which indicated that I was at all unsettled by what she was saying to me via her letters—hell, I didn't write enough for that—but I simply wasn't mature enough to appreciate a young woman's growing sexual feelings for me. Perhaps because my sexual encounters in the army had all been physical but never emotional, I misinterpreted Marilyn's letters to me. It's no tragedy, but it was strong evidence of how emotionally immature I still was in those days.

Let me tell you, the first time a nice Jewish boy from Manhattan's west side, a wonderful mixing pot of ethnic solidarity, left home to go overseas, he would expect to go to Europe, from where his parents or their parents or their parents' parents had emigrated to America. Of course, if he were in his right mind, he would not care to become an actor in what was then the major theater of war. In any case, no one *asked* me where I cared to go.

Our first stop was Oran, in what is now Algeria, on our way to India, and then we moved out into the Mediterranean again. While sailing through the Mediterranean, a bunch of us were up on deck watching dogfights between

110

Allied and Axis airplanes, ignoring the air-raid signals which meant we were supposed to be down below. We didn't see that we were in any danger. The hell we weren't!

The German planes were equipped with aerial torpedoes, and our planes weren't able to keep some of them from attacking the ships in our convoys and one of those bastard Nazi pilots was able to drop a torpedo down the smokestack of one of our sister ships. It was awful—the ship just exploded and fell apart before our eyes. Thousands of GIs and sailors were killed—they never had a chance—although, thank God, many others were rescued. It was a sight indelibly etched in my mind, and—apart from the deaths of my parents—probably the worst single moment of my life. One minute thousands of guys were alive—the next they belonged to the sea.

Furthermore, what I'd witnessed was not only a tragedy of epic proportions, it was a terrible historic occasion. We learned, a year and a half later via a small article appearing in a British newspaper, that that sinking had been the worst single transport disaster of the war because over four thousand men had died at sea. The article also said that this was the first use of that type of weapon—an electrically controlled torpedo.

So far as I know, the news of that sinking was never announced in America and the only reason it appeared in that British newspaper was that the ship was of British registry. A stamp commemorating that sinking, known as the Four Chaplains stamp, was issued after the war, in 1948.

An irony about all this is that I was up on the deck despite orders to be below. The danger, we'd been told, was from the enemy planes strafing our ship. But I'd seen too many submarine movies to go below deck, and if more of those poor guys on that ship that was hit had been on deck, more would have lived.

While we witnessed other aerial battles en route to India, our convoy wasn't attacked again and the biggest event on board our ship was the number of guys who finally stopped being seasick. One reason I stayed on deck so much is that it was often a nonstop vomitorium below deck. Another reason was that I played poker all day.

After an ocean voyage which took a total of ninety days (America to Africa to India) and which was the longest I've ever taken—and one I would never care to repeat— we finally reached India, and were informed that we were among the first thousand American troops to arrive there. Later on I learned, to my sorrow, that I'd be among the last thousand troops to leave there—being ordnance personnel, we handled all the military supplies for the Army and Air Force in India and Burma, and when the war was won, at last, they declared all of us essential personnel, despite our length of service, because we had to deal with all of the tons of supplies in India, Burma, and other parts of the Far East involved in the war against Japan. We were to categorize it and have it prepared to be sold, destroyed or shipped back to the United States. When I finally did come home, I had been in India for over three years.

CHAPTER 12.

Our unit was stationed in Calcutta, and while I of course missed my parents, my home, and my friends, being in India was truly an extraordinary experience. Nowhere else have I seen such natural beauty—and such beautiful architecture—side by side with such poverty and deprivation.

Once you have experienced certain sights, you will never forget them. Whenever there was an epidemic of cholera, which there was periodically, the bodies were piled up on the street corners. Eventually a truck would come along and collect them. Those who had been wealthy were burned on funeral pyres. The bodies of the poor were just dumped into the Hooghly river and floated downstream—I remember that what I first thought from a distance was a broad sandy beach turned out to be huge piles of skeletons that had been washed up on shore down the river.

Then there was the terrible starvation. Just thirty to fifty miles away food was rotting on the vines, but in Calcutta thousands and thousands of people were literally starving to death. There was only one railroad bringing food into the city—the few trucks and cars belonging to the Indians were used for official purposes—and everywhere you looked there were children with big, swollen bellies.

We deliberately ate less than full meals so we could give them food, but the daily, painful sight to which we eventually had to become accustomed was these hundreds of kids lined up around our mess hall waiting for the garbage to be brought out so they could go through the pails and satisfy a little bit of hunger. At first a lot of the guys actually broke down and cried when they saw these kids doing this, but finally we became used to the sight (but not hardened to the sight, that *never* happened) and we were grateful that we well-fed GIs produced a lot of garbage for these kids to scavenge through and find food. It sounds awful, but it helped them manage to survive. These kids looked old far beyond their years, and their parents, who were in their twenties and thirties, all looked like old people. But so few of them lived long enough to become elderly people—in those days the average life span for an Indian was probably twenty-nine or thirty years.

People in Calcutta worked for pennies a day. When we arrived there, the British were paying the equivalent of between eight cents and twelve cents a day for native labor, and we began paying twenty cents a day for the same work. For some laborers, it got up to thirty cents a day—yes, I know, *coolie wages*—which meant that their months pay wouldn't be much more than seven or eight dollars. But

113

pathetically enough, there was never any shortage of men to work at those rates.

When I went to work in the mornings the hills surrounding our depot buildings looked as though they were covered by white flowers—the coolies (the term refers to any unskilled Oriental laborers, in case it offends you) would be sitting in their white garbs, in hunched positions, all over these hills. We would strike a bell, and they would line up in teams of fifteen or so men selected by an overseer. And the overseers had overseers—one for every six gangs and then one for this level of overseer, and so on—in other words, a chain of command. And guess who was at the top of this chain command—yours truly, who was only a technical sergeant but who had earned at war's end a very rare M.O.S. number (Military Occupational Speciality). In point of fact, I was told that there were just five such M.O.S. numbers in the entire U.S. Army, and these were only assigned to noncommissioned officers whose job put them in charge of thousands of men.

On any given day I would be in charge, as warehouse foreman, of roughly two thousand coolies plus a certain number of GIs, and what I was running was probably the largest ordnance depot in the world. We were the only ordnance depot supplying the entire Allied war effort in the CBI (China-Burma-India) area of operations. The Burma Road, in a manner of speaking, was built from our depot and I was on one of the first convoys to use that famous highway when it opened up. It wasn't exactly a four-lane highway, I'll tell you, and if a truck broke down, we just pushed it off the road or over the cliff or into a river, depending on whatever happened to be handiest.

With all that equipment at our disposal there could have been an enormous temptation to steal, but I didn't—it would have been easy to sell high-powered rifles to wealthy Indian businessmen for over a thousand dollars—and I don't think any of the other guys did either, although once we did create our own kind of free PX (post exchange) when a trainload of candy, cigars, and other goodies passed through. When the company commander found out we'd "warehoused" some of this stuff for our own use, he lined

114

up all the noncoms and said, "Look, fellas, if you're using this stuff for yourself, okay, but don't let me catch you selling any of it." And he didn't—because *we didn't*.

Essentially we were a bunch of young kids, very few of us with any decent education—my New York City high-school education placed me among the intellectual elite of this group, which is one reason I was put in charge of things—and we were happy not to be in a combat zone, although we were certainly doing our share to end the war. Our reward for doing such a good job was to have access to jeeps and materials for personal use, but there *was* one instance when we decided that we should be receiving another kind of reward.

When other army units arrived in the CBI zone—they could be ordnance companies, infantry units, artillery, whatever—the noncoms at our depot would have to train their officers on how to meet their equipment needs for this theater of war, so I would have colonels, majors, captains, and lieutenants working under my supervision before they were sent, as we put it, "up country." (Calcutta is located in eastern India, just north of the mouths of the Ganges and the Bay of Bengal.) Sometimes we'd work around the clock, weekends included, getting these officers ready to do their job, and we felt that our pay as corporals and sergeants wasn't really very fair. So we got a little crazy and decided to stage a sitdown strike, perhaps the only one in World War II. We could have been court-martialed—hell, we *should* have been court-martialed, according to military law—but instead Uncle Sam sent two generals, no less, to talk to us, and I must say they were very fair-minded about the situation. From that point on we were paid on a per-diem basis, instead of a monthly salary, and that helped some.

In point of fact, we lived very well indeed—when we weren't breaking our humps to get equipment and materials where it was needed or to train these officers how to do their job—compared to any front-line troops. Our mess hall was pretty good, as mess halls go, and our first barracks were a group of buildings called the Dum Dum Orphanage, which originally had been a school for orphan kids. This proved to be inefficient because we were too

115

far from the depot, so we moved into the city itself, quite literally in the middle of one of the largest racetracks in the world—I'm pretty sure it was *the* largest clockwise racetrack in the world—which we called Hialeah although the actual name of the track was the Tollygunj Club.

Our barracks were now newly constructed straw huts, which were quite spacious and really not so bad. More important, they were close to the center of Calcutta, and when we had enough time off and some money in our pockets, we'd have a meal at a restaurant called Firpo's, owned by the former heavyweight boxer, Luis Firpo. It was also fascinating to explore the main business street of the town, Chowringhee Street, the Fifth Avenue and Broadway combined of Calcutta. This was where the best hotels, including the Grand Hotel, and finest stores were located, and the sidestreets led to the various government houses. One sidestreet in particular, however, led to something less fine—the infamous prison known as the Black Hole of Calcutta.

There was one place off limits to GIs—an elaborate whorehouse on Quire Road where beautiful European girls—Swedes, French and many other nationalities—living in posh homes and employing native maids themselves, catered to the sexual desires of rich and titled Indians. They also serviced not a few visiting dignitaries and U.S. generals who, immediately upon arrival in Calcutta, would have us chauffeur them over to Quire Street.

Whatever the privileges I'd managed, a personal visit to the Quire Street establishment was *not* one of them, and so I say, thank God for the USO girls and the Red Cross girls! At least some of them would go out with a guy who didn't have brass on his shoulders.

I dated some of the local American girls, but nothing interesting happened in my social life until I met a girl from Tennessee, whose nickname was, of course, Tennessee, and with whom a relationship developed that lasted off and on for about a year and a half. It wasn't love, certainly, and it wasn't just sex, but it was something in between—and very good, I guess, for both of us. As for its being "off and on," sometimes an officer would ask her

116

to go out and I guess she couldn't say, "Sorry but I'm shacking up most nights with a tech sergeant," so she'd go out with the guy. But I'd generally be back in her arms the next night. Thinking back on how many times I was A.W.O.L. in Tennessee's bed and never got caught by the military police at her place, I can only assume that we Geminis are luckier than we perhaps deserve to be.

Generally I'd meet her about nine o'clock, when she got done at the service club, and we'd go to her place—a small, kind of charming hotel near my own place of residence—and make love from nine P.M. until two or three A.M., and then I'd return to my home away from home for a few hours of much-needed sleep. Given my nocturnal activities, it's a wonder the war in the Far East was won when it was. . . .

If Marilyn had been my introduction to real-life petting, Tennessee was my post-graduate education—which, I suspect, is always going on—to grown-up fucking. To describe Tennessee in strict physical terms is not to do justice to her. She was in her middle twenties and was very tall and fairly lanky. In male-chauvinist-pig terms, she had fine legs, a great ass, and small but very perky breasts. Her face was pleasant—not pretty—but when she smiled and turned on that Southern charm she was one of the most desirable ladies in town, the expensive stuff on Quire Road not excluded. Tennessee had marvelous large brown eyes, brunette hair worn in a bun—almost made her look school-marmish, but how sexy when she let it down at night—and one of the most sensuous mouths in creation.

To put it bluntly, she taught me what a great blow-job was all about, and I can still recall her murmuring, in her delicious Southern drawl, "Really, Larry honey, it's such fuh-un sucking you back hard. I mean, young boys like you are—well, *just always hard*—but you do care to give a girl an even break." By this she meant that she'd taught me, and I'd learned, that sex is a matter of sharing pleasure, not just receiving it. The first few times Tennessee went down on me I just popped my nuts in what seemed like seconds, but I soon learned that it was just more fun to prolong things and to make love to her, and while I

117

wasn't as proficient at oral love as she was, I was sure a willing pupil.

I'd lie there with her long legs draped over my shoulders, and move my mouth over her vagina and try to use my tongue in ways which most pleased her, and she'd murmur, "Oh, yes, Larry, that's *real* good . . . just fine . . . but try to get at the clit, too . . . yesss, that's some real home cookin' you're doin' down there . . . yes, that's good, real good. . . ."

I must confess that I knew I was never as good at what we guys then called *cunt lapping* as she must have wanted me to be, but I'd bring her to orgasm and then she'd go down on me again and ask me if I wanted to come that way. Of *course* I wanted to come that way—it felt so good I couldn't imagine anything feeling better—but I would make her stop if I knew I'd be too tired to fuck her if I came this time, so I'd pull her up into my arms and we'd cuddle a bit and then go into a real "down home" fuck. I'd never met a woman with such long legs as Tennessee, and she'd wrap them around my back, which felt "real good," and—a first for me—over my shoulders, which felt even better because it allowed for deeper penetration and when she came she'd let out a kind of Rebel howl of pleasure that could have been heard back on both sides of the Mason-Dixon line. I sometimes wondered why no one ever complained about Tennessee's noisy lovemaking, but I supposed there were lots of couples fucking in that little hotel, and it was more fun than a nuisance to hear someone else having a good time.

Tennessee and I were simply too different as people for anything to have come of it, but I'll always be grateful for the steady sex I enjoyed with her and the "French lessons" I learned from her. And her main lesson—that kindness and consideration make sex ever so much better.

While my relationship with Tennessee was the highlight of social life during those years in India, a lot of my buddies had worked out a different kind of arrangement which reminded me of that Alec Guinness movie, *Captain's Paradise,* where he maintains a double life with double wives. They'd get friendly with the wife of an English officer or noncom, and when those gentlemen had to go "upriver" to check out the British outposts in Burma or Ceylon or wherever, the American would move in and play house with the British wife. And nothing was thought improper about it. I'm not saying they advertised that they were living together, but certainly there was no sneaking around on the part of the GIs.

When it was time for the limey officer or noncom to return, he'd give fair warning and the American would move out. And next time, the same situation, or with a different wife. If that's not "musical beds," I don't know what is.

Occasionally a high-ranking officer or visiting dignitary would come to Calcutta and want to go hunting, and we provided the jeeps and guns for them to hunt alligators in the Bay of Bengal or tigers in the surrounding jungles. I went along on a few of these trips, and at the time I thought it was fun. Shooting at alligators, I felt like I was in some Tarzan movie and half expected Johnny Weissmuller to surface from the waters and thank the Great White Hunter for saving his life. Now, with so many species of animals and other creatures threatened, I think hunting for sport is a rotten affair.

Living in a foreign country, it's of course fascinating to see the land and the sights, but it's even more interesting to get to know the people. During those years in Calcutta I became friendly with Indians and the British and—here's that west-side background showing—quite a few members of the Indian-Jewish population of the city. I'd go to their houses for dinner and spend the Jewish holidays with them, and to tell the truth, it made me a little less homesick.

However, the most memorable experience for me in India was to meet and become friendly with quite a few of the followers of Mahatma Gandhi, and through them with the great man himself, as much "the father of his country" as any man who ever lived. His real name was Mohandas Karamchand Gandhi, but it was as Mahatma that he was became known to the world. Gandhi of course was a Hindu nationalist and spiritual leader who developed the traditions of passive resistance—a tradition later so important to our own civil-rights movement—but I was in awe of him because he had seen so much and had fought so long for social and economic reforms for his country and for its independence.

Our conversations were always polite exchanges—he spoke very slowly, but was very articulate—and most often dealt with the subject of violence. As soldiers, he said, we were violent people and he would become upset whenever Indians became violent against their British rulers. And there were a few occasions when his followers would stop our trucks or cars, turn them over, and set them on fire. I know this upset him greatly because his defiance of authority was always peaceful, be it his own hunger strikes or his programs of civil disobedience.

My lasting impressions of Mahatma Gandhi were of this terribly frail man in his seventies who burned with inner strength and conviction. When I arrived in India he was being held, along with other Indian leaders, in the Aga Khan's palace in Poona, but he was released because of failing health and immediately went back to working for Indian independence. I think he always hoped the Americans would reflect upon their own struggle for independence from the British and support his cause—but nonviolently.

When you were with him, you were so concerned about how terribly thin he was, but he never hesitated to fast as a form of protest. After the war, when independence was close to becoming a reality and bitter fighting broke out between Hindu and Moslem factions, he vowed to "fast unto death" if the bloodshed did not stop.

In 1947, he fasted to stop Hindu-Moslem rioting in Calcutta and in early 1948 he was again fasting to end the violence between Hindus and Moslems. On January thirtieth of that year he was assassinated by a young Hindu extremist named Godse, and his death produced new waves of violence in India.

But he was mourned all over the world as a man of peace, and I remember that when I read the news I mourned not only for the world's loss, but—in some small way—for my own.

After all, the advice my father had given me when I entered the service was not so very different from what Gandhi preached, and for those who would listen, there was a lot to learn.

PART FOUR

BACK HOME: A CAREER, AND GIRLS AS A CAREER

CHAPTER 13.

When I left India I was returned to San Pedro on the West Coast and I had so many discharge points that the Army was willing to let me handle my release from the service in whatever manner was convenient to me. That is, if I wanted to spend some time on the Coast before going east to be officially discharged, that was all right. Since I had family in Los Angeles and since I had never spent any time in southern California, I decided to stay a week or so there.

My uncle, who had been the voice teacher for Enrico Caruso, was now working for MGM studios and he showed me around town and even got me some dates with starlets. No great romantic episodes there, though it was kind of exciting to be with a different great-looking gal every night.

I was having a grand time in Los Angeles, but the tug of going home at last became too great to resist, so I got on a train to Fort Dix, once again a civilian. As anyone who has been in the service can tell you, it's a strange feeling when you walk out those gates and know you'll never have to salute anyone again or say "Yes sir!" to some clown whose abilities and intelligence don't command respect.

As I was traveling on the train from Fort Dix to New York City I began to think seriously about Marilyn. It'd been three years, and while she wrote me regularly and had kept in close touch with my parents, I wondered how the two of us would really feel about each other. When I arrived home at my parent's apartment, there they were along with Marilyn's parents, but no Marilyn. After all the kissing and embracing and crying and shouts of "Welcome home!" I asked about Marilyn and was informed that we were all having a big dinner to celebrate my return home, and I was to go over to the Rabis' home and pick her up for dinner.

I didn't need a second invitation, as they say. I raced downstairs, jumped into my father's car, and tore over to the Bereford on Eighty-first Street. I don't recall how I parked—I sure didn't waste any time looking for a legal parking space—and I got up to Marilyn's first-floor apartment as fast as I could. When she answered the door, we melted into each other's arms and it was a few minutes before I realized that she was only wearing a thin wrap, open in front, and some very sexy lingerie underneath.

I assumed this delicious exposure of flesh was there for me to enjoy, and in a very few minutes both Marilyn and I were on her living-room carpet—it hadn't even occurred to me that someone else might be home—undressed and playing with each other, and she was sure ready to welcome me home in proper style when once again the jackrabbit in me took over; I came even before I could get inside her.

We laughed about it, but I could see that she was disappointed and I promised to make amends. But we were expected for dinner at my parents' home, so we'd have to postpone our great "welcome home" fuck for a little while, at least.

On the way over to my parents' apartment she put her head on my shoulder and we talked about the years we'd been apart. She asked me if I'd been faithful to her, and I said yes—feeling that my shack-up affair with Tennessee was friendship mixed in with a lot of sex—and I asked her the same thing, and she said that she was still a virgin. I believed her and I guess she believed me—*I* wouldn't have, frankly, although my performance in her living room was convincing enough—and we started to talk about the future and it was clear that we shared everyone's assumptions

124

that eventually we'd get married. And if there were any doubts in *our* minds, when we got back to my parents' place, both our parents announced that there was to be an engagement party for us in about a month. I found this a little overwhelming, my first night back from the service, but agreed that it was a good idea.

The engagement party, a giant blast with a band and tons of food and drink and all our friends there, was held at her parents' apartment, and in the midst of all the dancing and drinking and merriment, I took Marilyn aside and asked her, "Hey, are we really in a rush to get married?"

"I'm not," she said. "Are you?"

"No . . . I have the feeling that we're doing this for our parents. Hell, I've still got to go to college and it'll be years before I can support a wife."

"Well, it seems to me that things have gotten out of hand—here we are, at our own engagement party, and no one has asked us if we really want to be engaged."

"What do you want to do about it?"

"Gee, I don't want to embarrass our parents, but. . . ."

I took Marilyn by the hand and we marched up to the main table where the food and drinks were being served, and still holding her hand, I climbed up on a bridge chair —and almost toppled off I was so anxious to make my announcement— and called for everyone's attention.

You could see by their faces that no one expected me to say what I was about to say, but I took a deep breath, looked down at Marilyn looking up at me, and then told the entire room: "Look, folks, this has been a grand excuse to get together and see each other again after all these months, but Marilyn and I have been talking it over and we've decided . . . well, we've decided that we're not ready to become engaged, much less married, and so we're breaking the engagement—by mutual consent. We're not unhappy, so don't you be. . . ."

If the faces of our friends registered surprise, or disbelief, our parents looked as though they'd gone into shock, and Marilyn looked as if she wanted to be anyplace but here, so I jumped down off the chair and, still holding hands, we ran out of the party.

We walked up and down Broadway for a while, deciding we'd done the right thing, and feeling closer than we'd ever been before as a result of having shared a somewhat difficult experience and having made the mature decision. But we never did get engaged, we never did get married and, I'm sorry to say, we never slept together. Because of the awkwardness of the disengagement party, we decided it'd be difficult to see each other in a dating situation, and so we managed to stay good friends by talking on the phone or else seeing each other in a crowd of people.

Finally she met someone from Philadelphia, fell in love with him, and married him. I wasn't surprised not to be invited to the wedding, and I've never regreted getting up on that bridge chair.

CHAPTER 14.

Marilyn and I really had made the realistic decision, because for the next two years I went full time to City College, studying to be a civil engineer. But I was also resuming my social life, and found it kind of silly to be constantly asking my father for money to go out at night— ten dollars here, twenty dollars there—although whatever I asked for was never refused.

I earned some money working for him in his construction business, and since I found I enjoyed it so much, I decided to work for him days and continue my schooling at night. Of course it took a long time to earn a degree that way, but it didn't matter since I intended to remain in my father's business and use my engineering knowledge in that field. This was a wise decision because we had a wonderful relationship together and knew the day would come when he would decide to take it a little easy—and work for me, instead of the other way around.

During these years I finally outgrew what had kept me so thin and began to fill out so that my height and weight had some relationship to each other. In fact I looked older than my brother because not only was I no longer a skinny kid, but my hair had taken on a salt-and-pepper look which made me appear quite a bit older than my twenties.

I did eventually get married, but that was some time later. All I really want to say about it is that my wife and I had two beautiful daughters, whom we both love dearly; and that our marriage was a good one—while it lasted. Things were great for about nine years, then things just sort of fell apart.

What I had painfully learned was that I still wasn't mature enough to make any kind of long-term commitment. In the ensuing years, I would be, but as I've learned the hard way, a lot of us would be emotionally healthier and happier if we responded to our emotions with the right kind of courage at the right time.

I was now finally out of college and working as a full-time adult, and whether or not I was emotionally mature, at least I was financially secure. I no longer had to ask my father for the money to take a woman out and possibly start a relationship. As it happened, I was finding that most affairs started by chance—often by taking a chance—and you couldn't plan your affairs. They mostly just—happened.

For instance, Beryl, a slim, very entrancing dark-haired friend, I met by the sheerest accident. I'd been working on major alterations for a Times Square dance parlor, and when the day was over I had a drink or two with the owner of the place, who was interesting because he knew everything there was to know about Times Square area real estate. He predicted that one day Times Square would be mostly office buildings, with theaters and restaurants on the lower floors—a trend we now see developing—but he was also pretty intriguing because he played "Big Daddy" to a lot of women in the area, be they hookers or famous showgirls.

One day this guy—Dan—said he was going to visit a "poor wounded bird" he knew, and asked me if I'd like to tag along. At first I was confused—was there some sentimental side of him I'd missed, despite his Times Square trappings, and were we actually going to visit an injured blue jay or sparrow he cared about?—so if nothing else, curiosity took me along.

The "bird"—the term didn't become fashionable until at least a decade after—was Beryl, and she had just come out of the hospital after a brutal beating administered by a guy who'd taken her out, wanted to sleep with her, and she repulsed his advances. Unfortunately for poor Beryl, he didn't want to take *no* for an answer, and beat her into unconsciousness.

When we were introduced I felt awkward about the situation—she was such a slim, pretty kid and the black eye and the bruises on her face somehow made her even more lovable—but she put me at ease right away.

"Hello, Larry," she said, "meet 'Virtue Wins by Default.'"

"Boy, you should see the other guy," I said, kidding. "*He* has two shiners."

"It wasn't a fair fight," she said, soberly and a bit defensively.

"Well, he didn't know you could kick that high, now did he?"

We all laughed and I knew right away that I liked her.

Knowing that she had to subsist mostly on liquids and soft foods—among other things, her friend had broken her jaw—I began visiting her regularly with home-made soup, scrambled eggs, ice cream and other soft foods she could easily handle. She'd eat her food very slowly, and tell me about her erratic career as a dancer in Broadway musicals, and it was very, very easy to want to protect her and befriend her and make tender love to her. But when I finally slipped between the covers with her, was I in for a surprise!

Beryl was absolutely wild in bed—she wanted sex practically nonstop, none of it oral, and insisted on making

128

Micronite filter.
Mild, smooth taste.
For all the right reasons.
Kent.

America's quality cigarette.
King Size or Deluxe 100's.

Warning: The Surgeon General Has Determined
That Cigarette Smoking Is Dangerous to Your Health.

love frontways, backwards, sideways, lying down, standing up, at an angle, at the reverse angle, one variable position after another. It was great sex, if somewhat acrobatic, and I began to be grateful she wasn't a ballet dancer.

There were no tender, relaxed moments with Beryl, and since she wasn't using anything, I would go through three prophylactics in a session. There were moments when I could compare making love with Beryl to gym in high school, but every new position felt good and she never stopped moving. I used to be so grateful for my construction work keeping me in good shape, and there were rare moments when I was half convinced that Beryl hadn't been raped at all—she'd gotten that guy out on the high trapeze in some circus, and they'd both missed. . . .

At one point she got a call from her former admirer, which frightened her, so I moved her out of her tiny West Fifty-fifth Street apartment into the Hotel Latham, then a very lovely hotel just off Fifth Avenue on East Twenty-eighth Street.

For six months we saw each other almost every day—she'd make her rounds of the dancing auditions, then we'd have something to eat, maybe catch a show or a movie, then back to gym. The food was good, the show or film usually entertaining, and the sex athletic but invigorating, but the thing had to end—she was in love with show business and through her I met too many phonies to be entertained by those kind of people. And since she really wanted a career more than anything else, we drifted apart, with no hard feelings, I hope, and the knowledge that whatever company manufactures Trojans was now a lot more profitable for Beryl and me having known each other.

It was a funny time. I wanted to become serious with someone, but it didn't seem to be in the cards. Still, you never knew when. . . .

One day our firm received a call from Greenwich, Connecticut, to come up and make repairs on a home there which had been damaged by fire. The home was quite lavish, and the owner, a rich young guy named John Walton, was as charming a person as you might wish to meet.

129

Only trouble was, he drank all the hours he was awake and already had a very bad case of cirrhosis of the liver.

Living with him, and desperately trying to help him, was his girlfriend—mistress, roommate, lover, surrogate wife, you call it—Barbara, who was every Jewish guy's erotic vision of what the perfect WASP girlfriend would look like. She wasn't too tall and she wasn't too slim and she wasn't exactly beautiful, but she had blond hair and the largest blue eyes in the world and her figure was just perfect—not too much, not too little, of everything. She reminded me of a movie star of the forties, June Haver (who later became a nun, I believe), and was absolutely the perfect mother to their three-year-old son, a gorgeous little kid called Jamie.

Well, I planned, and then executed, the repairs on the house, and I felt guilty every time I accepted John's invitation to have a drink with him. However, if you didn't have a drink with him—this was always late afternoon, because John observed the rules about the "cocktail hour" for everyone but himself—he'd become surly, angry, hostile, and downright impossible to be with, and through these sessions I got to know, and admire, Barbara more and more.

One day John said in his slurred voice, "Hey, Larry, do me a favor—ole Barby hasn't been out of the house for weeks. Let her get a sitter, and you take her out to some nice dinner. She deserves a nice dinner, I'm never hungry at dinnertime. . . ."

Barbara protested, but when John insisted she seemed almost relieved. She looked really weary.

When the sitter arrived Barbara briefed her, and judging by the looks and whispers exchanged between the two of them, the sitter was well acquainted with John's drinking problems. I distinctly heard "Look out for cigarettes," which, I assumed, meant that John left lit cigarettes all over the place, and indeed, this may have been the cause of the fire.

At dinner, at a pleasant little re-creation of a nineteenth-century New England inn, I let Barbara do most of the talking and she seemed relieved to have a friendly ear. She came from a very well-to-do family of Scottish-English extraction, and had been married briefly to a spoiled college boy who'd loved her and left her—pregnant with Jamie.

Her parents, flinty New Hampshirites who'd never been friendly with anyone whose family tree in America didn't go back at least two hundred years, disowned her, and by chance, in Florida, she happened to meet John, who took her in strictly as an act of kindness. His wife had left him because of his drinking, he had no children and lots of room, and, Barbara admitted, when he was reasonably sober, could be a lovely man, kind and considerate and deeply affectionate.

As I heard her speak of John so tenderly, I found myself growing jealous, and wished that she felt this way toward me. She was so giving, and yet she needed someone so much. I know it sounds like a Hollywood tear-jerker, but . . . so does real life, if you've noticed. Still, I relished the time spent with her, brought her home, kissed her discreetly on the cheek, and saw her to the door. It was like my sophomore year in high school, all over. But somehow different—I knew that, too.

As the work on John's house was nearing an end, he seemed to suggest my taking Barbara out to dinner more and more, and she objected less and less, and I found myself becoming ever more emotionally involved with her. Finally, one night when I could listen no longer, I said, "Barbara, it's hopeless with John—he doesn't want to help himself. He'll destroy himself, you and Jamie—if he doesn't set the house afire, he'll do it by other means. He doesn't *want* to hurt anyone, but he can't help it—he hates himself so much that everything he touches is going to feel his destructive pattern. Leave him. . . ."

She began to cry, softly, but with so much feeling it wrenched my heart.

"Look, Barbara, we've never even made love, and this is really a gesture of friendship," I said, wanting to leap across the table and take her into my arms. "Come to New York, I'll get you a nice apartment, and stay there only as long as you want to. If you feel you have to return to John, you should do so, but I'm hoping you won't feel that way."

131

"Larry, he *needs* me so much. . . ."

"Yes, he does, but he needs Cutty Sark even more. . . I'm not knocking his need for booze, but it's going to destroy all of you."

Barbara flashed a brave little smile at me, and I knew she was going to come to New York. It was to be one of the more interesting periods of my life.

As tender and solicitous as she'd been with John, she was very demanding with me. I'll admit that most of what she asked for had to do with Jamie's needs, but she revealed herself as a very pampered young woman herself, one used to other people taking care of her needs.

She was very strict about my not living there, and I didn't even make a physical advance toward her until she'd been living in Manhattan for almost two months. But the moment we touched, an electric storm went off—she was absolutely the most physical woman in bed, including Xaviera—who can be pure kinetic energy in bed—I have ever met.

It wasn't like Beryl, who liked a lot of positions in rapid consecutive order—Barbara, who seemed so demure otherwise, was an absolute typhoon in bed. She's scratch and bite and at times, especially when she was coming, she was almost impossible to hold on to, and before then we'd have bounced off the bed, rolled all over the carpet, climbed up onto a chair, rolled off the chair, banged into the wall, fucking like two possessed animals, until we finally ended up in some corner of the room, utterly exhausted, and not necessarily liking each other. We were more like two tired animals.

I'd finally moved in three months after Barbara got settled in New York—among other things, I'd become very fond of Jamie. However, what I was learning about Barbara was that *she* found it hard to share love with others, and—now I can analyze this, although I couldn't have doped it out then—I feel she subconsciously resented anyone knowing what a wild sexual creature she was in (and out of) bed, resented anyone knowing what deep, almost animalistic passion lay just beneath that nice, demure, lovely exterior.

One day I came home from work to find out she'd gone

back to John. I was both pained and relieved—she was every bit as complicated as John was, and no easier to live with, but now I understood how they were mutually interdependent. Barbara finally got John to marry her, and I hope that was to her financial advantage because about a year later he died. When I learned of this I immediately thought of getting in touch with her, but something within me told me to drop this idea, and I wisely did so.

Quite recently I happened to see the society page of one of the New York papers, and there was Barbara in one of the photographs. She'd been the hostess for some charity function, and if the photograph told the truth, she was, if anything, more lovely than ever. In the photograph she seemed almost serene, and perhaps this was because she is now the wife of a very wealthy Stamford, Connecticut, real-estate man. I recognized the name of her husband, so I know that Barbara and Jamie don't want for material things.

So I hope the guy's a tiger in bed. . . .

CHAPTER 15.

Between these love affairs and my business affairs—in addition to running my construction business—I was studying to become a licensed public adjustor, which means I would be able to represent parties in their claims against the insurance companies in case of fire or other kinds of damage to a building—it's a wonder I've had any spare time for leisure activities, but I did—and they helped preserve my sanity when things got a little bit crazy, especially in the recent cuckoo years with Xaviera.

For instance, I inherited my father's stamp collection while in my teens, and I have been an avid collector all these years and have built up quite a valuable collection. Sometimes after having dinner with Xaviera I would go home and tinker with my collection until late at night. For me this is more relaxing than watching television or reading some junk novel. It's also an excellent way to take your mind off your troubles because there's just so much to *know* about those fascinating little pieces of paper and glue.

On weekends I used to be what they call a "pretty serious golfer." I have a handicap of fourteen—my usual game is in the low eighties—and I enjoyed the sport enormously, playing every weekend when weather permitted. But then I learned to fly—and that became my preferred weekend activity.

My love of flying began one weekend, about fifteen years ago, when a business friend asked if I wanted to go flying with him in his private plane, a Cesna Skylane. We just went up and flew around a bit, but I was already hooked—what a great feeling to be up there, the plane an extension of your body, the heavens above you, the earth below, your mood one of complete peace and serenity. I know racing drivers feel that they're part of their cars, but flying a plane has *got* to be more exhilarating.

I started taking flying lessons and on weekends my fly buddies and I would fly to various places just to have lunch and look around.

We'd fly to Boston to have lunch at Durgin Park or Anthony's Pier Four. We'd fly to Montreal to have lunch at the Queen Elizabeth Hotel. We'd fly to Atlantic City to have lunch at the Knife 'n Fork or the Neptune Inn. We'd fly to Cape Cod to have lunch at Provincetown's Ciro's and Sal's, or at an astonishingly fine little place a few miles out of Provincetown called Aesop's Table. Hell, we'd fly to Bradley Field in Windsor Locks, Connecticut, of all places, because there's a great restaurant there called the Airport restaurant. I know it doesn't sound like a great

134

restaurant, but you should try the lobster. And the pecan pie. Unbelievable!

Maybe this all sounds a little zany, but it didn't take any longer to fly to Atlantic City to have lunch than it does to drive into Manhattan from Long Island. And it's a much more pleasant way to travel, certainly.

I got my flying license and by now I numbered among my friends a terrific group of guys who owned planes, so we would go on some more ambitious flights than the lunch trips. We'd sometimes fly to Florida or Puerto Rico for the weekend, which was a ball. No women along— there'd always be women wherever we were going.

From these flights following the sun, it was a logical step to go on the first junkets to Las Vegas with my flying buddies. The bunch of us—Frank, Sidney, Mike, and I—had already flown out to the Flamingo three or four times when I received a call from Julie Weintraub, who represented the Dunes, telling me that he too was running a junket flight to Las Vegas. Now in those days Julie had his office in his hat, as the expression goes, and there was no Dunes Hotel office on West Forty-seventh Street as there is today. But Julie was serious—he rented an entire plane and proceeded to fill it up with gamblers—high rollers, as they are called. Julie, by the way, is one of the finest gentlemen I've ever met—a real host—and Man.

When we got to the Dunes we were asked to fill out forms for credit cards there, but none of us cared to make any kind of complete financial statement just to get the Dunes credit card. I just gave my name and the name and address of my business, nothing more, and when they asked for bank references, I refused.

In any case, the Dunes credit personnel were told to issue me a card without any bank references and I believe that even today my Dunes card—which is allows me credit up to four or five thousand dollars—only gives my name. No business name or bank references listed on that card.

When I was between women back in New York, I often went to Las Vegas by myself because there was sun and fun—and plenty of good-looking females—out there. At least once a month I'd take a four-day weekend there, and there were times when I was in Vegas every other weekend. If there was nothing to keep me in New York, why not go out there—to me, it had almost become a shuttle flight, despite the distance—where some excitement was guaranteed, and where I could always count on being with friends? I often went to Vegas with newer friends like Larry Ettinger, whom I met in Vegas and who has opened an art gallery in the Dunes Hotel, or old chums of many years like Larry DePippo.

The time in Vegas I'll never forget was when President Kennedy was assassinated—it was weird how they tried to suppress the news in all the hotels. Finally, five or six hours after the nation had been told the President was dead, it was finally official in Las Vegas. A lot of us thought that the hotel clubs and casinos should shut down, out of respect for our dead President, but I suppose there's some logic in believing that people needed to take their minds off the event. And of course I'm never one to underestimate the profit motive.

That evening the shows went on as usual, and I remember Sammy Davis, Jr., beginning his show by announcing that he would entertain us, but would refrain from any humorous routines—and no jokes or wisecracks! Later, in the gambling rooms, it was almost surrealistic. All people talked about was the assassination —that is, except for those people who were mumbling at the one-armed bandits or those surrounding the crap tables, screaming at the dice to turn up the right numbers.

It was the only time I've spent in Las Vegas when I *didn't* have a good time.

CHAPTER 16.

During all these busy months, with the flying and the weekend flings and the variety of things to do in Las Vegas, I knew there was a gap in my life. I still wanted to do different things on weekends, but I wanted to do them with the same person. It's great for the ego to go to bed with a gorgeous Las Vegas showgirl, but it doesn't do anything for the psyche. If the romance with Barbara had worked out, that would have been fine, but it didn't, and despite all my stunting around, I was very much ready for a permanent relationship.

And that's when I met Eileen.

Eileen was married, had two children, and was a budding account executive in a very large advertising agency. The world's second-largest ad agency, as a matter of fact.

Her marriage was bad. She was a very bright person, and knew her marriage was bad, yet she seemed powerless to do anything about it.

I repeat—she was a very bright individual. She'd read so much more than I had that I felt very much out of her league in that department. Instead of promoting the merits of pantyhose for an ad agency, she should have been teaching the history of Western culture at some good high school or small college. I stress *small* because Eileen had an intimate way about her, and she loved to share what she knew, and I couldn't see her lecturing before four hundred students.

137

I loved to listen to Eileen, whatever she was talking about.

However, being a man of physical needs as well, there were other things I loved to do with Eileen.

It's kind of strange—she was so physically different from anyone I'd ever been with before. I adore the female bosom. Eileen was as flat-chested as a high-fashion model. But so what....

I like some flesh somewhere on a woman. Eileen was as thin, all over, again like a high-fashion model. But she had the kind of beauty which was readily obvious when she was nude, because the curves of her body were subtle rather than voluptuous.

She also looked great in clothes. In fact she wore clothes with all the style of a fashion model. It's just when she was in her underwear that she didn't look so terrific. Just thin.

Had she ever been a model? No. Should she have ever been a model? No. She was far too clever to have settled for merely being a photographic image. But she surely did have an image. I was attracted to her the moment I met her, although I'd also have to admit that it would be a matter of opinion as to just how attractive Eileen was. Certainly she wasn't the usual pretty face.

Her hair was a muted red and her skin was very light. She had kind of angular features, and what it all added up to was a face which was quite striking when she was happy or at repose, and which could almost be homely, or unpleasant to look upon, when she was very tired or unhappy. Some men would call this a great face. I know I did.

Her eyes were deep-set, and an unusual shade of green-blue. Like everything else about Eileen, they weren't typically beautiful eyes, but you never forgot that they were there. Her nose was straight, not too long, and very classic. Her mouth was full, with well-defined outlines and contours, and I could never get enough of it. Kissing Eileen was a sensuous experience all by its very self.

In case you somehow haven't gotten the idea, I was not only attracted to Eileen, I fell madly in love with her almost from the first time I met her. It was on a blind

138

date, no less, at the Hotel Pierre. Eileen's husband taught American literature at Rutgers University in New Brunswick, and her nights out were no secret to him—the marriage had been a bad mistake, where intellects clicked but emotions didn't, and he recognized that they were both quickly becoming emotional cripples, but couldn't do anything about it. He wasn't a bad guy, to say the very least, and he loved the kids. But he simply didn't know what to do about his failed marriage. It was already a failure, and that's where I stepped into Eileen's life. She was openly dating other men.

A blind date for me? No way I would go out on a blind date! Yet some friend of mine had raved about what a terrific person was handling his firm's advertising, and how much I would enjoy her company. So we had drinks at the Hotel Pierre. That's all it'd be—drinks.

And 'enjoy her company'? I only loved her for the next eight years. From the first night I met Eileen, I wanted to have her where I could see her every day, be with her every day . . . have her *be* with me every day. I found her somehow—well, almost *necessary* to me, even at that first meeting, and I just talked about myself to her, and when the night was over and she had to go back to New Jersey (she refused my ride home)—I knew I wanted to see her again as soon as possible. Like the next evening. I don't think we even kissed good night, and I had absolutely no idea of what she thought about me but I was worried I'd made a fool of myself.

The next day she called me at work and my insides turned to honey when I heard her voice at the other end. Oh, Jesus, was I back to being a schoolboy again?

"Larry, this is Eileen."

"Oh . . . yeah. . . . HI!"

"How are you?"

"Just great—how are you?"

"Fine. I wanted to tell you I enjoyed last night very much."

"Oh . . . yeah, sure . . . so did I. Last night was the best time I've had in a long while."

"How so?"

Her question stumped me. We hadn't done anything beyond have two cocktails at the Pierre and a nice, but certainly in no way remarkable, meal at Le Alpi, a rambling Italian-Continental restaurant in the West Forties which is an old favorite of mine.

Lest I appear utterly stupid, I finally blurted out something, which, as it happened, was the pure and simple unvarnished truth: "Mostly I enjoyed being with you. I hope it doesn't sound corny, but I do mean it."

"I know," she said. "That's why I'm calling."

"Will I see you tonight?"

"I can't," she said. "My husband is on a university committee which meets tonight, and the only kind of sitter I might be able to get would have to be home by ten."

"Would you like me to drive out there? I can be there by seven-thirty or so."

"No, I'm afraid that would be awkward. I may go into New York to date, but I haven't had anyone to the house . . . we're civilized, but not *that* civilized."

"Oh," I said, feeling sort of defeated. "It would have been nice to see you."

"Hey," she said, "the world doesn't stop moving around the sun tomorrow—there *is* a day after tomorrow, you know."

'Right!" I said brightly. "Say, what are you doing on Thursday night?"

"I'm not sure," she responded in a low voice. "I'm hoping I'm having dinner with you—but right after work, because I *do* have to be home early."

"Great," I said. " 'Right after work' . . . 'home early' . . . great!"

"Well, not *that* early—but reasonable. Shall we meet for drinks at the bar of the Copain? It's a favorite place of mine, but if you don't care for it, there's no shortage of places in the area. Or we can meet on the west side if you want—you certainly know your way around that part of town."

"The Copain," I said, "will do just fine."

It did—a pretty restaurant on First Avenue and East Fiftieth Street, later famous because part of *The French Connection* was filmed there. We talked to each other as though conversation were going to go out of style the next

140

day, and it was a simple, beautiful evening. And I did drive her home that night. And many nights thereafter.

Within a matter of weeks I wasn't seeing anyone else, and Eileen certainly wasn't seeing anyone else, but it was a silly arrangement. There she was in New Brunswick and there I was in New York, and we wanted to be together.

One night we sat down and she said, "Look, Larry, this isn't good for either one of us. I've got to get a divorce."

"I know," I said calmly.

Without kidding you or exaggerating a bit, I'll admit that my heart leaped out into my dessert plate when I heard this, and the next day I called my lawyers and we worked out plans for Eileen to get a clean, painless divorce.

Her husband was very considerate about the whole thing and Eileen was soon living in her apartment sans husband. I wanted her to be in New York, but she wasn't ready to make that move just yet.

This wasn't a good arrangement, however, and we both knew it, and when she was emotionally ready to make the move, I got her a condominium apartment in Rego Park, Queens, and that was the beginning of a deep relationship which lasted almost eight years.

We never lived together when the kids were there, although I became as close to those children as a man could who isn't their natural father, and when the kids were away at camp, I did move in with her.

Why didn't we marry? It's a very good question.

For the first few years Eileen found the relationship absolutely ideal. She had a good job, she was in love, and her experience with being married had made her extremely leery of making that commitment again unless she was one hundred and ten percent sure that it was the right move. Remember how bright she was—well, she'd intellectualized this thing right out of proportion.

And, to be truthful, I didn't press the issue very much. It was a wonderful relationship for me as well. I had a wife, in effect, but I wasn't legally tied to her home and hearth.

Still, there came a time when I did think about settling down with her and suddenly there were new obstacles:

141

her career was blooming and so were her vistas. For two or three years we'd been going to shows and dinners and parties and she kept telling me that she was having the time of her life. She was like a transformed person—always radiant and secure in her new role.

What I didn't reckon with was that this new person was desirable to every man she met, and now that I was ready to settle down, she was ready to stay single. I'd been a jackass, I have to admit—I'd let her become a person radically changed from the woman with whom I'd fallen so much in love.

We continued to be together almost every night of the week, but it was different now—I wanted life to be more quiet and steady and she wanted all the thrills New York can provide.

It doesn't take a genius to guess what happened. My business was expanding and I couldn't be with her every night, and when I wasn't, someone else *was*.

There were some violent fights, and beautiful reconciliations, but I began to suspect that whenever I took her home early because I had business affairs to attend to, I wasn't her only date that night.

It dragged on for far longer than it should have—it wasn't doing either of us any good—and finally we agreed that the magic was gone. There was no point in my meeting her at her apartment around ten o'clock if she'd been having dinner with someone else. I *am* a jealous creature, and I couldn't live with the agony she was causing me. I'd loved her as one person—but now she'd become a jet setter, and I have to admit that I didn't care for the person she'd become. Where there'd been honesty, there was now deceit, and that's not the rule I care to live by.

If I seem to be skirting over a long period in a relatively few words, maybe it's because it's still a tiny bit painful to think about. What might have been . . . it's always easy to say what might have been. What's important is not to look back—always to be looking ahead.

And nowhere, even in my wildest dreams, could I have predicted what a dramatic turn my life was about to take, just a few months in the future.

142

PART FIVE

"THE SILVER FOX" GETS INTO THE SWING OF THINGS

CHAPTER 17.

To paraphrase ole Charlie Dickens, it had been the best of times and now it was the worst of times. In a way I was glad that the affair with Eileen was resolved, but I felt rotten that I hadn't seen the changes occurring in her a lot earlier and convinced her to marry me at that time. In effect what had happened was she'd changed from a woman with a budding career into a career business-woman—which was fine with me—and a regular jetsetter. We did love each other, and I should have *wanted* to marry her more than I did, and persuaded her that a life together would be the best future for both of us. I was closer to her children than their own father was, especially her son.

I began dating like crazy every good-looking woman I knew, but it was no good. Whenever the lights were low, and the mood right for romance, I'd start to think about Eileen and get depressed. So I began to drown my sorrow in a sea of activity—the weekend flights, going to Vegas, and sports. I avidly took up golf again, and I went to every sporting event in town—the Mets, the Giants, the Knicks, the Rangers, and I even went to college basketball games at the Garden if they sounded like good match-ups. Fortunately I had friends in the sporting world who could get me good tickets on short notice, but I didn't really care where I sat—I just wanted to be doing some-thing every night of the week. Sometimes I'd take a date to these games, but more often I was with some male friend who was as much of a "jock" as I am. But I'd be lying if I didn't admit that I also chose to be with male friends in whom I could confide about Eileen. What I wanted was for the Giants or Mets or Knicks to win, which made for an entertaining good time together, and then to have a male shoulder to cry on, if you will. I must say that my friends gave me a lot of comfort, with no superior bullshit advice added, during this period. I'll admit it—I needed all the help I could get.

About the only sexual adventure I remember from this period—it was no problem getting a girl to sleep with me; the problem was finding a girl I could really like—took place with Deborah, a girl I'd been dating who lived on West Fifty-seventh Street. She was a buyer for a large department store, very tall, and exceptionally beautiful. By all rights I should have been attracted to her, but on each of our first two dates, after dinner together at San Marco, which is a very fine Italian restaurant on West Fifty-fifth Street—and therefore not far from her apartment—I took her home and instead of even kissing her, I settled for a cup of coffee or a nightcap. She must have thought I was very timid—I left both times as though I were afraid she'd make a pass at me, instead of the other way around.

On our third date we had a quick bite, went to the Knick game at the Garden—it turned out she too was an avid "jock"—and then went back to her apartment. We were sitting on the couch, having a drink and talking about the game, which had been very exciting (the Knicks won, 128-124 in overtime), and I was thinking to myself, "Schmuck, this girl is very attractive and she seems to like you. Why don't you try to kiss her? Schmuck, *do* something!"

"Okay," I answered myself, "I will kiss her and we will see where that will lead."

But just then she slid over to me and gave me a little bite on my earlobe. "Larry," she whispered into my ear in a voice which sent chills down my spine, "have you ever raped a girl?"

I looked at her as though she were crazy and sort of shook my head to indicate *no*.

"Well," she said, ignoring my gesture, "*have* you?"

This time I was able to speak. "No, I've never raped a girl, because I've never *had* to rape a girl." Then I added, with a wide grin, "Why, do you have someone for me to rape?"

"Yes. Me."

I could tell by the seriousness in her voice that she wasn't kidding, so I listened carefully as she went on to explain: "The only way I can enjoy sex is if I'm raped—forced to have sex . . . so I want you to rip off every piece of clothing and force me to fuck you. Really *make* me do it—I want you to take me as painfully as you can. Because if you'll do this for me, we can have a wonderful relationship. I really like you, you know. . . ."

I was about to say, "This kind of lovemaking must be a little hard on your wardrobe," but without waiting for my reply she got up and disappeared into the bedroom. I didn't know whether I was supposed to follow her; so I just sat there waiting for further instructions from my rape victim-to-be. To tell the truth, half of me wanted to get up and get the hell out of there. This was a well-built plaster-walled west-side apartment, but suppose she started yelling "RAPE!" when I was raping her, and the neighbors heard her and called the police. On the other hand, she was very sexually attractive to me and I hadn't been laid in a while and she *had* turned me on more than a little bit.

While I was pondering all these considerations, she reappeared in the living room, wearing a skintight black leotard—I could see the outline of her bra under the top—the kind ballet dancers wear, which covered her body from neck to toes. And a very short skirt, which accented the marvelous profile of her ass. If you want to know the truth, I thought the skirt was a little bit superfluous since the leotard covered her entire body, but I guess a rape victim has the right to choose the appropriate costume for her rape.

I was debating how to begin the rape, but she suddenly pirouetted onto the couch and was all over me. I still wasn't sure how to manage this thing, but she was kissing my mouth in an absolutely violent manner—my lip

146

felt as though it was caught in a meat grinder, and I could taste blood—and something inside me snapped. I was furious with her for hurting me and wanted to get even with her, so I pulled her off me, picked her up, and threw her on the couch. Then I was on top of her, ripping that dumb skirt off. Somehow she wriggled out from underneath me and began to run around the room. I chased her, caught her, and forced her down on the carpet. Pinning her arms next to her body and straddling her middle, I ripped the top of the leotard right down the middle and pulled off her black silk bra by grabbing it between the cups and giving one violent yank. She had gorgeous breasts and I couldn't wait to get them in my mouth, but I turned her over on her stomach, holding her wrists together with one hand and ripping off the rest of the leotard with the other. The cheeks of her ass were so beautiful that I gave one of them a little love-bite, for starters, and from her wince I knew it was more bite than I'd intended.

Neither of us had said anything during all this, which somehow made it even more strange and violent, and now I had the problem of getting off my own clothes. So I tried straddling her again, and got my shirt and T-shirt off without any trouble, but as I was loosening my pants and underwear my cock jumped out and she lurched forward as though there were nothing she'd rather do than bite it off at the base. Instinctively I slapped her—pretty damn hard—and then turned her back on her stomach and held her arms together again while I managed to shed the rest of my clothing.

She was struggling like an insane person to get out of my grasp and I had all I could do to hold her down, much less screw her. At one point my cock—I had a tremendous hard-on, I must say—was near her face again and she looked at it with a crazed expression. I wanted to jam it into her mouth, I was so horny, but the fear that she might not return my cock to me made me think otherwise; I knew I'd better keep all parts of my body, including my mouth, away from those teeth of hers.

I decided to risk letting go of her for a minute, jumped up, and rushed over to the chair on which I'd hurled my pants. I separated my belt from the pants and went after her again. She'd gotten up and was heading toward the bedroom, and I actually brought her down with a flying tackle. It again was an instinctive thing—I simply leaped across the living room and cut her down with one arm around her legs. She groaned or made some animal sound, and I knew I must have hurt her, but I didn't care. I had her on her stomach again, with arms lashed together above the elbows, and then rolled her over on her back.

I was going to fuck her until she screamed for mercy, and I didn't concern myself one bit with whether or not it was going to hurt her. I forced her legs open and got ready to get into her. If she was tight down below, that was too bad because I was going to just ram it into her. But she wasn't the least bit tight—she was sopping wet and completely ready to receive me.

It was a form of sex I will never try again, but it was also a fucking session I'll never forget. She went absolutely crazy—without my touching her breasts the nipples were extended at least an inch—and the harder I fucked her the more excited she became. Despite her arms being tied behind her, we rolled all over the carpet, and she didn't come once or twice or three times—she seemed to be having one continuous orgasm. As for myself, I came very quickly the first time, but the second time was a half hour later, when I forced her over on her stomach and lifted her up by her middle so that I could penetrate her from the rear.

I did everything to her I could think of, finally dragging her over to the couch, forcing her to kneel in front of me and suck me hard again; to keep sucking until I came again, and to swallow every ounce of it. I had my hands behind her head and I was quite literally fucking her in the mouth; and the faster I moved her head back and forth on my cock, the more excited she became. Even after I came she kept sucking, until it finally began to hurt and I moved her face away. Not once during that final session did I worry that she'd bite it—she was so hungry to have my cock inside her, one place or another,

148

that she had at least one more orgasm when she was blowing me.

I untied her and slumped back on the couch, utterly exhausted, and she just lay there on the carpet, looking up at me gratefully. She finally said, "That was great, Larry," and I suddenly felt a little sick to my stomach.

I didn't feel superior to her or anything like that—I just realized that she'd managed to turn me into some kind of unfeeling animal, and I didn't feel very good about that. She came up on the couch and cuddled against me, and because I felt very sorry for her I stayed a while longer. We got dressed—she put on a bathrobe this time—and had a drink together; and then I left. "Will I see you again?" she asked.

"Sure," I said, not meaning it for an instant.

I did see her again, however, though not under any circumstances I'd planned. It was about a year later—and I was walking into the Hotel Americana in San Juan with Xaviera on my arm and saw Deborah in the lobby, standing there with some tall guy. She saw me as well, and I excused myself from Xaviera for a moment to go over and say hello.

When I got about five feet away from Deborah, a smile on my face and ready to extend my hand, she turned away from the guy she was talking to and gave me a withering look. I'll tell you, if looks could kill I'd have been an instant corpse. The expression on her face had stopped me in my tracks, and then came the worst part. Still glaring at me, she snarled, "Get lost, baby. You're last week's news." Embarrassed, I turned around to rejoin Xaviera, who was to hand me more grief.

I told her how I happened to know Deborah, and she didn't buy a word of it. She was sure that this was one of the great loves of my life, and I couldn't tell whether she was genuinely jealous about it or just being bitchy. I found out a few minutes later. When we went up to our room she started throwing at me everything that wasn't nailed down. To escape her wrath I went on the balcony, and she threw one of the glasses from the bathroom there. It hit the floor and shattered; and before

I knew what was happening she'd locked the door—and there I was out on that balcony, standing there with cut feet.

"Xaviera, open the damn door—I've got cuts on my feet!" I said, but there was no answer. Then I heard the door inside slam, and I knew she'd gone out. I don't know whether she left me marooned on the balcony to teach me a lesson, or whether she grabbed the first guy she saw and fucked his brains out, but it was at least an hour before she returned and let me in off the balcony. Fortunately the cuts weren't bad, and my feelings went deeper than the cuts. Now it was my turn to be in a huff, and I didn't speak to her for another hour. Finally we made up the way we always did—in bed.

And that was the last time I made the mistake of recognizing, while in Xaviera's company, any woman I'd known previously.

CHAPTER 18.

I met Xaviera about three or four months after the final break-up with Eileen. When she returned from Puerto Rico and we started seeing each other regularly, I found that for the first time I was no longer thinking of Eileen, and I was grateful for that.

Perhaps I was no longer moping over Eileen because there was no time to remember her or to feel sorry for myself—being around Xaviera was like being part of a three-ring circus all day long. Something was always happening, and I found myself always looking forward to the next day with Xaviera, to the crazy times and the quiet dinners and, later, even to the daily problems. It was actually fun helping her to solve them.

And the sex—I must say that was highly therapeutic. And it was good for her as well as for me because it was sex with great feeling behind it.

I make no claims to having an extraordinary penis. It's the only one I have. But it seems to do the job of making people happy; I know that it surely made my Xaviera happy—there were times I afforded her so much pleasure that she would end up almost fainting, and want me to stop making love to her.

I tell this not out of any arrogance—I was proud and delighted that I could give her so much pleasure, and I'd be the last to deny that she taught me many, many things about the human body and its areas of sensivity. After I started sleeping with Xaviera I realized that I'd really known very little about the ultimate joys of oral sex before, and she has told me that I was the best pupil in the Class of 69 she'd ever had.

She also taught me a great deal about the importance of foreplay and how, when arousing your partner, your hands and mouth should never be inactive. Regardless of whatever position we were in, my hands would roam and my lips would explore, and we were able to create unbelievable pinnacles of pleasure in bed. I remember the two of us lying side by side, my mouth nibbling the side of her neck and my hand massaging her clitoris while our bodies moved together in a slow but delicious fuck. This doesn't sound very exotic, I know, but it brings great satisfaction to both partners. It makes me horny just thinking about it.

Yet there were times when we were tired or not feeling horny and there was no pressure on either of us to sexually satisfy the other. We would go to bed and sleep in each other's arms, like two kids, until the morning, and when we woke up, refreshed, making love would be a great way to start the day.

But there were other times when we couldn't seem to get enough of each other, especially on vacations, and

151

not only did we do it in that plane going from Los Angeles to Las Vegas, we also did it in the toilet of a plane going from New York to the Islands. And in a phone booth in Penn Station while waiting for a train to Philadelphia. Xaviera loves the challenge of doing the unexpected and of doing something forbidden in public, and I think you'll agree that making love in a plane or phone booth fulfills both categories. Half the thrill, I have to admit, is doing something outrageous right under people's noses and not getting caught. The danger of getting caught makes for an atmosphere charged with excitement, though I have to admit that it was only afterward, when we'd succeeded in not getting caught, that I was able to relax and be glad we'd done something outrageous again.

Of course it wasn't always ecstasy and the outrageous. There was aggravation, too. One time I took Xaviera to Las Vegas with me and I couldn't get her to stop handing out her business cards. This was bad enough, but most of these guys were there with their wives or girlfriends and the women were becoming incensed by Xaviera's actions. One of them really blew her top and went over to the manager to complain.

The next thing I knew he called me over—we'd known each other for years—and said, almost apologetically, "Listen, Larry, you got to stop that girl of yours from handing out all those little pieces of paper—know what I mean?"

I knew all too well what he meant—if a lot of wives didn't want to come out to Vegas anymore, a lot of husbands wouldn't be coming out either, and a lot of business would be out the window. So I got the message and told Xaviera to stop advertising herself. If I'd known she was going to do this I simply wouldn't have brought her out there in the first place.

Xaviera didn't get the message right away, so I had to say, "Look, if you keep on handing out your cards, we're both going to be kicked out of this place, so unless you stop I'm going to put you on the next plane back to New York. Let's have fun here, and not cause any trouble."

So she stopped with the self-advertising campaign, and we did have fun.

One of the heavy rollers there on this particular weekend was a friend of mine, Larry, who is not only a very big gambler but also a very big man—he must weigh close to three hundred pounds. Since it was Larry's birthday, I arranged for him to have dinner with us at the fine rooftop restaurant at the Dunes, where they serve over thirty different dishes featuring duck. When it was time for dinner we told Larry that we'd do the ordering—that we'd called his friends back in the city to find out his favorite dish, and the chef here was preparing it especially for him.

However, what we'd done was to have the maitre d' make a big production out of coming out of the kitchen with a big silver platter, complete with silver cover, and present it at our table as though it were the crowning culinary glory of his kitchen. And under the cover, Larry would find a small kitten—alive, of course—and we'd smile at him and say, "Ah, Larry, just what you want for your birthday—pussy!"

Unfortunately, when Xaviera and I had arranged for someone from the hotel to buy a kitten we'd forgotten to warn him *not* go buying a black cat because there of the old superstition about a black cat in a gambling casino. And of course when Larry lifted the cover off the platter that's exactly what was looking up at him— a cute, all-black kitten. Larry took one look at that little animal, leaped back in his chair about twenty feet, and left the room in a considerable hurry. The destruction he left in his wake was almost unbelievable—it was as though a Sherman tank had moved through the room— and the whole sight was so funny that everyone whose table had not been rocked by Larry's considerable girth rocked with laughter.

Larry decided he had to get even with Xaviera and me and even if it wasn't Xaviera's birthday, he would celebrate it anyway. He invited us to dinner that night— to prove to us that he was a good sport, he said—at the Dunes's Dome of the Sea restaurant, which is a very elegant arena-style room with an actual canal in the

153

centre and tables at various levels. We were seated near the canal, which conveys a harpist in a small boat around the room, which are considered the best tables, and thoroughly enjoyed our dinner. Everything was firstrate, and we were awaiting our dessert course when the maitre d' approached our table as part of a small procession. He was carrying the same type of silver tray with dome cover as we'd used the night before, and in front of the procession were two busboys, each carrying sparklers in their outstretched hands, and singing "Happy Birthday."

Every person in the room was looking at us, and I was pretty certain that Larry had paid the chef to bake some crazy kind of cake. In fact I was really curious to see what he'd dreamed up. The maitre d' stopped at our table and made a great show of placing the tray in front of Xaviera. Then the maitre d' joined in singing "Happy Birthday" and there were two hundred pairs of eyes looking at our table as Xaviera lifted up the silver cover.

And there, all by itself, was a six-inch penis-shaped vibrator. The place broke into an uproar—it was like a World Series game when someone on the home team hits a home run.

Xaviera took it all good-naturedly, holding up the vibrator for everyone to see and announcing, "It's the biggest one I've seen in a long time." That got a lot more laughs.

Later Larry confided to me that it had taken him several hours to find the damn thing. In those days sex shops weren't very common and you generally had to send away to get a vibrator or dildo.

Later that night, when we were in the casino, Xaviera leaned over and whispered to me, "I may have to try that thing out tonight."

"I sincerely doubt that," I said, and we both broke up.

CHAPTER 19.

Xaviera would often kid me about being a one-woman man, but that's the way I am. I was able to participate in swings with her, partly because she'd educated me to regard these as social occasions where the object was to have some fun of a sexual nature, but not to start up any new love affairs. Swings are actually very impersonal affairs and you can generally count on the couples who arrive together going home together, or else finally going to sleep with each other, not someone else, at the end of the night. Besides, with Xaviera there was no way to keep her from swinging, and at least we went to them together. The first few times I was pretty uptight about swinging, but I finally learned to enjoy myself and not regard Xavier's body as something I owned that no one else could touch.

But that didn't change my feelings about caring for only one woman at a time—not dividing my affection, as some people can—and it's why I never felt it necessary to cheat on her. Hanging around that apartment of hers, with all sorts of sexy ladies on the premises, there was never any shortage of temptation—but I never laid a loving hand on one of them. I'm not flattering myself when I say that more than a few of them indicated a lively curiosity as to what Xaviera's boyfriend was all about in bed, and there were others, I'm sure, who thought that by fucking me they'd be "fucking" Xaviera—getting back at the boss

155

through her boyfriend. But I never cooperated on that score either, although there were times when I was angry at Xaviera and might not have turned down the right kind of turn-on.

Much later, when Xaviera had to leave the country, I was besieged with phone calls, all from girls, both at home and at the office. These calls almost always fit into one of three categories.

Group one consisted of girls who either knew me through Xaviera or else knew of me through her book, and wanted to find out what Xaviera and I did between the sheets that kept us together for more than three years.

"Is this Larry the Silver Fox?" a demure voice on the other end might say.

"Yup," I'd reply in my best Gary Cooper manner.

"Are you the friend of Xaviera Hollander?"

"Yup."

"Well, are you wondering why I'm calling?"

"Yup."

"I hope you're not going to think badly of me as a result of this call. . . ."

"Nope."

"I was wondering if you'd like to go out?"

" 'Go out'?"

"Well, if you're busy I suppose we could go straight to bed."

"Lady, I don't even know your name, and you're inviting me to bed?"

"Yes, I suppose you could put it that way—does the idea appeal to you? I'm considered very attractive, and my hus—"

That would be the end of *that* conversation, but I have to admit that a few truly nice voices did intrigue me. However, I figured I was a little old for blind dates—look what happened the last time I'd gone out on one, with Eileen!—and if I wanted to see someone for an evening, I wanted it to be someone I knew and liked. But my heart, if not my head, very much belonged to Xaviera.

The second category of caller would be a would-be madam. They felt that since I'd eased Xaviera through so many problems, I'd be a great guy to know and could turn them overnight into wealthy women. And of course they'd be only too happy to express their gratitude to me in any way I deemed suitable. "No thanks," I thanked them, ending the conversation. I had never wanted Xaviera to become a madam, and I wasn't about to get involved with any lady with similar ideas in her head.

This may surprise, or even shock, some of my readers, but I don't think prostitution should be legalized. Tolerated, yes, and not prosecuted—if it's a crime, it's a victimless crime, and I'm sure our law-enforcement people have more important areas of crime to concern themselves with—but I'm far from convinced that the legalization of prostitution would be a good thing.

I believe that if prostitution were legal it would be an invitation for organized crime to move in and "unionize" the profession. Right now there are so many girls on Manhattan's east side operating out of their own apartments, or else for small madams, that it's almost impossible for mobsters to gain any control over them. But allow prostitution to become legalized, and I predict a very fast takeover by the mobs or by very powerful pimps.

Xaviera, in her speaking engagements, has argued that with prostitution made legal, taxes could be collected, pension funds could be arranged, and day-care centers established for the kids of working girls. I don't say that any of these are bad ideas per se, but I can't imagine any hooker I've met publicly identifying herself as a prostitute and paying taxes to the Internal Revenue Service so that she could continue functioning as a prostitute. I may be completely wrong on this question, but I don't buy the theory that legalized prostitution would necessarily be a good thing for society. Society—at least American society —will have to undergo a giant change in its attitude about women who sell their bodies for money before legalized prostitution would make sense to me.

The third category of caller would be girls who'd been giving freebies all their lives and had now decided that their talents could be turned to business advantage. I discouraged all these callers in no uncertain terms, in more than a few cases having to hang up on them because they wouldn't get off the phone.

Xaviera would have the world believe that her girls were all wonderful creatures who knew what they were doing by being prostitutes, but having spent a lot of time among these girls I can't recall one of them who could truthfully say to me, after a year in the business, "Boy, Larry, this is the life. Am I having a ball! Have I made a lot of money!"

True, there were a few nymphomaniacs who found in prostitution a way to go to bed with ten men, and occasional housewives who actually did become call girls for a few months to supplement their incomes—but usually these women got out of "the life" as soon as their bank accounts were properly swollen. But most of the girls who fucked for money also had fucked-up lives, and those who believed that prostitution was a sure, safe route to making a lot of money in a short time seldom found that belief to be justified by what actually happened to them. A number of them didn't save a dime—they'd spend their money on clothes and guys, and the clothes on their back were *all* they had to show for all the hours spent on their backs.

Anyone who envies the life of a prostitute is naive or misinformed. True, the smart ones, like Xaviera, who become madams, may make a good deal of money, but I don't believe they're ever really happy at what they're doing.

I've said I didn't cheat on Xaviera with any of her friends and/or "associates." This is true. However, there was one occasion where opportunity knocked—Miss Opportunity had great knockers, as it turned out—and I didn't decline.

When I'd been dating during the months immediately before I met Xaviera, there was a young blonde of whom I'd been fond. Her name was Bertie—for Beatrice—and she was twenty-three years old, with a great figure—especially her breasts, which were large for her size and very pliant to the touch. She looked so young that I thought of her as a terribly cute little blonde rather than a very pretty young woman—which she certainly was.

When I first met Bertie, her husband, who was a jockey, had left her with three children, no less—each one cuter than the next. She'd been married at seventeen, and still had the bloom and optimism of youth on her side. Because I was trying to get over Eileen, I found her spunkiness very refreshing, and enjoyed our evenings together, including the few times we made love. But nothing very special, and when I started seeing Xaviera there was no time for Bertie.

I must have been going with Xaviera for about a year when suddenly little Bertie showed up in my office. She was moving to Florida to be near her folks and, being in my neighborhood, had stopped in to say goodbye. Since it was late in the day I told her to wait around for twenty minutes or so and then I'd give her a ride home to Long Beach, where she lived, and we could have a good talk. The office, I explained, was just too frantic, what with phones ringing all the time, to have a civilized conversation.

This was fine with her, and I cleared up the day's business affairs as quickly as I could and then we were on our way. On our way over the Brooklyn bridge Bertie decided to stretch out, putting her head on my lap and curling up on the front seat. I put my hand on her shoulder, feeling almost fatherly toward her. We talked about what she had been doing, about her kids, and I was very pleased she'd stopped in to see me.

After about ten minutes of this conversation I realized that she had taken her right hand and moved it onto my crotch. This didn't especially surprise me, although I hadn't expected any such attentions—Bertie had been free 'n' easy on our dates, and whether or not we made love had been left up to me. She was always willing. Well, now she was giving my crotch area a rubdown and of course there was a member of my family rapidly responding to her touch inside my trousers.

Laughing at the growing bulge in my pants, she zipped open my pants and took out my penis, which by now was fully erect. I started to complain that the zipper of my

159

fly was rubbing against it, so she undid my belt buckle and, with some cooperation on my part, slid down both my pants and shorts and put her head back on my lap, where it had been, with one slight variation. She had taken my cock and put it into her mouth, so while I was calmly driving along, or trying to, wonderful Bertie was giving me a succulent blow-job while I played with her breasts with my right hand and drove with my left.

After about ten minutes or so of having my cock kissed and lapped and sucked, I couldn't hold back any longer and I came in Bertie's mouth.

Knowing that she didn't mind swallowing sperm, I didn't even offer a handkerchief—with one gulp, everything was gone.

I thanked Bertie for having quite literally drained the day's tension out of me, but instead of leaving me alone, she said she's like to try for a double-header, and five minutes later her mouth was back sucking on my penis. I didn't believe anything was going to happen for a while, but it surprised me by getting hard again. Still, I knew this time it would require quite a lot of oral artistry on Bertie's part for me to come again.

She didn't seem to mind the work load she'd taken on, and I was beginning to feel the faint stirrings of another orgasm when we arrived in Long Beach. Because her head was down on my lap she didn't know we were near her home, so I drove past her house to a very quiet section where most of the houses were summer homes.

"Bertie," I said, "stop it—I'm going to come."

"That's the general idea," she said, her lips poised just above the head of a very horny penis.

"No," I said, "let's take it easy for a few minutes, and then we can fuck. Okay?"

"Okay," she said, grinning up at me.

She sat up and I moved over from behind the steering wheel, and we kissed, then I removed her sweater—and since she wore no bra, I was able to kiss and lick her breasts to my heart's content. I was also playing with her clitoris, and caressing her ass, and finally she moaned a little and said, "Oh, Larry, let's get on with it—I'm about to come."

I lay back toward my side of the car, and she straddled me and we managed to maintain a really strenuous pace for about five minutes. Then I had to jam her all the way down on me because I was experiencing an orgasm which seemed to start down at my toes and move through my entire lower body before I exploded inside Bertie. At the same time she came more than once herself, so I guess you could say we were glad we'd had a chance to say good-bye.

The next day I had a little surprise. I noticed a discharge stain on my shorts. I didn't know what to do. I certainly didn't relish going to Xaviera and telling her about my pleasant ride home with Bertie. Come to think of it—whoops, sorry about that!—there was no need to tell Xaviera about Bertie because you can't contact venereal disease overnight. On the other hand, there was every reason to speak to Xaviera because she's been the only other woman I'd had sexual relations with in a long time.

I was a bit embarrassed about calling my family doctor —which is silly, I know—because he's a strait-laced Park Avenue type who would really regard venereal disease as a social disease. So I asked a close friend of mine to refer me to his physician, who, he'd once told me, was a regular guy.

My examination consisted on his asking me to drop my pants and shorts and to squeeze the head of my penis. To my horror, I saw a thickish white fluid come out, and I was certain I had the clap or something equally unpleasant.

The doctor captured the discharge on a slide and said it would take until the next day for the laboratory results to come back. He'd let me know then. That put me into a panic—I just couldn't wait another twenty-four hours to learn what was wrong with me.

While I couldn't explain to the doctor the exact nature of my predicament—the doctor had already assured me that it could not have been caused by my contact with someone the day before—I prevailed upon him to rush the test results so I could have a verdict in the latter part of the afternoon. He recognized my sense of panic and said he could get the tests back in a matter of hours if I was willing to pay for a "rush" report. I told him I'd be only too happy to cover any extra fees incurred by the same-day service.

For the rest of the afternoon I moved around like a guy in a bad dream. If I was infected, I had been infected by Xaviera. This also meant she would have to call up every John she'd been with in recent weeks and inform them she may have given them a present, and to see their doctors at once. I didn't relish being the bearer of this kind of news—I was sure, in one way or another, the thing would get turned around so that it was my fault.

Around five o'clock that afternoon the doctor called my office and asked me to see him in half an hour. Uh-oh, I figured I had it for sure. If I was all right, he'd have told me over the phone, wouldn't he? So now the fun would really begin.

At exactly 5:30 I walked gingerly into the doctor's office and took a seat. He asked me to drop my pants and shorts again, and I did so, and then he applied some salve to the head of my penis. Oh Jesus, I thought, this really looks bad. What the hell did I have!

Then he gave me some pills to take.

And then he said, "Don't be alarmed—you have no infection. What you have is an inflamed penis—which can be caused by over-use."

" 'Over-use'?" I repeated.

"Yes—just like your body can be overworked, your penis can be physically abused . . . have you indulged in any excessive sexual activity very recently?"

"Well, nothing I'd consider 'excessive'. . . ."

"How about letting me be the judge of that?"

I thought about that week. "Well," I said, "two nights ago I made love to someone twice and last night a young lady performed fallatio on me for over an hour."

"I'd say—"

"and then we made love," I continued.

He uttered an expression in Yiddish which meant *hog!* or something close to that. "Listen, my friend," he then said, "that organ between your legs isn't made of foam rubber, you know. And it can't be replaced. That discharge produced by your inflamed penis is its way of saying: 'Help! Slow down. Let me have a little bit of rest.' "

At first I thought he'd been kind of cruel for not letting me know over the phone what the problem was, but now I could see the value of getting me over here to give me a lecture. I got his message, and avoided any sexual contact for the next few days. When Xaviera asked me if I'd be staying over, I pleaded tiredness and went back to my own place.

"You're acting strangely," she said, because she knows me so well.

"Just tired," I said. "I've been working too hard lately."

Little did she know which part of me had been working too hard lately, and when she reads this it will be her first knowledge of Bertie and the knight with the white discharge. . . .

CHAPTER 20.

One of the most frequent questions I get asked about *The Happy Hooker* is to what extent is it actually Xaviera's book.

It's essentially always the same question but it takes several forms:

"How could a hooker write a book like that?"

"Did Xaviera have anything to do with the writing?"

"Did Robin Moore write the whole thing?"

"I've heard that Yvonne Dunleavy did all the writing —is that true?"

Robin Moore has recently published a dreary little rip-off of a book entitled *The Making of The Happy Hooker*, which purports to tell the entire story of how the book came to be published. I will have quite a lot to say about Robin's recollections later on in this book, but suffice to say that these few pages will tell you as much about the creation of that book as Robin's entire book.

When Xaviera purchased the infamous black book we've all heard so much about by now, she would make fifteen to twenty phone calls a day to men listed in that book. There was an entry under Moore, and when she called that number, the voice on the other end belonged to a gentleman named Moore, all right, but it wasn't the same Mr. Moore listed in Xaviera's book. It was, by complete coincidence, our friend Robin speaking at the other end.

Xaviera made her usual pitch for business and Robin was intrigued, he later told me, more by Xaviera's voice than by the opportunity for some professional sex. I happen to know whom he was romantically involved with at the time, but that has nothing to do with our story here.

Robin did pay a visit to Xaviera, and he was immediately intrigued by her—as a possible subject for a book. His interest in her story had been additionally whetted by an hour spent with her in the bedroom, for which he was charged, of course. I arrived not long thereafter, and was introduced to him as the author of *The Green Berets*. He seemed to be a pretty nice guy, and Xaviera was obviously turned on by the idea of doing a book with him.

Nothing was even remotely formalized then, and it's my own opinion that Robin's suggestion about a book— although in recent years he always seems to be working on several books at once—was something of a lark for him. By this I mean he was far from persuaded that a good book could result from Xaviera's experiences and her knowledge and opinions about prostitution. After all, she was hardly a veteran madam—or prostitute, for that matter.

Robin, on the other hand, is a veteran researcher, and I frankly think he relished the idea of hanging around a business establishment where the business is sex. Hell, what writer wouldn't find this an interesting area for research!

164

In any case, the way it was left was that Robin would provide a tape recorder for Xaviera, and that he would also provide for the transcription of the taped stories Xaviera produced. It seemed a good way for her to work, I had to agree, because I couldn't envision her sitting down at the typewriter—despite her typing skills—and producing a book-length manuscript. She had neither the training nor the discipline for that—then, too, English is not her native language, although, I must say, her letters written in English are well-expressed and enjoyable to read.

When Robin left I sat down with Xaviera and we discussed the pros and cons of doing a book. I had a funny idea—not funny *haw-haw*—but just an idea based on a hunch of mine that not only could a book result from this collaboration, but that it would be successful. (Although no one in his or her wildest dreams could have predicted just *how* successful—as this is being written, the covers of the latest edition of *The Happy Hooker* proclaim "Over Six Million Sold!")

By the end of our discussion Xaviera had definitely decided to try and do the book—which made me glad, for another reason. You see, I had a very personal motive for pushing for the book—I knew that if it came out it would almost surely put Xaviera out of business. For a year now I had tried unsuccessfully to get Xaviera to cut back as far as her business was concerned, and the only concession I'd won from her was a promise of less personal involvement with the Johns.

The early taping sessions with Robin generally followed this procedure: he'd come over once during the week, in mid-afternoon, and on Saturday afternoon, when things were almost always quiet. Xaviera, with some help and prodding from me—her memory is not always the best— would have decided what areas she was going to discuss and the actual sessions would often be three-way conversations between Xaviera, Robin, and myself.

When the conversation would turn to something Xaviera preferred not to discuss in front of me, or else dealing with the great love of her life—Carl—I'd be asked to evacuate the premises for a while so Xaviera could do a tape with-

165

out worrying about my reactions to whatever she had to say.

Somewhere along the line Yvonne Dunleavy was introduced into the picture as Robin's collaborator. Yvonne was an Australian journalist who'd met Robin through a mutual friend, June Collins, who was also Australian and with whom Robin was finishing up a book called *The Khaki Mafia*. Yvonne's contribution, Robin explained, would be to bring a female viewpoint to the book, but my own less than flattering (to Robin) viewpoint about this arrangement was that Robin's role would be to make the book happen and get it published, and Yvonne would take over the hard work.

Xaviera and Yvonne didn't hit it off at first, but no one can deny that Yvonne worked very hard on the book, getting Xaviera's story out of her and then rewriting it so it would read smoothly. What I didn't like about Yvonne's approach to the book was that she was using the words *fuck* and *suck* as though they were soon going out of style, but a lot of the four-letter words were eliminated, except where they occurred in dialogue—which is certainly legitimate.

Xaviera was provided with parts of the manuscript to go over and correct as it progressed, but I don't think she was ever allowed to see the complete manuscript before it was sold to the publisher. My suspicion is that Xaviera was shown pages to pacify her and make her think her editing requests would be followed, but when I later compared the original text and the pages Xaviera had edited, quite often her changes had not been implemented. Later on, when a Dell editor took over the book, Xaviera was treated as an author should be—like a gentleman, female version—and changes were made both at the manuscript stage and in galleys. I know Xaviera felt a lot better about that.

But I am getting ahead of my story. At this point there was no complete manuscript and no publisher, but the book was really starting to take on some form—I honestly don't know to whom the credit here belongs, to Yvonne or Robin or to both of them—and it was time to formalize the working relationship between Robin, Yvonne, and

Xaviera. This would turn out to be an arduous procedure, and I'm not going to bore you with the grim business details—except to say that in my opinion, Robin's share was larger than he deserved in terms of the actual work he did on the book. But then again, he was the "name author" connected with the book, and his agent sold the book, and Xaviera and I were then just two newcomers to the publishing game.

To get away from the grim to a grin, the lawyer who was brought in to arrange the legal relationship between all the parties involved at that time regarded the whole project as something of a joke, in publishing terms. A whorehouse book? *Another* whorehouse book? Was the world waiting for another whorehouse book?

Of course that lawyer—he is today Xaviera's literary lawyer—hadn't seen any of the manuscript, and he'd been thinking of books which promised a lot of candor but didn't deliver, and which dealt with sex but weren't sexy. *The Happy Hooker* delivered all it promised, and *more*. Today he freely admits that his opinion of the book's prospects was one of the two big mistakes in judgment he's made as a lawyer. But fortunately for everyone concerned—because he's a very sweet guy—it was an error in judgment which didn't hurt anyone, financially or otherwise.

Xaviera's editor for *The Happy Hooker* attributes the success of the book to a number of factors: (1) It was the most candid and open account about being a madam ever written; (2) It was a helluva sexy book, but the sex was legitimate—there was no need to drag in any sex because it was always there; (3) Xaviera comes across as a super-sexual creature, and her expressed attitudes about sex and her sexual feelings are remarkable for their honesty; (4) the Knapp Commission publicity and Xaviera's own publicity tour were great boosts for the book; (5) No one could say *The Happy Hooker* was just a "dirty book"—it has information, real information, controversial disclosures and opinions, news impact, and the tangled, sometimes sordid, but certainly powerful, story of a young woman who never came to America for any purpose but to marry her man; and (6) there were great elements in the book which smacked of soap opera, be it Xaviera's bad luck in finding happiness or just her unrelenting troubles with the New York City Police Department. There was also the major love affair with Carl, which was a soap opera without many bubbles, after the first six months.

Xaviera's first editor also feels that the time was right —and ripe—for such a book. Freedom of expression allowed for the book—it became *the* book of the early seventies—and the recent U.S. Supreme Court decision might have put the book in jeopardy of every local "know-nothing" vigilante group in the fifty "feelthy" States.

His greatest difficulty in editing the book, he later told me—quite apart from the fact that the book was edited and prepared for the printer in so short a time—was that there did seem to be three different voices in the book. The beginning of the book, he said, really sounded like Robin Moore, but a lot of the writing was clearly Yvonne's, and it was just obvious to him that a number of people had worked on the manuscript. Thus, his job was to try to make the book's style seem consistent. Xaviera was some help there, he recalled, because she helped him eliminate expressions she simply never used.

P.S. He also cut out some sex scenes, believe it or not. . . .

When *The Happy Hooker* was first published it climbed atop the New York *Post*'s nonfiction best-seller list and stayed there for months. We were told by the publisher that it was the New York *Times* paperback list which really counted, and this appeared but once a month—but it, too, had gratifying news. I know Xaviera has written of her joy about bestsellerdom, but you would have had to be there to see her, a grown woman, yelp for joy as each week's list confirmed the continued soaring success of her book. I had made only a peripheral contribution to that success, but you can imagine how good it made me feel, as well! I gave away so many *free* copies that Xaviera began to complain I was hurting sales of the book.

As for Xaviera's second book, I must say that I like it even better because there is nothing about Xaviera's previous career in it—apart from the "Question & Answers" section, which has proved to be very controversial—and the large initial printing (1.4 million copies) and subsequent large printings have boosted the book to the point where it may well be the most successful sequel book by any author in history, not excepting such "biggie" novelists as Harold Robbins, Irving Wallace, and the like. I'm not sure about this, at this writing, but it's very possible.

So—just as a well-intentioned phone call to a cop friend helped ensure the success of Xaviera's literary career, so did a call to the wrong "Moore."

CHAPTER 21.

The time was drawing near when Xaviera would be leaving the country, and whenever she wasn't off on a publicity tour on behalf of *The Happy Hooker*, we relaxed and had a good time in New York. Dinners, parties, evenings on the town, whatever struck our fancy.

One weekend I got a call from a friend of mine, Billy, who was a fellow junketeer to Las Vegas. It's odd how some friendships are—I think I saw more of Billy in Vegas than I did in New York—but he now had a suggestion for an offbeat evening in Manhattan together which definitely appealed to me. At least it appealed to me when I got used to the idea.

"Hey, Larry," Billy said after the usual "Hello, how are

you," . . ."how would you and Xaviera like to go to a massage parlor?"

"Why, you got a coed massage parlor in mind?"

"No, seriously—I belong to this place, a club, really, and there are plenty of girls who come with their guys for an evening."

"What do the girls get out of it—a Lesbian experience?" I asked. So far the idea didn't much appeal to me.

"No, dummy, that's not the way it is at this place. This isn't one of those one-hour-to-get-your-rocks-off places. It's a really classy place where you go to spend the evening. I told you it's a club—you go swimming, have a few drinks, and some time during the course of the evening, you get a massage."

"And what happens when you get a massage?"

"That's up to you . . . there are no rules about what can and can't go on in the massage rooms, but this is a completely respectable place."

"Sure, it sounds like fun. I'll ask Xaviera if she wants to go."

Ha, ask Xaviera if she'd like to be one of a few females among a small army of guys—I knew the answer before I asked the question. Her eyes lit up like Times Square at ten in the evening when I casually mentioned the idea.

That night, Billy, Xaviera, and I arrived at his massage club, which was located in a large apartment building on West Fifty-seventh Street just off Eighth Avenue—a very fine neighborhood, as it happens, with Carnegie Hall and the Art Students League near by. As we entered, we were greeted by a pretty young woman who asked to check Billy's membership card. He then explained to us that cash couldn't be used to pay for any of the regular services here—we were his guests and he would sign for everything. He'd be billed by the club at the end of the month, he said.

Billy then led us to a large dressing room with lockers, where he said we should strip down to the altogether—I was suddenly glad for my nudist-camp training—but that we could wear towels to the pool. But swimming had to be in the nude, he said—that was a club rule.

"Don't worry," he said, "it's all very relaxed here."

170

"Who's worried?" Xaviera said, flashing that famous lascivious grin of hers.

Billy then explained that we'd spend some time at the pool, and then our names would be called for a massage appointment. If we didn't want a massage, that was fine, too, just let them know.

"I *definitely* will want a massage," Xaviera said, still grinning.

"Me too!" I chimed in, sounding like a kid who was afraid that the supply of lollipops was about to run out.

Billy left us alone, and Xaviera and I changed from being completely clothed to being completely nude.

"Where's the towels we're supposed to get?" Xaviera wondered.

"I guess we get them on the way out," I said. And that's the way it did work. As you left the (un)dressing room, a girl attendant—again young and pretty—gave us large towels to wear, and we wrapped ourselves in them. Just then Billy showed up, also in a towel, and took us to the main pool—an Olympic-size affair with a very handsome bar on one side.

I was surprised to see everyone, including a lot of women, standing around casually nude, and Xaviera, rapidly getting into the spirit of things, dropped her own towel and pulled mine off me, and said, "Come on, let's swim."

We dove into the pool and swam back and forth, stopping to catch our breaths and to talk with anyone who cared to talk with us. Here we were in the middle of New York City, without a stitch of clothing on, chatting as though we were at a cocktail party. I wondered how many of the folks passing by on West Fifty-seventh Street could even dream what was occurring on one floor of this elegant apartment building.

When Xaviera and I had had enough of the pool for a while, we climbed out and dried off. And we didn't put the towels back on—we walked over to a couple of beach chairs and plunked ourselves down in them. Xaviera wanted her usual orange juice, and I was thirsty too, so I got up and went to the bar and ordered soft drinks for us, indicating that they were to be put on Billy's bill.

"Of course, sir," said the bartender, about the only person in the place who wasn't nude.

"You know something," I said when I returned to Xaviera with our drinks, "you couldn't use money if you wanted to—no pockets."

We both laughed, and I was glad we'd come. I felt very relaxed and was enjoying the hell out of Xaviera's observations as she checked out nearly every person in the room. She was being a visual *yenta*, if you know what I mean."

"Look at the size of that guy's cock," she was saying, adding an "Ummmm" to express her admiration. "And just *look* at the beautiful body on that girl—what legs, what a great ass she has!"

"Nothing wrong with her bustline, either," I commented laconically.

"I'll say—boy, how'd you like to be close to *that* for a few hours?"

"You or me?"

"It could be both of us, for all I care," she answered me, "just so you kept your sperm out of her and I got my licks in." She enjoyed her pun while I groaned.

"Look at that fat, dumpy guy," she continued. "Isn't he embarrassed to be nude with all these great-looking people around?"

"Xaviera, for all you know he's a wonderful guy and the biggest stud in town . . . besides, he's got as much right to be a member here as anyone else. You pays your money and you shows your pee-pee."

We both laughed, and it went on like that, our just carrying on a happy, kind of silly conversation until our names were called.

"Massage, anyone?" I said, getting up.

"No fucking around in there, you hear," she said, walking away in a different direction. I didn't bother to answer her. I had read some things about massage parlors, but I really didn't know what to expect.

I was led by an attendant into a nice-sized room with a large table and introduced to my masseuse, a honey-blonde in her early twenties who looked about fifteen. She had a moon-shaped face, with very big blue eyes, and a pouty little mouth. But she filled out her polka-dot bikini very nicely—no childish features there, I can tell you.

"Good evening, sir," she greeted me, "my name is Linda." Her voice was very high and reminded me of the old movie-cartoon character Betty Boop, and that's how I continued to think of her.

Betty Boop indicated that I was to get on the table, stomach down, and she proceeded to give me a fairly decent massage, rubbing the oil into the skin around my neck and shoulders and working on my back. Then, wiping off the oil which hadn't been absorbed, she gave me a cooling alcohol rub. Her hands weren't very strong, but it felt relaxing just the same.

While Betty Boop was massaging me I asked her what she did, and she replied that she was an actress. An "actress"—the world is full of attractive young women who believe they are actresses. I'm glad that some of them have jobs which take them away from "actressing," or else the unemployment rate would be even higher.

Betty Boop finished with my back, then asked me to roll over, and gave the front of my body the same treatment. To my surprise, I didn't get hard, and for all I could tell she didn't even notice I had a penis between my legs. Well, if *she* didn't care, then *I* didn't care. . . .

Just then, as my skin was cooling off from the alcohol rub, Betty Boop said, as though she were ordering a frankfurter at Nedick's, "Now, sir, would you like your penis massaged as well?"

Aha, I thought, at last she's trying to get a rise out of me, but I said, sort of timidly, "Well, er, what do you have in mind?"

"I could rub your penis for you, sir. . . . I'm sure it would feel good."

"You mean, you would use your hand to make me feel good?"

"That's right, sir, I would use my hand."

Hell, I wasn't interested in a hand-job. "Listen, Linda," I said in what I hoped was a warm, comforting voice, "don't you think you could use something else?"

173

"What precisely did you have in mind, sir?" Her expression didn't change a bit when I responded, "What I had in mind is *precisely* what is beneath your bikini bottoms which I am sure is very cute and furry and cuddly and which would feel very good if you were to place it over my penis. It goes by many names——"

"Oh, you mean my cunt!" she said brightly.

"I was referring of course to your vagina," I said trying to keep from laughing "but if you want to call it your cunt, that's fine too. Yes, as a matter of fact, I would like my penis and . . . your cunt to get together for some mutual pleasure."

"Oh, I can't do that."

"Why," I said, "is it against the rules?"

"No, it's not against the rules. We can do anything so long as we are discreet about it."

"Then what's the problem?"

"My boyfriend forbids me to screw with the customers."

"Oh . . . *well*, bully for him."

To tell the truth, I was getting a little weary of this conversation. She had a very lovely body, and since Xaviera was undoubtedly balling someone wherever she was, I certainly didn't feel guilty about wanting to ball Betty Boop, but if all Betty was willing to do was play rub-a-dub-dub on my cock, I guess the massage was over.

I had forgotten a possible alternative, but Betty hadn't. "Oh, sir, how will it be with you if I blow you instead?"

"It will suit me just fine, but how come you're willing to blow me, but not have intercourse with me?"

"Well, sir, that's just it—if I screw you, I'm making love to you, because my whole body is involved in the act, but if I blow you, well, it's just my mouth—it's really much more impersonal that way."

"Your boyfriend doesn't mind you using your mouth on other men's penises?" I asked as she poured a little oil into her hand and began to "massage" my penis into a state of readiness.

"He minds," she said with a little smile, "but I gargle after every act of fellatio, and I promise him I won't fellate more than seven or eight men during the course of a working session."

Oh, so now she wasn't blowing me after all . . . she was going to fellate me. During those few seconds her hand was working on my penis to get it hard, I kept waiting for her to say something along the lines of "Excuse me, sir, but before I begin fellating you, I had better inform you of our rates for fellatio." For all I knew, she would charge by the minute, but no mention of money was made, and now she couldn't talk if she wanted to. Her mouth was full of cock, and her head was bobbing up and down at a fantastic rate.

I'll say this for Betty Boop—if she didn't take lessons from another Linda—Miss Lovelace herself—she sure could have fooled me, because she got an amazing amount of penis into her mouth.

At this rate I was going to come in less than two minutes, and I tapped her on the shoulder to slow her down, but if anything she went up and down even faster—her spinal cord must be made out of elastic—and I couldn't have held back if I'd wanted to. Just as her mouth went down almost to the base of my penis, I exploded a small gusher of jism inside her mouth, which, since she was holding my balls in one hand, she had to know was about to happen. But she kept her mouth all the way down while I kept coming, and only when the spasms had stopped did she slowly come up for air. Then down once more, and back up again, to clean it off.

I just lay back and relaxed for a few minutes, while Linda excused herself for a minute and left the room, presumably going to wherever it is she goes to gargle. When she came back, I expected some mention of money—of course I didn't have any on me, but I'd bring back whatever she asked for—but all she did was smile at me and say, almost hopefully, "Well now, sir, I certainly hoped you enjoyed that."

"It was very, very good, Linda. You have quite a talent in the fellatio department."

"Thank you," she said. "I really do like to please, even if it is impersonal. . . ."

"Where did you learn to . . .eh, well, take so much penis in your mouth?"

"My boyfriend taught me," she giggled, and then her

175

face turned crimson as a deep blush took over. "Oh, Jesus," she said, "he doesn't want anyone to know that! It's our secret."

"Your secret is safe with me," I said, "and my compliments to your boyfriend. What does he do for a living?"

"He's an apprentice plumber," she said proudly.

"It figures," I said, holding back the laughter until after I'd left the room.

When I got back to the pool area Xaviera was seated at the bar, completely nude, discussing her problems with the Immigration Department with some people there, and she sort of waved hello at me and kept on talking. Billy was on the other side of the pool, chatting with some friends, and I joined that conversation for a few minutes.

Finally he asked me, "How'd it go?"

"Swimmingly," I responded, giving him a big wink. Then the two of us went back to the bar and had a drink. I was feeling pretty hungry after my great orgasm, and suggested that Billy go out to dinner with us. Xaviera agreed it was time for dinner, and so I asked her what kind of a tip she wanted to leave the girl who'd given her a massage. I couldn't believe she hadn't carried on with her girl in one way or another.

"What do you mean?" she said.

"Well, I'm going to go back to the locker and get some money to give my girl a tip, and then go back and get dressed. I'll bring back money for you, too, so I don't have to make two trips. I don't want to come back here after I'm dressed—it's too hot here."

"Well, never mind me," she said.

"What do you mean?"

She looked at me, and if there is such a thing as having a lascivious twinkle in your eye, that's what Xaviera had as she said, "Larry, *she* should tip *me*."

"Do you mean what I think you mean . . . ?"

"I mean that I already took care of her—she should pay me for the 'fastest flick in town.' " She stuck out her tongue at me, in a naughty way, lest I not get her meaning.

I went back, got enough money to give Linda a nice tip, asked one of the attendants to call Linda out so I

176

could make sure she actually received the money, then went back and pulled Xaviera away to get dressed.

"How was your massage?" she asked me as we were getting dressed.

"Okay," I said, "How was yours?"

"Delicious. . . ."

"Naturally," I said.

"Well, she *was*," Xaviera insisted.

"I hope you've left some appetite for dinner," I said, not a little sarcastically.

"I'm really famished. How 'bout you?"

"Oh, I've worked up a little appetite," I said, looking as mysterious about it as I could manage.

"Well, I bet I eat more than you!"

"I'll bet you do, too," I said, half teasing her. "Just don't eat too fast—it's bad for your digestion."

We ate Chinese that night.

But you know what they say about Chinese food.

So later on that night, the two of us had a little snack. I ate Dutch. And Xaviera ate American.

CHAPTER 22.

The day came for Xaviera to leave and you have read, I'm sure, about all the newsmen pursuing her like leeches.

I missed her almost from the start, but fortunately she loves to write letters, and we stayed in close touch that way. That is, I wrote cards or called, and she wrote letters.

Here are some brief excerpts from letters Xaviera wrote me during the first month or so we were separated:

Dated May 1, 1972

"My Dearest Larry, My Schnooko,

"My God, do I miss you! I never thought I had been so attached to you. It is at present midnight Monday night, and I just congratulated my mother on her birthday, and will take her shopping tomorrow afternoon to buy her a nice present. . . . Larry, at least I have plenty of time to work on my new book. I've done a hell of a lot so far. If and when you decide to come, try to do it in a cheap way with an eight-day-tour package deal. Maybe it would be better if you just keep staying in the U.S. and meet me in Canada. And then maybe we can take off for a week, providing you make the arrangements since I have not got a clue where to go. Maybe we should meet someplace in Spain, in case you come to Europe. However, I am too confused now to think it over. I wish you would come and marry me so we would not have to go through any more hassles. . . . My love, don't cheat. I do love you more than ever and I'm dying to be with you again. I did sort of get to like you, you silly dummy. . . .

"Love and kisses,"

May 3, 1972

"Hi Larry,

"It is presently Wednesday morning. Yesterday was my mother's birthday. There are dozens of flowers from friends all over the country. . . . Larry, I desperately need the following, strange as it may sound: Two douche bags, one to hang and one with a ball that squeezes. They do not even exist here, and I would hate to eat a girl here. Have no intentions, but for my own hygiene I want to be clean . . . . Also, I do need quite a few more sheets and pillowcases. We have big square pillows here, queen-size sheets. . . . Boy, such a long letter you wrote. Please write two more lines next time. Type it even?

"Love and kisses,"

Undated, early in May, 1972

"My dearest Larry,

"Thanks for the check from the magazine sale of part of the book and the two letters. By now you must have received all my letters, which I send daily. You see, I do not neglect you and, after all, they are a lot longer than your little scribbled notes. . . . Look up your calendar when the next big American long weekend is coming up. However, I'd hate to stay in Europe too long, and wish the hell you'd marry me. I think I can pretty much manage to stay faithful. Have done it so far . . . all you need now is a business in Holland. . . . Next week I intend to buy a motorcycle since the car here is not available a lot of the time, and I live far from the city. I will return from Paris this coming Sunday. . . . Love you and miss you.

"Love, love, love,"

May 6, 1972

"My dearest Larry,

"Finally I get some more complete letters from you. . . . I LOVE PEOPLE but here in Holland all I do is stay home and work on my book. . . . Just paid another $100 for Bagel, who is locked up in quarantine until May 25. That damn dog, I wish I had given him his shots earlier. One of us should have thought about it. . . . Far away from the

179

whole mess in the States, I seem to realize that a lot of people have been very good at bullshitting and stepping on me. I don't mean you in particular, because you have taken an awful lot of crap from me. Why, God only knows . . . maybe an ego trip. After all, not every man in N.Y. City could call himself the only steady boyfriend who lasted through thick and thin, heaven and hell. Forgive me, Larry, but I am just basically very depressed. . . ."

Undated, but around mid-May, 1972
"My dearest Larry,

"It was awfully nice to hear from you again by telephone. It seems that you are a millionaire, talking for that long. . . . Went out with a nice chap from South Africa, also a Dutchman, thirty-nine years old, but all uppity-uppity, no hanky-panky, and maybe you will meet him someday. . . . When you come, bring along a few typewriter ribbons for this IBM electric, some more tape casettes, and the flash attachment to my camera. If possible, also bring some Soft & Dry or another good deodorant (here very expensive and not so nicely perfumated), some soap (tax-free), a good adjustable shaving razor, and all the pussy spray there is left in the house. Hope the douche bags will arrive, feel uncomfortable without them. . . . Bring a nice bottle of perfume for my mother, a few cartons of Pall Mall without filters, and some gin, tax-free. Also, I think somewhere at Bloomingdale's or a store like that you can buy a little note-pad for taking down messages. They come in all sorts of colors. They're very cheap, but look nice. . . . Also if possible, take along my muskrat fur coat and I will keep it in storage here in Holland. Take that over your arm, and try to find a pair of colored slippers, the same type as the dog bit to pieces, but with flat heels, at Bloomingdales, ground floor or the one below, size 7. . . . Please bring along the new *Cosmopolitan* and *Harper's Bazaar*. And all the newspaper clippings you've gotten lately.

"All my love and kisses,"
May 17, 1972
"Hi there,

"Had a marvelous time in London and would really love to live there at least during September and October, since

180

that is when my book is coming out and I want to do some publicity. The *Penthouse* issue will be the September one as well and Bob Guccione is planning a great press party, an introductory party, in my honor so that the world will know that Xaviera Hollander is going to join *Penthouse* as a regular contributor with her own column. . . . Also received, the day before I left for London, the new part of the manuscript with the typed-up sections about Debbie and the kid, Phillip Roberto. . . . Got me rather excited remembering those moments. . . . Meanwhile, you crazy stupid son of a bitch, of course I love you and miss you. Have not had one orgasm since I left, except for this morning in the bathtub. . . . I will have an awful lot of work to do as far as the new books are concerned. I need more letters-to-the-happy-hooker material. Just bring the whole stack along, and I will choose. . . ."

Undated, but around May 20, 1972

". . . When you finally get here, I will buy you a birthday present, namely one of those blue jeans-type suits. . . . I will now retire myself to tape some answers to all the letters. Have just finished editing another section about Phillip Roberto, and have received another lovely letter from him—an adorable letter and great for the book. . . . Maybe you will appreciate it finally that you are having a Dutch girlfriend who can eventually show you a bit of the world other than Curacao (though that is Dutch, too), Puerto Rico and Las Vegas. I miss you, you silver fox, and am getting horny like hell. . . . You'd better stick to me, I hope, because I am not about to share you with anyone, especially after not having seen you for so long. I miss you and my watertap in Amsterdam. Joke, but true."

Dated May 24, 1972

"My dearest Bubala, maybe this is what I will call you in the future. . . . As far as Bob Guccione is concerned, he is dying to see me and to discuss all sorts of interesting things. Instead of writing for them, I might suggest doing some public relations work for them, which might mean traveling around Europe, etc. I think I'd rather do that, and some writing independently, rather than have to function with a monthly deadline on my back. . . . I am spoiling you by writing so much. . . .

181

"Love and many kisses,"
Dated May 31, 1972

"Hi there, my dear darling. Received your envelope with the text of David's story and the Miami material. I think I will redo this some so people will understand that these things went on at the same time. . . . I met Monique van Cleef yesterday, that famous Dutch slavemaster who got raided in New Jersey. Jesus, she really had some equipment in her house. Her book, the one that Bob Abel showed us, is coming out in September, and is called *Pay for Pain*. I believe Olympia Press is doing it. . . . Yesterday Albert took me shopping to a lovely boutique in Amsterdam, the most expensive one of all, and he bought me over two hundred dollars' worth of clothes—darling clothes, a black pair of elegant summer pants and a bright-colored peasant-style blouse, real silk, and a lovely long purplish silk wrap-around dress, which will be great for St. Tropez, and a beautiful big blue chain for around my neck. I felt so embarrassed—I was only used to YOU doing such things for me. That is awfully nice of him, and his wife appreciated the gesture. Any other normal woman would have thought her husband is crazy to spend so much on another woman, no? They really are groovy people and I am sure you will enjoy being with them. . . . Okay, write me soon."

Dated June 2, 1972

"Hi there, dear Bubala, it is at present Saturday afternoon, June 2, 1972. Tomorrow will be your birthday. I will definitely think of you. Hope you received my card in time. Meanwhile received the brochure from that lecture bureau and also some of the bookings, but really, Larry, I am NOT going to lecture for less than at least $800 or $1,000. . . . Monday I am leaving for London and will be back Wednesday late in the afternoon. My back has been killing me and Thursday next week I will get a complete checkup, with X rays. PLEASE, if you get this letter in time, call me Friday night around six P. M. to let me know exactly what is happening and when you are coming to St. Tropez and for how long. I miss you, stupid. . . . Meanwhile I worked those two days on the book. Received all the material on the girls and on Hector and the deejay. I really don't know where this is going to fit into the book,

182

but Bob will find a way to make it all fit in. On my new tapes, I have gotten as far as Paris. . . . It is now Sunday afternoon. Will leave for London tomorrow at one P. M. Party last night was great. Had a swing afterward with eight people, all NEW to it. Some girls cried for jealousy (like you and me, at first). They will learn soon. . . . Please call me either Friday afternoon or keep on trying."

An early June letter

"Hi there, my dearest darling. It is Sunday night and we are all in St. Tropez. . . . The people whose house this is were here until this afternoon and there were six other people here as well. No swinging going on. Just good friends and the owner of the house cooked a great spaghetti dinner. The French are really nice people and very hospitable, so long as you don't leave their house a mess, and we will see to it that it will look prim and proper when we leave. . . . This is really a fascinating little city, with the most beautiful shops you have ever dreamed of in the world. THIS IS WHERE THE LATEST FASHIONS EXIST AND START. Today I bought myself two lovely pantssuits . . . look adorable, but all I need now is a good suntan. PLEASE DON'T BUY ANYTHING FOR YOURSELF OVER THERE. This is where it is all at. For men as well as women, so you better take a lot of money along (for yourself, I mean) . . . bring along all kinds of Flair pens, too. . . . I have been behaving well and went to sleep both nights alone so far. Have no need for sex yet and would rather wait till you are here. I am building you up tremendously, so you better look real nice and most probably you will have an even better suntan than we have. . . . Please call Robin Moore and get back those tapes he promised us . . . also call the district attorney and get my books back. He doesn't need them anymore. And he promised to return them. . . . Love you, miss you, worked till three A. M. on my last tape. . . .

PART FIVE

HAPPY DAYS ARE HERE, AGAIN— I GO ABROAD AT LAST!

CHAPTER 23.

I hadn't seen Xaviera in over two months, although our correspondence was practically on a shuttle basis back and forth across the Atlantic. So I finally picked myself up and boarded an Air France plane and flew to Nice. It was the Fourth of July weekend, and I was going to take three solid weeks off.

In Nice I rented a Volkswagen, got directions to St. Tropez, and away I went to be reunited with Xaviera. She had prearranged to move out of the house in which she'd been staying with friends, and to get us a hotel room. I drove the distance between Nice and St. Tropez in no time at all—a beautiful drive taking me past Antibes and Cannes and St. Raphaël. As I was driving into the parking lot of the De Paris Hotel, where Xaviera had booked us a room, I saw her sitting on the hotel's front porch, waiting for me. She must have seen me at the same time, because a second later we were running to meet each other. Then we were in each other's arms, hugging and kissing. I didn't realize until that moment just how much I'd missed her. I had missed her a lot. Really a lot.

After we finally stopped hugging and kissing, Xaviera showed me to our room—which was a lovely, sunny room with plenty of bureau and closet space. The De Paris is ideally located, right in the center of St. Tropez, and while you need transportation to the beaches, all the shops are

185

close and it is a very pleasant walk to the boat basin and harbor.

After I got unpacked Xaviera showed me some of the town and then we had dinner. That night, you can bet we made love—mucho love.

The next morning we got up feeling great, and went downstairs to the hotel's restaurant at about 8:30 for eggs and marvelous croissants, made even more marvelous when accompanied by rich, creamy French butter and delicious orange marmalade. Then it was time for the beach—and the two sun-worshipers jumped into the rented Volks and were off to Tahiti beach, as though it were vitally important to be the first persons there. It wasn't even 9:15.

When we arrived near the beach, Xaviera showed me a parking area where the car would be shielded from the sun by a kind of leafy netting, hung there for that purpose, and we parked there. The walk to the beach was just a short block, and I was anxious to see this fabulous beach Xaviera had been raving about. I'll say this—she hadn't exaggerated one bit. This was a truly spectacular hunk of God's earth, with silvery white sand and clear blue water. The only beaches I've ever visited which merit any comparison with Tahiti beach are the ones in the Virgin Islands.

However, that's where the comparisons end. As people began to arrive, I had to admit that Tahiti beach had the most attractive people I'd ever seen in one place, with most of the women topless, and it was a strange feeling to be introduced to women with bare breasts. You do your best not to let your eyes dip down to their breasts, but I must admit that I flunked the test a lot of the time. After all, when you meet a pretty or attractive woman, you try to visualize what she must look like with no clothes, and here were women, one better-looking than the next, with only a sliver of a bikini between them and total nudity.

In addition to the gorgeous men and women on the beach, there were some hippies too, some of them *not* so gorgeous-looking. I got the impression that they were allowed to spend their nights on the beach as well, that the local police didn't bother them so long as they behaved themselves. On the way to the beach one day we passed two hippie boys hitchhiking, so we gave them a lift and they proved to be nice kids. I sometimes wish I'd had their sense of freedom when I was a kid.

Xaviera and I spent a good part of the daytime hours on the beach, because you could eat there as well, at a spacious restaurant with excellent food and pretty people. Or maybe it seemed so good because we were always so hungry after three or four hours in the sun and surf. Then, too, we generally didn't take lunch until two or three o'clock, so we had plenty of time to work up an appetite.

One day, after our lunch at this restaurant, we passed a small stall where two young girls were selling bikinis— not the elaborate, multicolored, elastic type of bikini, but crocheted bikinis or bikinis made out of bright solid-colored patches of material. I think these kids made the bikinis themselves, but they were certainly reasonable and I think Xaviera could easily have been persuaded to buy out the "store," so we settled for two suits, which I bought, and made it back to the beach to take a swim before the sun disappeared behind the mountains.

I guess every resort town on the ocean has an "in" beach, and we were *on* it. Tahiti was jet-setter territory, and so it also attracted the would-be jet setters—those who follow the fashions, which in this case was topless bathing. So the people Tahiti beach didn't attract were the tourist couples or groups of girls who felt uptight about the topless situation. On an adjacent beach, we bumped into a couple we knew from New York who both felt that way —he didn't want his wife to be showing off her boobs, and she felt shy about it herself, so it was perfectly logical that they should avoid Tahiti beach, because there a woman with her top on might be considered square or old-fashioned. In any case, our friends from New York were having a ball with their tops on, so that's all that really mattered.

Xaviera had briefly introduced me to Leo and Marika, about whom I'd heard so much—from Xaviera's letters, I knew they'd done a lot of swinging together—and also to Freda, a German girl staying with Leo and Marika who turned me off completely. Xaviera had described her as a very cold creature—I also felt she resented Freda's closeness with Leo and Marika—but that wasn't what I reacted

187

to. Freda had a beautiful body with large breasts and great legs, but there was something wrong in her skin pigmentation which produced livid white spots on her skin, and this physically repulsed me.

In any case, while we conversed with a great number of people in St. Tropez—naturally Xaviera already knew the whole town—we didn't socialize much during the day, being content to be by ourselves. One really wonderful thing about this beach was that it didn't get crowded like most American beaches, and you could put down a blanket and not have to worry about someone settling practically next door to you.

Inevitably, sometime during our hours at the beach, Xaviera would decide she had some phone calls to make —in New York or wherever, Xaviera always has phone calls to make—and we'd have to walk down to the next beach, Morea, where there was a restaurant—the Malaya —with a phone. I'd go along with Xaviera to keep her company and to keep her in phone change—no small feat. While she was making her calls I'd chat or kid around with the people at the bar of the restaurant, but we never made any formal plans to meet these people later. You could generally count on their showing up at a restaurant called L'Escale, because that was *the* place in town to gather, so it really wasn't necessary to make definite plans for the evening.

Besides, Xaviera and I were perfectly content with each other's company. When we'd have enough of swimming and sunning ourselves, we'd have our late lunch and then decide whether or not to head back to the hotel. The vote was generally to head back to the hotel for a shower and some sweet, sweet lovemaking. Then, instead of our usual nap, we'd throw on some casual clothes and go out for a walk.

My favorite place to visit was the boat basin, which was really a treat for me. I have always had a thing for boats, and the larger ones here were the most exquisite yachts I have ever seen. I think one day I counted over a hundred boats that were seventy-footers or larger. And what was even better than just gawking at these splendid yachts was going onboard them, because Xaviera seemed to know

188

someone on half the yachts there, and we were able quite literally to walk from yacht to yacht meeting people. The owners of these yachts were millionaires, but they were all gracious and cordial to us, and I think one evening I must have been introduced to fifty people in the space of a few hours. These were the real "beautiful people," because whatever their ages they looked well tanned, fit, and well cared for—which is hardly surprising. Anyone who can afford one of these gorgeous yachts can also afford to take very, very good care of themselves. And others.

Thus it was a bit perplexing to me one evening when Xaviera and I stood on the deck of a yacht belonging to a wealthy American watching a small cabin cruiser which was on fire. It wasn't moored anymore, and was floating around as it burned itself down to the waterline. But what was truly strange to witness were the people on all the yachts who stood around watching the small boat burn. If it happened to get close to their own yachts, as it drifted around, they'd dispatch part of the crew to shove it away, but no one on any of the boats did anything to put out the fire. It was as though the little boat were the "ugly duckling" of the boat basin.

In addition to its natural beauty and the smashingly attractive people who come there, St. Tropez has a lot of man-made beauty. Here I am referring to the absolutely fabulous shops in the heart of town, which are the blocks next to the boat basin. Xaviera had warned me not to bring along a lot of clothes because (1) dress in St. Tropez is very informal and (2) we'd be going on shopping binges, which both Xaviera and I love to do. So I'd packed very lightly—no suits, no sport jackets, just some slacks and shirts and bathing suits.

So quite apart from the sheer fun of it, there was a logical reason to go shopping most afternoons, and Xaviera bought me two voile shirts at a very smart boutique, and they are still among my favorites to this day. She also had a good friend, Lothar, who ran a very chic shop featuring tie-died suits for under forty dollars, but I'm afraid my waistline wasn't designed for the really narrow French cut. I would have enjoyed owning one of his suits—they are well-known in fashion circles the world round—and

189

when I was eighteen or nineteen and all skin 'n bones, it would have been a perfect fit for me. But with maturity, alas, has came a few inches in girth, and I think any guy with a waist larger than twenty-eight inches would have trouble looking good in these suits.

I liked most of the clothing styles I saw in the St. Tropez stores—with one exception. It had become very trendy to put studs on blue jeans and denim jackets, and all types of designs—eagles and stars and everything imaginable—were created by riveting these studs onto clothing. The first thing it reminded me of was the dress of the Hell's Angels and other motorcycle gangs, but here you'd see multimillionaires walking around with stars on their asses or eagles on the backs of their jackets or names spelled out in studs.

Aside from this one uniform, though, everyone did their own thing and dressed in very individualistic fashion. Each shirt or blouse was different in design and style and color, or so it seemed, and all the people looked as good in clothing as they did in bathing suits. My own preference among the females were the girls in see-through blouses, or in skimpy bare-midriff blouses which tie in front but leave little to the imagination. I found this even more of a turn-on than the bare-breasted beauties on the beach. You'd be standing a few inches from some great-looking creature, inhaling her heady perfume, and looking down upon her sumptuous bosom. It was a great sight, a beautiful sight—better, even, than Tahiti beach. I think that by the time we left St. Tropez I'd gotten a little used to it, but it was a lot of fun until I did.

If I ever did. . . .

I know this—if I hadn't been with Xaviera I might have gotten myself arrested for trying to make love to the entire female population of St. Tropez between the ages of twenty and thirty-seven-and-a-half because I found one more attractive than the next. And when you looked at them, they looked right back at you, and I'm sure that had I walked up to any one of these wonderful-looking females and put my arm around her waist and said, "May I buy you a drink?" I'd have had a companion for the evening.

But I *was* with Xaviera, constantly with her, and despite

my erotic daydreaming, I wouldn't have had it otherwise. I had been anticipating this vacation as a great time, and it was exceeding my expectations.

In addition to being in Europe for the first time and the sun and the beach and the breasts and the yachts and the shops, another reason I was having the time of my life in St. Tropez was the pure delight of having a car there. In New York and most American cities, owning a car is usually a hassle except for weekends, when the traffic, at least, is light, but here people seemed to regard a car as a pleasant convenience and not a problem. Most of the cars were small European models or else sports cars, and drivers parked them wherever there happened to be an open space —in front of the boats, on the sidewalks, wherever. You just parked. Period. No one argued with you. If some guy's car blocked our car, someone would help you push that car a bit so you could get out. And you'd do the same for someone else. No one rushed around in their cars. No one seemed in a terrible hurry. It was a pleasure. My God, having a car was *fun* in St. Tropez.

Evenings we usually drove over to L'Escale to enjoy the crowd there. (We ate there once, and it was fine, but so were the other St. Tropez restaurants—the food there is every bit as good as in Paris, I feel.) The scene there, I must say, was unique to my experience—we'd have barely gotten through the door when people would be greeting us and putting drinks into our hands. If memory serves me correctly, I never got a chance to buy a round of drinks there because whenever I needed a refill, there one was, plunked into my hand, and my protests—everyone spoke some English—would be ignored, in the nicest way possible. Still, since Xaviera seemed to know everyone in the place, I had to wonder, each time some new good-looking guy became my friend on the spot, how many of these laddies had enjoyed her favors. Things, I'd learned, were very, very casual in St. Tropez, and people went to bed with each other as easily as they took a dip in the blue Mediterranean together. But that had nothing to do with the place itself—it really was one of the most cordial and friendly places I've ever frequented.

People didn't come to L'Escale in groups, but rather by themselves or else as couples, and the mood was always relaxed and most genial. People here didn't get hung up on planned evenings, and it made for a very loose, swinging—in the old-fashioned sense of the word—atmosphere. You didn't come to L'Escale to prove anything—except that you knew the best place in town to go for some relaxed fun.

There were other spots which Xaviera and I liked. The Le Gorille cafe, down by the boat basin, served sensational cold fruit drinks and you could sit there and admire the yachts and watch the world walk by. We also liked some of the discotheques for after dinner, and one night, just as we walked into Papagayou, we ran into Leo and Marika, who seemed rather cool to us.

I knew that Xaviera had had a falling-out with them, which I'll let her tell you about in her new book—because it's quite a long story—and I also knew, from her letters, that they had been quite close, and now she felt badly about the misunderstanding, or whatever you cared to call it, between them. But she didn't seem to be able to do anything this night to patch up things, and Leo and Marika weren't being very helpful in that regard, either. After a few minutes of small talk, we each went our own ways, and I knew it bothered Xaviera.

"Look," I said, "if you want to be friends with them again, why don't we spend an evening together with them?"

"No, I'd rather have you all to myself," Xaviera said. "We can always see them another time."

"But I thought you wanted me to get to know them?"

"I do, but. . . ."

I knew Xaviera well enough to recognize that she really did want to make up with Leo and Marika, and perhaps I'd given her the opening to make it happen. She could always say I'd heard so much about them and wanted to spend at least a little time with them while in St. Tropez, so why not have dinner? If they declined, well, then that was that. They'd never become friends of mine, and the friendship with Xaviera was definitely over.

So Xaviera did call them, and to her pleasure they really accepted and we had a very nice evening together, with dinner at my expense and the rest of the evening on them. The friendship seemed to be blooming again and I guess I made a hit because, unbeknownst to me, Leo invited Xaviera and me to their farewell dinner party in St. Tropez. She accepted on behalf of both of us, but asked Leo not to mention it because with swingers like these, any big bash was also sure to turn into something dealing with other appetites as well. Xaviera, I later learned, also felt it would help matters considerably if I felt obligated to attend because of her.

Frankly, I was surprised when Xaviera told me two days later that we'd been invited to a swing party, because we had so conspicuously been avoiding that kind of thing here in St. Tropez. Also, the rules were different because she'd been building me up as a lover to her friends. Why, I could even come inside a female at this event! She said it, but I wasn't convinced by her tone.

As the night of the party grew closer, I grew more apprehensive. Part of me was dying to go to this party but Xaviera had put all this burden of reputation on me. Suppose I came in half a second? Suppose my cock didn't stand up to the test to which, I'd gathered, Leo and Marika were sure to put me? On the other hand, suppose I was in terrific form and all those delicious fantasies about the St. Tropez women were materializing in one night, and Xaviera became enraged by my running after everything attractive and female in the room?

However, there was another side of it. I'd come to St. Tropez to be with Xaviera, not to go to a swing. Sure, I could be turned on by watching her make love to another woman, but I didn't particularly look forward to watching her fuck with another guy. How jealous would I be?

At this point I was really anxious to chicken out of the party. I didn't need voyeurs, or other participants, in my love life, and anyhow, it looked as though Xaviera and Leo and Marika were going to be friends again.

Then I had another thought, or inspiration, if you will. There were going to be perhaps fifteen other couples at this little affair, and that was a lot easier to handle, in many ways, than a swing with just one or two other couples. There had to be people there who would please both Xaviera and me, and after it was over, if we still dug each other, then the experiment would have been worthwhile, proof that our feelings for each other went a lot deeper than sex. Or was I just trying to talk myself into something?

CHAPTER 24.

The day of the party, I was demonstrably tense and nervous. Xaviera noticed it and suggested we go back to the hotel earlier than usual and get some rest. Neither a shower nor trying to take a nap helped any, so we decided to try some foreplay for relaxation purposes. We caressed each other, most tenderly, and I ate her and made her come while she sucked my cock and made it grow to twice its usual size. Xaviera, however, wanted me to hold back—"Don't spill it, do not spill it, save it," she kept telling me as she played with my cock and ass and balls.

Well, I realized that she wanted me to live up to the advance billing she'd been giving me, and you can imagine how horny I was when we finally got to the party. We brought along presents for Leo and Marika—a thick leather belt for him with a devil's head brass buckle, which we'd bought on the beach, and a mock chastity belt made of linked chains going around the waist and between the legs (which I'd actually given to Xaviera as a gift) for her—and when we arrived, I was glad we'd brought the presents along (they were peace offerings, really, for Xaviera's sake) because the party wasn't anything like I'd expected.

For one thing, by now I was so used to the casualness and easy-going style of St. Tropez life, and this wasn't, by any kind of measure, a casual party. Leo, for instance, greeted us in an elegant Morrocan caftan with a big heavy buckled belt, which we made him take off and replace with our belt. He seemed very pleased with the present, and Xaviera quipped, "The devil in you is outside now, so you'd better put an angel inside."

He then escorted us into a gigantic living room—remember, I'd never been to this house before—in which there were no electric lights on. A large fireplace in one corner of the room, and huge, fantastically shaped candles lit up the room in an exotic way. Most of the guests had already arrived, and I immediately got the feeling that part of the "formality" of the evening could be attributed to the fact that a lot of these people didn't know each other, their only link being Leo and Marika. And, to a degree, my own friend, Xaviera.

Marika came over to greet us, and she looked spectacular—she is a tall, truly handsome woman who could cause stirrings in any man—and then Leo and Xaviera took me around to make introductions.

I met Ahmed, an Egyptian Jew in the export business whom they knew from Paris. He was a big man with a strong-featured face. He reminded me of Omar Sharif.

Marika's sister, like her sibling a tall pretty girl with a splendid figure, hardly looked like she belonged at this event. She seemed very nervous.

Freda was there, with a girl, but made no effort to speak to us.

There was a huge handsome bull of a man, very Scandinavian-looking—he reminded me of some Viking god of old—who turned out to be completely French. With him was a girl who looked to be still in her teens, a pretty brunette with a pageboy haircut. She wore blue jeans and a white see-through blouse which revealed two pert little titties with erect nipples.

Xaviera got into a conversation with them and Leo then brought me over to a corner of the room to meet Nicole, a very elegantly dressed woman in a long black evening gown, cut very low in back, who was most striking. Black hair, green eyes, a patrician face. My guess was that she was in her late thirties or early forties, but her age hardly mattered—she had extraordinary presence, almost a mystique, about her and you knew she would always have an air of mystery about her that would prove compelling to men. The equally patrician gentleman with her was Robert, her husband, who was clearly a good deal older than she was, but a superb tan, good muscle tone, and well-chiseled features made him a fit companion for his remarkable wife.

"Ah, Xaviera's friend from New York," he said, giving me a warm but very practical handshake. "We've heard so much about you."

"I hope it's been the sort of thing I'd like you to hear," I replied, grinning slightly. "Xaviera can be quite a biased reporter. . . ."

"Oh, it has, it has," he said. I smiled at his wife, and she smiled back, looking as mysterious as ever. As Leo led me away to meet the actual owners of this glorious villa —Xaviera had raved about the place, and especially about the pool, but we hadn't been invited—he mentioned that Nicole and Robert were among the wealthiest people on the entire French Riviera, both of them coming from rich backgrounds. "Old money," he added, with a little smirk, as though to say, "Old money, new money—what's the difference, so long as it's *there*."

What I was thinking about, however, was not the amount of money in the room, but what an odd collection of people for a swing. Take Francois, for instance—he had to be possessive about his wife, and yet here he was. Was he wondering, as we shook hands, "Will this American of Xaviera's come back and make love to my wife better than I can?" Or would he feel angered, or turned on, by the sight of his wife sucking my cock? And what about that giant Frenchman who looked like Leif Eriksson—he could probably break me in two if he didn't like the sight of his little lady friend riding up and down on my cock. The room was full of very attractive women—a few, like Nicole, simply stunning—and I was so horny that just thinking about making love to these new women was really getting to me. I'd either be a magnificent flop, in which case this might end up being the shortest swing on record, or else it'd be a magnificent night.

Then it finally occurred to me what the real allure of the evening was—I didn't know any of these people well, apart from Xaviera, and I'd only just met Leo and Marika. Then, too, they were all Europeans, and that somehow made them more glamorous and intriguing. And they were all so different.

Just then Xaviera came over. I'd been chatting with Marcel and Brigitte, our actual hosts—a very pleasant couple in their early forties, they were the owners of this villa—when Xaviera whispered something in my ear. I told her I couldn't hear what she'd said.

"Come along with me," she repeated in my ear. "I want you to meet some people who are really different from anything you've ever experienced." What? Had she been reading my mind?

She took me toward the corner of the room where there were three people—a guy and two girls—sitting on the edge of the fireplace, watching the open fire, and just before we reached these people, she whispered, "*These* are the girls with the rings. . . ."

I didn't have the slightest idea of what she was talking about, but it was too late to ask her because we were already there. The guy's name was Mark—he was a slim British playboy in his late twenties who looked as though he could afford a little sun—and the girls, who also looked pale in comparison to the other people in the room, were named Lori and Julie, and they didn't impress me either. Both were far too slim and flat-chested and looked like a couple of teenagers.

As we moved away to make some other introductions, I asked Xaviera what the "girls with the rings" business was all about, and she informed me, to my complete surprise, that Lori and Julie were considered by some of the people in this room to be two of the most erotic creatures on earth.

" 'Erotic creatures'?" I said. "They look as though they should be babysitting for the kids of some of the people In this room! Are they hookers or what?"

Xaviera fixed me with a look which said I didn't know anything about anything, and then went on to explain that Lori and Julie were not hookers, just a couple of fun-loving freaks who'd had holes drilled in their nipples and through their outer vaginal lips and could put rings through these holes, just as a woman would wear earrings after getting her ears pierced. But instead of earrings, Lori and Julie had hung chains or keys on their rings and could twirl them around.

Boy, that certainly sounded erotic to me—maybe we could get them on the Johnny Carson show. "Xaviera," I said patiently, "I am not impressed."

"You'll see," she replied. So then I asked what Mark's role was in all this—did he keep a supply of keys available for them to twirl at all times or what?—and Xaviera, either missing or else ignoring the irreverence of my question, explained that Mark was their "old man," their protector, and that his little clan had formerly included three girls, but one had left to get married. Mark was independently wealthy and was keeping both girls, although occasionally they picked up a little money working in porno movies.

"Yes, I know," I said, "I saw their last film, with Gregory Peck—*The Keys of the Kingdom*." Xaviera, who isn't always up on the old movies, didn't laugh, so I asked another question: "If they're such super swingers, why don't they look happier here? Are they jealous of everyone else's tans?"

Xaviera gave me another of those looks which said "Dolt!" and explained that the three of them had been here before—which is where she'd met them—and the girls were the stars of that party, the belles of the ball, if you will. But tonight nobody seemed to be paying much attention to them, which probably accounted for their baleful expressions.

Suddenly Xaviera stopped to introduce me to a really fine-looking woman with short brown hair who was having an animated conversation with Ahmed, whom I'd met earlier. Hmmm, I thought, making notes for later, really good-looking chick—but it was not to be. The woman's name was Nina—she was Dutch-Belgian—and she was

198

obviously very emotionally involved with Ahmed. So far as I could tell, they weren't out of each other's company all night, although someone might have stuck a rigid tongue one place or another in Nina sometime during the night, when my back was turned.

"What's *her* story?" I asked Xaviera as we continued our tour around the room.

"She lives in Antwerp, her husband is in shipping, she's thirty-four, has four kids and an awful marriage. . . ."

"So why doesn't she take her four kids—if her husband's wealthy—and end the marriage?"

"He won't give her a divorce," Xaviera said, "but he lets her come to places like St. Tropez whenever she wants to and fuck her brains out, while he stays home with the kids."

"A nice arrangement," I commented, "Very 'modern.'"

We were passing by the patrician-looking couple I'd admired before, Nicole and Robert, and Xaviera stopped to chat amiably with them in French. Nicole shyly whispered something to Xaviera, and she in turn whispered something in Robert's ear, and he nodded his head appreciatively.

"What was that all about?" I asked as we walked back toward the bar.

"Oh," Xaviera said casually, "Nicole was admitting to me that she has never made love with a woman, and"— I could see Xaviera's eyes sparkle as she contemplated this—"I told Robert that I would eat Nicole up and that he could either watch or he could make love to me doggie-style."

"Oh," I said. So much for any notions that this patrician couple wouldn't be up to the demands of the evening. "Listen," I continued, "are there any rules for this special occasion that I should know about?"

"Yes," she responded without expression, "I must make love, as a courtesy, to the host. . . ."

"Let's hear the 'and'. . . ."

"And *you* must make love to the hostess."

Well, if I was going to play the game, at least I knew what the rules were.

The rules were to be very, very courteous.

CHAPTER 25.

Yes, there would be some "eating" going on this evening, but in the meantime I was hungry. So I was grateful to see Leo and Marika and her sister, plus some other women, now appear in the dining room, bearing what appeared to be tons of food. Great platters of cold meats and cheeses, several different kinds of salads, bowls of celery, hearts of palm, tomatoes and other vegetables, various relish dishes, several kinds of bread, and platters heaped with delicious-looking pastry. Plus one of the largest serving bowls I've ever seen, heaped with spaghetti, and two separate bowls of sauce for it.

Dinner was being served buffet--style, and since there was so much great-looking food spread out, I thought I'd just skip the spaghetti. But when I passed where the spaghetti was being served, Leo, who was in charge of serving it, took my plate and said, "With . . . or without?"

"You mean one sauce is a lot spicier than the other?" I asked him.

He gave me a look which made me feel I'd asked a stupid question, then said, patiently, "I want you to know there's plenty of spice in both sauces, but this one —over here—has a different kind of spice in it. It's called hashish."

I looked at Xaviera, who looked a bit surprised herself, but she nodded—which meant Leo wouldn't be kidding about the hash sauce—and we both decided to try it.

We'd never been stoned together before. However, since Xaviera has little experience with drugs. I told Leo to go easy on her sauce. As for myself, I told him, "Pile it on," because I was sure the hash would help me lose any inhibitions I had about the rest of the evening.

We found a spot to sit down and eat, and both remarked about how good the spaghetti was. It didn't taste any different from other excellent spaghetti sauces I've had, and so far as I could tell, was having no effect on me. But then I'd never had hash in food before, and didn't quite know what to expect.

I don't know if this was the case or not—that the hash increased my appetite—but I really ate a hearty meal that evening, even finishing a little bit of spaghetti, with lots of sauce, left on Marika's sister's plate. Then, as I was helping to clear away the dishes, and since no one was looking, and that sauce was so darned good, I finished Xaviera's spaghetti, I also had some more salad, fruit and cheese, and felt really content. I'd already had a perfectly swell time, swing or no swing.

I'd been about an hour since we'd started eating, and I asked Xaviera if she was feeling anything, and she smiled a cute little smile and said, "I'm feeling groovy." Come to think about it, I was feeling a little light-headed myself —though maybe not "groovy"—and I had attributed this to the hash, because I deliberately hadn't had any wine with the meal.

Just then a new couple arrived at the party, a Dutch couple in formal dress, whom I vaguely remembered from the beach. Leo and Marika didn't seem to know them, but since they were Dutch, welcomed them in. He offered them a drink, then had some spaghetti—which had been warming over a fire in the kitchen, brought out, along with both bowls of sauce. "With or without?" he said, asking his usual saucy question.

This didn't register on them any more than it had on me, so Leo explained what the secret ingredient was in the second sauce. Since they were speaking in Dutch, I was relying on Xaviera for a simultaneous translation, and she told me that the woman, who was a blonde in her late thirties, seemed outraged by the suggestion they "eat an illegal drug," and that they'd been told this was an official dinner party, which is why they were in formal dress.

It was obvious that they'd gotten the wrong address, or some other misunderstanding had taken place, and Leo was very politely trying to explain this to them. In the meantime, a few people at the party were moving all the furniture from the center of the room and placing big foamy pillows all over the living room floor. I didn't know where all these pillows were materializing from, but the expression on the face of the Dutchman's wife was rapidly changing from distaste to disbelief to near-hysteria as she watched the living room being transformed into a sea of pillows and saw Marika and the girls with the rings and some of the men being disrobed.

Even to me it was an astonishing scene. Men and women both were helping each other out of their clothes, almost regally planting kisses and caresses on the magnificently tanned bare flesh which was emerging from the clothing, and the sight was one great body after another emerging into nudity in a loving process which reminded me of some coronation. At the same time, half the party group was still talking and chatting as though this were some tea social.

If I'd been in a normal cogent state, I might have felt sorry for the Dutchwoman, but I was really flying now and the whole situation—this completely "straight" couple arriving at the wrong place at the wrong time (just when a swing was about to begin)—struck me as really quite funny. Finally Leo, to put her out of her agony, quietly pointed out to her that "a hell of a party was about to start in five minutes, and did she want to stay or not?" She yelped out a stuttering kind of "No!" and rushed for the front door. But her husband, a slightly balding blond guy just beginning to show his age, seemed in no hurry to follow her. In fact he stood there, sipping on his drink, watching closely as Marika made an elegant show out of removing her clothing. He seemed almost hypnotized.

His wife reappeared and said, this time in rather good English, "Come on. Come on. I don't want to be any part of this. Let's go!" He heard her, all right, but he

202

didn't budge. Then she went back into Dutch, telling him she was leaving with the car, and he could walk home if he didn't get his ass into high gear and leave with her (Xaviera's translation). He stayed put. She'd lock him out of the house, his wife screamed, and then slammed the door. Not a move from her hubby.

Then Marika, who had been the object of his fascination, came over and explained that he'd better go if he wanted to stay on good terms with his wife. And that if she drove off with their car, he'd be in bad straits because it was already too late to call to cab. To me, the sight of tall, succulent, nude Marika standing there next to this guy in his formal dress and Leo in his North African caftan was absolutely a howl, and I found myself giggling like crazy. The hash, I knew, was really working now, and I felt just great.

The poor guy, knowing what he *should* do, just stood there, and said, in English instead of Dutch, "But this looks like a pretty nice party . . . I sort of like it here . . . I'd like to stay, if you don't mind."

Aha! A conversion! However, Leo, speaking with a real edge in his voice this time, began to deliver a lecture that was so severe that just about everyone in the room stopped what they were doing and started listening to him: "Look, I guess you don't know anything about swingers or, more important in this instance, about swingers' own code of etiquette. But don't think we *don't* have them. So let me tell you these few things. If you arrive with your wife, we expect you to leave with your wife . . . if you arrive with a partner, a companion, a date, or whatever, we expect her to be your responsibility at night's end—a swinging party is *not* the occasion to end your emotional responsibilities to that person. . . . Yes!—a swing involves changing partners, but it does not involve hurting anyone. No one here would ever enjoy himself if it involved hurting someone. We're going to be having a lot of fun, but always fun with all the rules observed—we're not here to form new alignments. So I suggest you return to your wife as soon as possible. Unless I misunderstand you, I suggest you take advantage of the fact that your wife has not driven off—we would have heard the car, I daresay—and keep your marriage intact. . . ."

Our friend looked meekly at Leo, and said, "But I *did* really want to stay. . . ." Leo looked at him, and said, not without warmth, "Look, if you want to come here, you have to bring a companion—so you talk it over with your wife, and then decide if you've learned anything quite apart from the fact that there are lots of beautiful women in St. Tropez"

Leo then took our friend by the arm and escorted him to the door. "Dear boy," Leo then said in a voice so unctuous that it reduced a lot of us to laughter again, "please don't come back until you have a beautiful woman with you . . . or else a complacent wife . . . *you* decide."

As the poor man left, we could hear his wife screaming outside, and then their car screeching off. At the first sound of their screaming, we all relaxed and laughed.

This was a party—no outsiders allowed.

CHAPTER 26.

It took a few minutes after the abrupt departure of the uninvited guests for the mood to become completely relaxed again, but the hash was working an everyone, and soon the living room was full of nude people settling down, in various combinations, on the large foamy pillows.

I looked around, and didn't see Xaviera in the sea of bodies. Because of the candlelight—the open door had caused a few candles to blow out—my vision wasn't too terribly sharp, but my mind wasn't so blurred by the drug that I was about to grope my way among all these bodies looking for the one I knew best. After all, this was a swing and the idea was to have a lot of partners.

I sort of drifted around until I saw somebody available—Marika's sister, lovely in her nudity, was lying back, being eaten by Marcel, her long legs draped over his rugged shoulders. She seemed to be enjoying herself, not nervous as she'd appeared earlier in the evening, and so I wasn't hesitant about offering my cock to her mouth. Turning her head, she took it greedily, and held it with one hand as she sucked on it, and while it felt good, it wasn't anything sensational. I kept thinking of Xaviera doing the same thing, and hoped our paths would soon cross so that we could finish what we'd been doing back at the hotel.

Our paths were to cross, right then and there, because suddenly there Xaviera was, hovering over me as Marika's sister was sucking me, her long hair loose and hanging down over her face, among other things tickling my balls. I don't think I'm flattering myself when I say I saw an angry look of jealousy take possession of Xaviera's face. I would have tried to get up and join her, but there was a female mouth keeping me where I was, and before I could even say anything, Xaviera had moved away and purposely gotten herself into a cosy little threesome almost next to me. She had draped herself over someone's lap—the guy's back was to me, so I couldn't see his face but from his blond mane and the size of his shoulders, I knew it was the Viking—and he was spanking her. Meanwhile, kneeling in front of her, was this well-known fashion designer who enjoyed the reputation of being a regular fucking machine. Not only did he have great endurance, Xaviera had told me—he'd arrived late at the party, and I inquired about him because of his striking appearance—but he had a rule about never fucking the same woman twice. In her case, she implied with a cocky little shake of the head, he'd broken his rule.

Well, he wasn't fucking her now, he was on his knees in front of her, his big dick sticking out, while she played with the head of it and caressed him. Then she began moving her head up and down on his cock, and I could tell by the content expression on his face that she was giving him a very good time. Now and then she would glance at me.

If she had staged this little scene, as I'm sure she did, to get me uptight—and very aggravated—she'd succeeded very well, but because now I was wishing I was back at the hotel, or somewhere else. It's not easy to disengage your swollen penis from an eager feminine mouth, and maybe it's not even polite to do so, but I gently pulled Marika's sister's mouth off my penis, whispering something like, "Excuse me, I have to get up for a while . . . er, thanks very much for the nice blow-job. I, uh, enjoyed it very much." She must have thought I was crazy, but after staring at me for a few seconds, she relaxed and let Marcel's agile tongue in her cunt occupy her complete attention. And I began to hear moaning noises begin to start from deep within her. Oh, well, somebody had satisfied her.

Feeling very moody, I went over to the bar and poured myself a Coca-Cola and smoked a cigarette, all the while watching Xaviera work on this stud's cock as though it were the last penis on earth. I watched the other fuckers and suckers, too, and I must say that there were incredible combinations of people doing things to each other. But mostly I just watched Xaviera and felt very alone and miserable.

I was having my second or third cigarette when the little girlfriend of the Viking came over to me, her body looking very cute to my hashishy gaze and without saying a word dropped to her knees and began sucking me hard. It didn't take long, I'll say that, and I sort of eased myself down into a 69 position with her and teased her clit with my tongue until we were both ready to fuck. I lay back on my pillow and she climbed over my cock and, cooing little French sounds, lowered herself down on it. Because she was so tiny, I could put my hands under her ass and move her up and down on me, at the same time using one finger to hit her anus on the downward strokes, regulating the speed of our lovemaking to suit both to enhance and prolong it, but now she was having

206

what seemed to be a series of orgasms, and was all over me, kissing my chest and sucking on my nipples in gratitude, I guess. I wished like anything I could be coming inside her at the same time, but I knew that it wasn't going to happen even if we kept at it for an hour. So I held her close to my body until she finally stopped shaking and quivering, and then, giving me a big wet kiss on the mouth, she moved off me and on to somewhere else in the room —and no doubt onto someone else.

I had hoped Xaviera had been watching me perform with that cute little piece of French pastry because all the while I was fucking her I could hear the sounds of Xaviera being spanked resound throughout the room. But no, having doubtlessly satisfied the fashion designer with her mouth, she was now between the legs of the Viking, trying to get him up for her and—very little was happening. His penis, though erect, was about the size of someone's small finger, and there just wasn't anything for her to fuck, so she got up and left him there with his pathetic little hard-on. I don't know if it was the hashish or my emotional state or what, but I found myself laughing so hard I had to hold my stomach to keep from hurting. I couldn't come, and he couldn't grow a decent hard-on. What a couple of swingers we were!

Later, I found out from Xaviera that the poor guy is basically impotent—perhaps because of the miniscule size of his penis—and that spanking is his thing, spanking others and being spanked. Xaviera hadn't known this when she went down on him, and she felt slightly mortified because she had wanted to get into a good fuck with him because she knew I'd be watching.

However, she didn't stay mortified very long. I watched her as she went over to Nicole and Robert, who were still together and still partially dressed, watching what was going on all around them with a kind of fascination, but also, I felt, with a certain kind of anxiety. Xaviera also sensed this, I think, and she took Nicole into her arms and began kissing her on the neck and face, at the same time caressing her shoulders and lower back. Xaviera said something to Robert, who was standing there looking slightly in awe of Xaviera, and he helped her finish undressing Nicole, who was wearing a special kind of bra arrangement because her evening gown had been cut so low in back. Xaviera slipped Nicole's panties off her, and then eased her back onto a cushion.

I've seen Xaviera make love to many a girl, but I don't know if I've ever seen her so intent on turning another woman on. She began to devour Nicole's vagina, and Robert—pardon the pun—was eating it up. Now, instead of penetrating Xaviera from behind, as they'd agreed to do, he pulled the top of his wife's body closer to his middle and, bending over her face, put his cock in her mouth. Not wanting to spoil his fun, she began sucking on him, but after a minute or so she pushed him away. Unless I'm crazy, she felt awkward and uncomfortable with what Xaviera was doing to her and I certainly didn't feel superior to her—indeed, the look of shyness on the face of this mature woman was really beautiful to behold, although I was probably the only one in the room seeing it.

After another minute or two Nicole also pushed Xaviera away, gently but firmly, and got up and walked over to a chair by the side of the room. Xaviera looked at Robert, and Robert at Xaviera, and then he followed his wife, sitting down by her feet and putting his head in her lap. It was really very tender—either swinging wasn't his bag, either, or else he cared too much about his wife to desert her at a time when she was upset, and, possibly, embarrassed as well. Every time I looked at them they were in the same position, his head on her lap, her hand on his shoulder, each comforting the other, and many hours later they got up together, got dressed and quietly left.

Meanwhile Xaviera spotted me and, crawling on hands and knees over the pillows, we finally got together. A number of things might have happened but none of them did. I just put my arm around her shoulder, put her head on my chest and was content to hold her in a warm close embrace. She hugged me periodically to let me know how glad she was that I was there, next to her. The hash was still very much in control of my senses and I felt as though I were floating there, that those pillows were really clouds, and everything felt light and euphoric.

Somebody started to eat me, and I didn't pay attention

208

to whoever it was down there. If they wanted to blow me, they could be my guest. When the time came, there'd be plenty for Xaviera, and until then, I was happy to be lying there with her, knowing she was with me and not someone else.

After a while—hash changes your sense of time completely—I got the sensation of different mouths working on my cock, and through the pleasant fog I was in I could hear Xaviera whispering what sounded like instructions in French and Dutch. Finally I lifted my head a little and realized that both the girls with rings were blowing me, and that Marika was also there, occasionally getting her mouth on me as well, and that nothing was happening. Mr. Softie was in charge down there, and these girls not only couldn't get a charge out of him, they couldn't even persuade him to rise to the occasion.

If I had been less high, my inability to support an erection might have bothered me, but it simply didn't—the sensations being produced by their wet mouths on my penis were very good, and I hoped they were having some fun down there, but I felt miles away and for all I knew, that semi-limp penis down there belonged to someone else. I didn't learn until later that Xaviera had said some very flattering things about me to these women, and not only was I letting them down, but I was letting her down as well.

These thoughts may have crossed her mind as well, but just then Marcel came crawling by and, seeing Xaviera's cunt unoccupied, pulled her out a bit, get between her legs and jammed his cock into her. As soon as he was securely moored to her he put her legs over his shoulders and, raising himself up, began a kind of rapid, brutal, pumping motion. Xaviera just closed her eyes and snuggled her head a little bit more into the crook of my shoulder. I know if she had wanted to aggravate me she would have made a great show out of what a great fuck this was, but she didn't moan and groan and scream in ecstasy.

What amazes me is how calm I was through the whole thing. Despite my fuzzy state, I realized that the rules of the swing permitted Marcel to take Xaviera, unless she objected—and I think that since she was pretty high herself, he was inside her, pumping away, before she could realize what had happened. In any case, he didn't take very long and in another minute or two he'd had his kicks and returned Xaviera's body to my custody.

I wasn't completely aware that he'd done that because Marika's sister and the two girls with the rings were having a little huddle on the pillow next to me, and Lori and Julie apparently decided that my cock was a lost cause because they crawled away to find some more rigid member of my sex. However, Marika's sister, interested in finishing what she'd started before, was all over my groin trying to produce something tall and hard down there. She was sucking away so energetically, my entire limp penis engulfed in her mouth, that I wished I could produce an erection by mind control, just to please her and reward her for her hard work, but she was more eager than expert, and it wasn't working. Xaviera was watching this with amusement, and I was wondering why she didn't help out—then it dawned on me, the light at the end of the tunnel, if you will, that she might be glad that none of these women could produce an erection in me. It said something about something. . . .

About then, Marika's sister got up and gave me a small shrug and a kind of innocent little smile, as if to say, "Well, I *thought* I knew what I was doing," and moved away. I turned my full attention to Xaviera, but she was about to wiggle away from the protective custody of my shoulder. "Hey, where are you going?" I said, my voice sounding very strange to me—as though I were a 78 r.p.m. record going around on a 45 r.p.m. machine. Then I realized that I hadn't really talked to anyone since the swing began, and perhaps that was why the hash was making my own words sound slurred to me. However, she obviously was able to understand me because she whispered back, "I'll just be gone ten minutes—I have to pay a 'politeness fuck'—I'd forgotten about it. Don't worry, I'll be right back. . . ."

"But you fucked Marcel—just now, don't you remember? You're not *that* stoned, are you?"

"No, I let Marcel fuck *me*—I didn't fuck him, if you understood what was going on—because he's the owner
210

of the house, and I might want to visit with them sometime when Leo and Marika are not here."

"Then who—?"

"Leo, of course. He's the host for the evening, not Marcel."

"Oh, yeah . . . say, you really are a very 'polite' person, aren't you?"

"Don't be mean. Go find a bathroom and clean up, and I'll do the same—after I've been 'polite,' that is."

I knew, as usual, that there was no use arguing with Xaviera, especially since *I* hadn't done my job of exchanging amenities with Marika or Brigitte, the owner's wife, so I groped my way over the pillows and found the first-floor bathroom. There was a bidet in it, and I must say I had a pleasant time cleaning up whatever parts needed freshening up. The sensations produced by the warm water spraying up on my balls and ass felt almost as good as the feelings produced this evening by numerous mouths on my penis.

When I returned to the living room I looked for Xaviera and saw her energetically balling with Leo. Nearby the legendary stud, the fashion designer, was screwing Brigitte from the rear, and she and Xaviera were close enough to each other to exchange a few "polite" kisses. I still wasn't having any normal reactions to this scene, which was just as well, but I knew I didn't want the fashionable fucker to have a go at Xaviera.

As it happened, he was now finishing up with Brigitte, and he was soon seen to get his clothes, put them on, and depart the premises. He hadn't had any of the magic spaghetti and, accordingly, he was able to do exactly whatever he wanted to do whenever he wanted to do it—which, in this case, was to fuck the owner's wife and then leave. He was pretty "polite," too. The room was full of the most "polite" people in town.

At last Xaviera was done with Leo and waved at me as she went off to visit the first-floor bathroom herself, as she'd instructed me to do. By now the evening seemed to have been twenty-four hours long, and when Xaviera returned we cuddled again and there seemed no need to make love. She, of course, had just been laid twice in the

211

last half hour, or what I thought was the last half hour, but I had yet to have an orgasm this evening. I may have been fucked up by the hashish—I wasn't sure—but in no way was I fucked out.

Yet I somehow wasn't feeling insecure about not having come yet this evening. In fact, having Xaviera back in my arms made me feel content to continue to watch the proceedings in the room, although I was also slightly amazed to see that people didn't seem to be stopping their sexual activities. Instead of continuing in threesomes and even foursomes, some people were now swinging with just one other person, fucking on the couches and in the chairs alongside the sea of pillows and so, if nothing else, it was easier to see who was doing what to whom on the pillows. They were almost empty.

Marika had her mouth wrapped around the long, skinny joint of some guy I didn't know, and Nina and Ahmed were still together in a far end of the room, and Leo, who seemed to have a perpetual hard-on, was looking for someone he hadn't had yet. He saw Marika's sister lying by herself on a pillow, and like a lion spotting his prey, he went after her.

"Oh, oh," said Xaviera, who had been watching the scene as closely as I had.

"What do you mean?" I asked her.

"Leo has never swung with the sister, and as long as Marika is busy with that guy, he's not going to miss this opportunity." She was right, because Leo was kind of hovering over Marika's sister like the title character in *Dracula*, and she was looking up at him with an expression which was half innocence and half invitation. Then Leo dropped himself on the pillow and as he began to eat her, her thighs closed around his head and there was no question that this was an experience *she'd* wondered about, too.

Xaviera and I, as if by signal, turned toward each other and hugged even more tightly, and it felt as though we were melting into each other. Of all the people in the room, only *we* counted. My body felt numb, yet tingling all over, and her body felt soft and pliant and wonderful next to mine. Without even realizing what I was doing, I had begun to caress Xaviera and kiss and suck her nipples and move my

212

mouth down her body toward the place my mouth wanted to be. But, Jesus, when I reached Xaviera's lower stomach, I opened my eyes and realized that somebody had beaten me to her vagina. It was Julie, one of the two ringers in the crowd, and she was eating away at Xaviera with great abandon—as though the whole fucking evening was just getting underway.

The extraordinarily good mood the hashish had produced in me all the long, long evening disappeared like a candle being snuffed out, and I took hold of Julie, with all intentions of removing her to another part of the room. But nothing happened—I couldn't budge her. Now really angered, I tried to get up, the idea being to take this little quiff with the rings in her nipples and twat and play horseshoes with her. But I couldn't get up. It wasn't just the giant pillows making it difficult to get any leverage—*I couldn't get up!* My God, that hashish could prevent warfare from ever breaking out again, if my response was any indication!

Feeling helpless, but somehow not feeling badly about it—the hashish, again—I just sort of plunked myself down next to Xaviera and let things happen. I watched Julie work on Xaviera—no ordinary cunt-lapper, this kid—and Julie saw me watching her, and then began to work on me as well, hoping to have better luck than the last time.

It was a crazy scene, her frantic but expert mouth going from Xaviera's cunt to my cock in a matter of seconds, and I stretched out my hand toward Xaviera and held her hand, and a wonderful feeling soared through my body.

What was this wonderful feeling? A fantastic orgasm, with jism spurting as high as the ceiling? No, nothing was happening down below, and it could have been the hashish—I'd had a great deal of it via the sauce—but I prefer to think it was a spiritual thing, a reaffirmation of my feelings for Xaviera. This may be corny, or totally unrealistic, but the strong evidence in favor of this explanation was my perpetually limp penis. It has never happened before—or since.

Looking up, I saw that Marika, still very stoned herself, judging by the intense gleam in her eyes, had joined our little party and was ready to make things happen. So while

Julie continued to eat Xaviera, she also took turns on me, alternating with Marika when *her* mouth got tired. And nothing happened. My cock simply refused to defy gravity by rising off its launching pad.

Again it dawned on me that, whatever feelings Xaviera might now have on the matter, these women were still trying to figure out what the hell she might have been bragging about before I'd arrived, and they both worked on me like you wouldn't believe, and still nothing happened.

I looked at Xaviera helplessly—by now it had really gotten to me that I'd been erectionless for hours—and she looked at me as if to say, "What do you want from me? I can't do anything about them." However, after about ten more minutes of mouth-to-penis resuscitation and the patient still hadn't revived, Marika and Julie got bored—justifiably—and left us alone.

When they went ashore from the sea of pillows, Xaviera and I were the last survivors of the swing through eternity—everyone else was now exhausted at last—and I was terribly conscious, despite still being very high, of the eyes of everyone in the room bearing down on us. Suddenly I wanted to prove, if only to Leo and Marika, that I was a good lover, that the reports had been true, that perhaps I could only perform, in certain situations, with a partner I had great feeling for.

And then the hash took over my head again, and I couldn't care what anyone in the world thought because I was now feeling too groovy to care about anything except the here and the now of Xaviera and me. And Xaviera must have picked up my vibes because she was now kissing my body and caressing me and moving her mouth down to the source of the trouble, and in less than a minute I had the largest erection since the Sears building in Chicago. It felt as though it were the acummulation of all the erections I *hadn't* had all night, and it also felt as though it might be around longer than the Sears building.

Oblivious to everyone around us, oblivious to the world at large, oblivious to anything other than our two bodies together, Xaviera and I moved with almost startling grace into the most sensational fuck of all time.

We fucked and fucked, and when we got done with that, we fucked some more.

She was up above me, riding my cock as she'd never ridden it before.

I was above her, driving into her with a glorious rhythm I had never achieved before. I was holding her shoulders in a vise, I was putting my nails into her back, I was stroking her clitoris as I drove again and again into her body, relentless but adoring, and the closer and closer I came to a climax, the higher I rose above her, and the deeper I plunged into her, never hurting her, but never failing to touch her at the most inner spot of her being. Deeper and deeper, higher and higher—*now* I can understand that the hashish was heightening everything, yet prolonging the sense of time devoted to each sensation—but then it seemed like we would be fucking until the end of time, and when we came, the world would have to end. There'd be nothing left to know. . . .

Suddenly the world was moving inside me, and around me, and through me as I experienced the beginnings of a crashing orgasm which seem to build and build, never ebbing, until I wasn't sure I could stand it any longer. But despite the tidal wave of sensation that had overtaken me, I had opened my eyes because of Xaviera's screams, and saw tears streaming down her cheeks, and it seemed as though each time my body rose to plunge down inside her again, the screams grew more wild and her eyes were erupting in tears, and then we both came, in a convulsive, never-ending wave of sensations. We'd done it—we'd stopped the world so our orgasm would go on forever and ever. . . .

If I had ever felt a part of the universe, it was during that orgasm which took over my entire central nervous system and put it into "Tremble" for about ten minutes, and it seemed to me—I really can't be sure—that Xaviera didn't stop crying until long afterwards, and we held and comforted each other without ever saying a word, and when finally we returned to some state of realistic consciousness, we both realized that we'd taken a very profound and truthful trip together. If there was never anything else, we'd lived a small lifetime in those twenty minutes, or however long it took to travel the universe.

Xaviera pulled herself up on her elbows and looked into my face. She is not a beautiful woman, but she seemed almost ethereally beautiful to me, and with one hand I wiped the tears from her face and neck. I didn't ask her why she'd wept so—I hoped I knew.

I then asked myself if *I* was still high on hash—and answered, "You bet your ass you are!" However, I managed to stand up, for a change, and go over to the bar to get Xaviera and me a drink. She was tired and terribly thirsty—and I needed some liquid refueling myself. We still hadn't talked to anyone, and as I was pouring a cold soda for Xaviera, and a cognac for myself, it occurred to me that we had just put on a performance—which is what it had been for the others—second to none this evening, and so far as I was concerned, second to none at any swing anywhere. For that matter, the people who had disappeared into bedrooms were now beginning to drift back into the living room, their faces tired and exhausted, but the sounds and erotic mood Xaviera and I had established had prevented them from going to sleep for the night.

And little did I know that the best was yet to come, in a manner of speaking.

Xaviera and I continued to ignore the world, or at least those directly around us. Because we both were still very high, we made light talk—she knew I was a sneak when it came to watching her and so she discussed everything she'd done that evening, using her own funny version of utter candor, leaving out several events I'd witnessed—we kept playing a game where we raised our arms together, and then dropped them to see whose arm would hit the pillow first. It didn't matter who won each round—we always laughed like two happy children—and I'm not sure I've ever felt so completely relaxed, before or since.

We must have carried on like that for at least half an hour, ignoring all about us, and yet conscious that all eyes were upon us, and there came a moment when I knew we were back into lovemaking and I wasn't at all sure when or how we'd gotten there. My body was still feeling both numb to large physical demands and hypersensitive to every touch, and I felt delicious tingles as Xaviera crawled down over my body and began sucking my large toe. Then her mouth moved up my instep, which also felt great, and up my calf and lower thigh and then captured my crotch. ("We surrender!"). Her head was resting on my abdomen, and as she bowed down to take my balls in her mouth, and treat them like some delicious meatballs meant to be savored but not swallowed, she moved her body around so that her cunt was next to my face and I began to nibble at her in the most discreet way, as though trying out a new delicacy. Then our feelings took over and I was eating her as never before, my tongue flipping around her clitoris and into her vagina. If anything comparable were possible, Xaviera was accomplishing it at my end of the current physical setup, but for strange reasons I won't atempt to fathom, I knew I was safe from coming, while at the same time I was able to bring Xaviera to at least two body-shaking orgasms.

Then it was time—no one tells you it's time, you just do it because it's *time*—to resume fucking, and now it was more varied, more knowing of each other, yet despite the drug having worn off a little bit, no less intense, and Xaviera and I fucked away without stopping for what seemed like half an hour (though I'm sure it may have been for only twenty-nine minutes or so). And *all* the frustration and expectation and excitement of the evening boiled up inside me, and I achieved two orgasms without leaving her body, and once again she screamed and cried and went out of control in a way I'd never experienced before, except this time I cried as well, and laughed, and so did she, and all I truly remember from this unprecedented height of feeling was one point when we both screamed and laughed for happiness. I remember Xaviera yelling out to me, "I want to go home! I want to go home!" and then we both came together again, and she was weeping again, and then I don't remember anything for a little while.

When we both came back to our senses we were surrounded by everyone in the room, everyone turned on and passionate as hell once again, and the sea of pillows once again rocked and waved to an armada of happy couples.

Days later, when I could think about it, I understood that Xaviera's own feelings of insecurity had come out in

217

our lovemaking—she was a flying Dutchwoman, a person without a real home—and that the hashish had intensified everything in our private relationship, the love, and the troubles, including being apart.

As for myself, I was stoned, true, but I was making love to the only woman I'd loved that deeply, and yet I realized that this was temporary, that we'd always have to say good-bye and to find our own way.

But I'll never forget that night, when drugs and need and despair all got wrapped up into one extraordinary emotional trip, and I'll let Xaviera confirm the depth of what went on in a letter I received on August 7, about a month after that weekend:

"What a difference it makes to be a woman thinking of her man. Love you, you silly old bastard Silver Fox. If you ever forget it, just think how much we loved each other when we were stoned."

And she wrote a Dutch friend in America, around the same time, a card he later showed to me. It said, in part: "Had a fantastic orgy two days before we left for Yugoslavia. Leo put some hashish in the spaghetti sauce for 20–30 beautiful people. I never take drugs, but this was way outtasite. The beautiful thing of all was that Larry could only make it with me and no one else, so stoned we were. I cried, screamed, laughed and went off my rocker for hours and hours. . . ."

CHAPTER 27.

We stayed at the villa, sleeping until late in the afternoon and having our first meal of the day—either a very late. lunch or a very early dinner—around four o'clock in the afternoon. Some of the people from the night before were still there, and everyone seemed to be in a really fine mood.

Except Marika. Of course she knew that Leo had made it with her sister at the swing, but what she'd hadn't known was that Leo had also slept with the sister a few days earlier. And apparently this didn't sit too well with her. She was a very liberated woman and a dedicated swinger —you had to be, I gathered, to stay with Leo—but in this instance she may have felt that she was being used by Leo to get at her sister, because he had insisted on inviting her sister to St. Tropez. And one of the rules in a swinging marriage is: No siblings allowed.

Xaviera and I talked about the night before and she admitted the hashish had really gotten to her and that the best times, apart from our actual lovemaking, were when we were just lying there together—that it felt so good just to touch my body and know it was there.

I'd be the last to claim that Xaviera's screams and crying the night before were entirely on my account, because I realized that she did have insecurities. It's okay to say that any place I hang my hat is home, but sooner or later we all want one spot on the globe—be it New York or London or Toronto—that we can return to, that *is* our

219

home. I of course feel this way about New York, but I don't know if Xaviera has a place she regards as home—it's not Amsterdam, I do know that.

I also talked with Leo, toward whom I now felt a lot warmer—later, in the States, we became fast friends—about the potent effect the hashish had had on Xaviera and myself, and he felt that both Xaviera and I had taken an honest, and therefore partly painful, trip into ourselves that might never have happened had we not been under the influence of the hash. And, of course, the sexual tension set up by the swing: being liberated enough to tolerate—indeed, approve—someone you really care about making love to a lot of other people had a good deal to do with the intensity of our feelings for each other. Xaviera wanted to show me off and at the same time keep me for herself. At least that's the way I saw it, and I think Leo agreed.

Before Xaviera and I left—we'd be leaving for Yugoslavia the next day and had to start packing—Leo and I made plans to get together in America the next time he was there on business, which we did.

As I was driving back to the hotel with Xaviera I asked her what she'd thought of Nicole and Robert, the handsome couple who'd ended up spending so much of the evening comforting each other. So far as I was concerned, the sight of the two of them like that was one of the memories I'll hold longest from the evening. And if my own ever-loving hangups hadn't prevented me from being an effective swinger, Nicole, to me, was certainly one of the most desirable women in the room, and I'd like to have known her better—in the biblical sense, of course.

However, Xaviera viewed them differently. "They were party poopers," she ruled, "and they won't be invited again."

Ah, yes, once again I was reminded that Xaviera and I can be so close, yet at the same time worlds apart. Maybe nobody loves a "party pooper"—but *I* could have. . . .

CHAPTER 28.

We were off on a kind of whirlwind trip through part of Europe, and I was very excited. This was my first trip to the Continent, and while St. Tropez is a truly wonderful place, I wanted to see as much of Europe as we could comfortably fit into the remaining vacation time.

We landed in Italian Trieste, and learned that there were no direct flights to the Isle of Krk—our first destination, since Xaviera had been invited by *Penthouse* magazine to attend the official opening of the Penthouse Adriatic, its hotel and gambling casino there. So we tried to fly to Zagreb, one of Yugoslavia's larger cities—but no direct flights there, either.

So we said, "What the hell, we'll just drive there." And that wasn't so easy to arrange, either. The Hertz people would be happy to rent us a car, they said, but we couldn't drop it off in Yugoslavia. We'd have to hold on to the car and leave it in some other country because, while trade relationships between Yugoslavia and the Common Market nations were opening up, Hertz still felt nervous about having its cars left in a communist country. The reasoning was that if political relations between Yugoslavia and the neighboring countries ever hardened again, Hertz would be out a lot of cars.

So we agreed to drive in—and out—of Yugoslavia with a Hertz car, and off we went. I'd expected the roads to be not at all comparable to American highways, but they were surprisingly good. We hit Customs after only a ninety-minute drive, and my American passport got us through without even one suitcase being examined.

Now we were heading south, the beautiful Adriatic on our right as we took the route along the coastline. The only large city we passed through was Fiume and while the drive took quite some time, it was so scenic along the way that we didn't mind. Finally we reached Kraljevica, from where we would take a ferry to Krk.

The ferry itself was a pretty ancient affair, and not too large, and there was a long queue of cars waiting to get on the damn thing, so it took at least half an hour before we were actually on the ferry. As we drove off the ferry Xaviera saw Molly McKellar, who is the public-relations person for *Penthouse* and the clubs, and we stopped to chat with her. She is a very lovely and charming young woman, and for the first time since leaving St. Tropez, I felt a little bit at home with people. We talked for about twenty minutes and then, because she had to wait for someone on one of the incoming ferries, we took off for the hotel.

However, this feeling-at-home feeling proved to be rank optimism, because when we got to the hotel and asked for our room, the desk clerk looked at us as though we were two creatures from Mars or someplace equally exotic. In the most haughty voice possible, he announced: "I'm very sorry, sir. We have no reservation for the young lady or, for that matter, for you, sir."

I got the distinct impression that he expected us to turn around, get on the ferry, and leave the country, so we asked to speak to Bob Guccione. He wasn't there, but his girlfriend, Karen—whom Xaviera knew well from London—was on the premises, and a few minutes later we were on our way to our room.

Well, another unfortunate surprise! The room we'd had to struggle to occupy was about one-third the size of any normal American hotel room—it was the smallest room I'd been in since staying at the YMCA in Middletown, Connecticut, as a teenager—and there were no closets, just a plain pipe rack about two feet long. And one bureau.

It had been a long day, and I wanted to make a very large complaint over these crummy accommodations—

after all, Xaviera was an honored guest at the opening of this place—but she didn't feel like making any waves.

"Look," she said, always the practical one, "we're guests of *Penthouse* and we have to accept whatever type of hospitality they offer us."

"Do we have to accept such hospitality without closet space?"

"Yes—we don't have a closet, but we're not paying for one, are we?"

The discussion was closed.

Afterward, I learned that most hotel rooms in Yugoslavia are built on a small scale—smaller even than the typical European room—and that we hadn't been singled out for discrimination. As for the rest of the hotel itself, it was fabulous. The Penthouse Adriatic overlooks Malinka Bay and provides a panoramic view of the Adriatic Sea and the surrounding islands—Krk is the northernmost of a series of islands known as the Dalmatian Islands—and while one side of the island, where the ferry lands, is very rocky and without vegetation because of the brutal winds which batter the coastline there, the hotel was surrounded by rich, lush foliage. It was a great setting for a hotel *and* for a gambling casino.

The casino itself was located in the heart of the hotel, and was open every night from eight until four in the morning. There were twenty-one, roulette, and dice tables —since there were only two crap tables in the place, players were shelling out twenty-five dollars just to get near the dice—and private *chemin de fer* salons off the main room. To me, the real novelty of the place was the sex of the gambling personnel—they'd all been imported from London and it was the first time I'd ever seen female croupiers, and all of them very attractive young ladies. By the time you got done checking out their faces, breasts, and legs, you didn't have much passion left for cards.

The Penthouse Adriatic has indoor tennis courts and an outdoor pool, plus all the usual facilities—sauna, steam room, gym, and the rest—but the unique sports facility there is the bowling alley—actually three alleys—in the basement. I'd never been to a hotel with bowling alleys before.

223

We took most of our meals in the outdoor dining area in order to enjoy the sublime weather. Besides, the main dining room inside had slow service, although nobody really seemed to complain—the only impatient guests being the Germans. We personally found most of the waiters and waitresses to be great kids, and whatever they lacked in finesse and experience, they more than made up for in friendliness and their eagerness to please.

As per usual, Xaviera and I tried to explore as much of the island as time would allow. About fifteen minutes away was a lovely little fishing village, and ten minutes away, by car, was the main city of Krk, which had some small shops worth browsing, plus many little outdoor stalls where you could buy native handicrafts at very reasonable prices.

The most interesting part of the island, in some ways, was the beach near our hotel. You got there by walking through the gardens adjoining the hotel toward the ocean and there was a strip of shoreline, perhaps six hundred feet long, which the islanders had cleared of rocks and filled in with sand. This part of the island was used for swimming and boating during the daytime, and for fucking at night.

One night Xaviera and I went with the pit boss of the casino—a handsome young Italian she'd known (again, in the biblical sense) in London—to the fishing village for a dinner of native seafood—fish dishes I have had nowhere else—that was spectacularly good. On the way back, walking along the edge of the beach, we heard unbelievable noises—it sounded as though the entire island was out there, fucking their brains out, and the moonlight reflected off the water allowed us to catch glimpses of asses and legs and breasts. The subliminal effect of this audio-visual show turned on Xaviera and me but good, and while we didn't run back to the hotel, we went straight to our room when we got there.

Arriving in our room, we threw open the windows—our room overlooked the tennis courts and gardens—took off our clothes, and jumped on the bed. I was feeling marvelously horny, but I didn't want to come too quickly, so for the only time in our relationship, I allowed Xaviera to wrap a rubber band around my erect penis and balls. This prevented me from coming but it also made my penis grow larger, and when Xaviera started to suck me, I almost went crazy. Then she got on top of me and fucked me for the better part of a hour, enjoying two orgasms in the process. Finally I couldn't stand it anymore and when Xaviera removed the rubber band, I drove into her and had a body-jarring orgasm within ten seconds.

I never let her use a rubber band on my penis again, because truthfully, I was afraid it might lead to some kind of physical injury, but I'll admit that it did the trick that night —it, *ahem*, stretched out our lovemaking so Xaviera was able to have more satisfaction before I came. Without it, I'm sure I would have popped my load in about twenty-six-point-five seconds.

We'd been at the Penthouse Adriatic for three days already, and still hadn't seen the phantom Bob Guccione. Quite apart from the fact that Xaviera was there to help celebrate the hotel's opening, I was there as her business manager because we hoped to negotiate all the details of her writing a column for *Penthouse* while there, and no one could finalize anything except Guccione, who is the sole owner of the magazine. We kept asking about him, and were assured that he was on the island, but we never got to see him and were beginning to wonder if he weren't patterning himself after Howard Hughes. Run an empire, but don't ever get seen in public.

However, on the fourth day, we finally did meet Bob, and he immediately apologized for having been too busy to see us. Bob grew up in Brooklyn, so here were two native New Yorkers shooting the breeze right away, and I found him a "regular guy," as we used to say. I liked him. Not that it matters, but he's also physically a much more imposing man than his rival, Hugh Hefner, whose career he has of course emulated.

Because we soon became good friends, Bob confided to me that he was having lots of problems with the Penthouse Adriatic. A major problem was the lack of air conditioning —which made it uncomfortable for the usual American visitor.

To make this point more dramatically, Bob told me a horror story about a gambling junket to Krk which had

225

originated in Miami, Florida. The chartered jet, a Yugoslav JAF plane, had taken off with its load of passengers on what turned out to be a twenty-four-hour-long nightmare. Before the plane had even left the continental United States, one of its key operating systems wasn't functioning and the decision was made to land at Jacksonville.

As it turned out, the repairs were going to take hours, and no one was being allowed to leave the plane, which sat there with its air-conditioning system off, of course. Some of the passengers were just about ready to fight their way off the plane, but the exits were being guarded by two husky Yugoslav stewardesses. If they'd been men, some of the passengers would have rushed them, but the male passengers felt reluctant to have a fist fight with women, whatever their sizes. Yes, I know—male chauvinism strikes again!

So they sat there for hours, frustrated, disgusted, and very sweaty, while the plane was being made airworthy again, and finally they did take off. The flight was uneventful, but when they approached the airport at Krk, the strong winds on that side of the island—the rocky side, which has no vegetation—made a safe landing seem very difficult, so the plane went inland, four hours away by surface travel, to land. Then there was a wait of hours to round up enough buses to transport the high rollers to Krk, and they reached the ferry slip at Kraljevica around midnight, too late for a ferry.

Okay, high rollers, wait some more while special arrangements are made to get the ferry rolling again, and so when the four buses finally pulled up in front of the Penthouse Adriatic, the people who staggered off them were a little upset, to say the least. And when they saw the size of their rooms, and felt how warm it was this particular evening, and realized that there was no air-conditioning, they were even more upset. And when they learned that it was too late for dining room service, or for any kind of food to be ordered—they hadn't eaten in twelve hours—they were about ready to burn the place down, or else eat the Penthouse "pets"—Guccione's answer to Hefner's "bunnies"—alive.

Fortunately Bob had the good sense to open up the

226

kitchen so that sandwiches and cold food could be served to the exhausted party—after all, if you don't feed a gambler, he's not going to have the energy to toss any dice around the next day. Also: so far as anyone knows, no "pets" were eaten (alive) that night.

"Bob," I said when he was done telling this story, "were those the bleary-eyed guys Xaviera and I saw stumbling around the place this morning?"

"Yeah . . . how'd they seem to you?"

"Ready to gamble tonight, and have a helluva time— once the blood reaches their head."

Bob also tells a funny story about how the hotel has to work under normal conditions. In an American hotel, if some minor management decision has to be made, there are always two or three people empowered to make that decision, whereas in Yugoslavia there is a whole small army of bodies to be consulted and a formal meeting has to be called to render that decision. That's the socialist system, so whenever Bob had a problem he wanted to discuss with the hotel, he'd so inform the hotel manager and he in turn would call a meeting of the hotel's board of directors.

The next morning, no matter how hot the weather, Bob would attend a meeting of the board of directors, each member dressed in white shirt, black tie, and formal evening clothes, outside by the pool. He and Jerry Kurtz, who'd organized the Miami junket, Bob told me, had wanted to show some feature films to the high rollers as part of the Penthouse Adriatic entertainment, but the board of directors' meeting was so complicated that the idea was dropped.

So, as it happened, was the idea of finalizing the details of Xaviera's contract with *Penthouse,* because Bob was so busy taking photographs—if *Penthouse* is discernibly different from *Playboy,* it's because of Bob's much lustier and kinkier photographs of women—and I ended up talking with Al Freedman, one of Bob's top associates. We had lengthy discussions, which included some book projects as well, but we both agreed that the final contractual arrangements would best be worked out in New York. Guccione was just too preoccupied with the hotel, and its "official opening," and its Yugoslavian quirks, to be able

227

to give us his full undivided attention, and since I'd be back in New York in another week or so we decided to wait until then to iron out the final details.

As I have inferred, the Penthouse Adriatic "pets" were all gorgeous girls, about half of whom were recruited from the Penthouse Club in London, and half from local talent. Whatever the source, it didn't matter, because these were really fine-looking females. And, of course, their sexy costumes accentuated everything there was to accentuate. Which leads me to a kind of funny little story.

At the hotel were two Jewish couples with whom Xaviera and I had become quite friendly. The husbands were nice guys, and the wives were natural-born sexpots. The two girls—girls, hell, they were in their thirties—appeared one night as our waitresses, and I must admit that their "pet" costume, which takes a woman's body and rearranges it to best advantage, showed them off to *considerable* advantage. They may have been a dozen years older than the regular "pets," but they looked every bit as ravishing and sexy—all tits and ass!—and they had no greater admirers than their own husbands, who drank in the sight of these community chests raised to heights not enjoyed even when the gals were sixteen years old. And I kid you not—every guy in the place found these two wives sexy as hell in their costumes. The two women were sexually showing off, and all the men—including their admiring husbands—loved it. Gradually Xaviera and I recognized them.

I wonder how many friends mentally raped these two women that particular evening.

P.S. We never got sexually involved with the two couples.

However, wherever Xaviera goes, there goes sex, and our little "pet" project, if ever it existed in her mind, didn't go completely unfulfilled.

Well, at least imagine my surprise early one evening, while I was getting ready for dinner, when Xaviera arrived in our "locker room" with a delectable-looking "pet" in tow. Dark hair, dark eyes, and the most perfect mouth for kissing ever seen east of the Alps. Her name was Marie, she was Yugoslavian, she spoke quite good English, and she had an hour-glass figure which was only slightly magnificent.

After only a few minutes of preliminaries—Christ, would you believe she drank orange juice in the same quantities as Xaviera herself . . . I mean, *who* gets horny on vitamin C?—Xaviera had pulled her down on the bed and was kissing her. At first Marie was able to push Xaviera's mouth away from her, so Xaviera merely switched to Marie's ear lobes, starting to gently nibble on them, with an occasional tongue darting in and around the ear, and her hands lightly caressing various parts of the girl's magnificent body. You could actually mark the point where the girl decided to succumb, or where her central nervous system decided for her, and Xaviera was able to gently ease her back upon the pillow.

Once Marie had fallen back on the pillow again, it was no contest, and I don't think it took Xaviera more than thirty seconds to get her down to bra and panties. Her bra was a skimpy affair which barely encased her large, jutting breasts, and it took another few seconds for Xaviera to have her completely nude, and spread out on the bed. Then Xaviera began to kiss and tongue her from neck to breasts to crotch.

I kept waiting for Xaviera to order Marie into the shower, but Xaviera had gotten herself too turned on to wait, and she soon began eating Marie with such extraordinary passion that I finally woke up to the fact that I was sitting there like some "taxi squad" player on a professional football team who wishes he could play but knows the coach won't let him into the game.

But, hey, *I* was really a close buddy of the coach this time, and she'd let me play. I knew she would! Hey, Coach Hollander, call for a center plunge, and here I'll come.

So I got out of my clothes as fast as buttons and zipper would allow, and charged over to the bed as hard as the stupendous hard-on waving in front of me would allow. I didn't know where to begin, the girl's body was so beautiful, so I decided just to cop a feel and see how such substantial breasts could defy gravity, and just as I was being terribly impressed as to how this could happen, and was thinking of slipping my throbbing cock between those breasts and pointing it toward Marie's mouth, Xaviera's hand shot up and grabbed my penis in a no-nonsense grasp.

That'll teach me not to wait for the coach's instructions! I'd been sitting on the bed, and Xaviera's hand on my cock persuaded me to stand up. Then she took Marie's head and placed it along the side of the bed, all the while continuing to work on the girl's cunt in a way which permitted no outside thinking. So when Marie's head was two-thirds off the bed, and she was lying there with her mouth panting and open, I realized what Xaviera wanted to happen. She didn't want me to be eaten by Marie because I'd surely come pretty quickly that way, but it was okay for me to diddle around a little in Marie's mouth. So, very gently, I eased my penis into Marie's mouth, and if Xaviera didn't think Marie was going to work on me in that position, she was crazy. In fact, in some ways it was sexier than usual, as Marie's lips clasped my cock each time I tried to withdraw it, so I lifted her head back fully upon the bed and began to slowly extract my penis from her mouth. Just then *she* began to have an orgasm, and her mouth closed over my penis as though she had decided that it was her favorite piece of candy.

It felt great, and I of course kept hoping I wouldn't come—at the same time praying that I would—but as Marie's body relaxed, so did the grip her mouth had on my engorged penis, and I was able to slip out of a situation which was not exactly no-holes-barred. There was at least one opening which wasn't open to me. But the coach called the signals in time, and told me to keep the ball. Good thing, too, because in another minute or so all my good intentions would have gone down the drain.

Now I was really in the game for real. Sending Marie to the bench, Xaviera was now on top of me, pumping away for a first down. Then it was my turn to go for the bomb, and as in all our best games, we crossed the goal line together.

That was our only extracurricular sex while in Yugoslavia, and after the scene in St. Tropez, I think that that was a very good idea. We had a grand time at the Penthouse Adriatic, enjoyed all the people we met, and if there was any complaint to be made, it would have to be made by Xaviera, because she wasn't able to make one international phone call while there. She tried to call her parents' house in Holland several times, but apparently the only way you can get an international call through in less than eight to twelve hours is to declare it an emergency. I tried to call my office for four days in a row—I placed the calls the night before—but the closest I got was to hear my office manager yelling, "Hello . . . Hello? . . . HELLO?" So while he talked to me, I never got to talk to him, which was all right, too. I'd made the gesture, but I needed the rest. As for Xaviera, it was probably the first time in recent years she didn't improve the local economy of wherever she was staying by making several thousand phone calls a day.

CHAPTER 29.

Because of the grand weather, we'd stayed at the Penthouse Adriatic longer than we'd intended, but now it was time to hit the road again. We took the ferry and spent a few hours in Kraljevica to see how the people lived there —among other things, no one seemed to be remotely as casually attired as we were—and talked with some of the ubiquitous American hippie kids whom we found sitting in the outdoor cafes or else congregating in the various squares. No one seemed to mind their presence and I must say the people seemed happy and content. So, saluting Kraljevica with two ice-cream cones—pretty good, too, I have to concede, for communist ice-cream cones—we headed back up the coast of Yugoslavia for Trieste, and then down into Italy for Milan, where Xaviera had a good friend.

Because this was quite a long trip, I shared the driving with Xaviera, and with Grand Prix driver X. Hollander at the wheel of our Fiat, we passed everything on the road. Each time X. Hollander, driving the Fiat like a Ferrari, passed someone, she waved happily at them, and *I* was happy I couldn't hear the curses as we tooled it into Italy.

Our first stop was Verona, home of Romeo and Juliet. We drove around for a bit, then headed for a hotel which had been recommended to us. It was almost time for dinner, but we went out and visited a few of the city's historic churches before heading back to a restaurant near the hotel. We didn't know anything about the place we picked for dinner, but it turned out to be beginner's luck—the help and the customers were enormously friendly, and the veal piccata was exceptional. Then we decided to forego any night life, even if there was any, for a good night's sleep.

The next day we headed straight to Milan. My time was growing short, and I wanted to get to know at least one of Italy's main cities. But Xaviera wanted to reestablish her friendship with Fiona, a lovely ex-model who had worked for her briefly in New York when a bad love affair had left her strapped for funds. Fortunately, Fiona had a lot of free time and was only too anxious to serve as our (my, really) tour guide through the city. Of course we visited La Scala, the famous opera house (I said I wouldn't leave until Maria Callas showed up and sang "I Get A Kick Out of You" or else "Oklahoma," from the Rodgers and Hammerstein musical of the same name, but I got no cooperation from the girls), the Duomo, Milan's cathedral and the the second most famous church in all of Italy, and the fabulous Galleria shopping arcades, where you're walking on a sidewalk beneath a wonderful glass ceiling six or seven stories high. This was where, in a corner shop, Xaviera and I saw her first Leonardo dress. The price, as I recall, was one hundred eighty dollars, and we were both aghast at the notion of people spending that much on a dress. Later on, Xaviera came to own several Leonardo dresses bought at prices up to three hundred dollars, and I—the big spender from the city—bought about half of them.

We had a lot of fun in Milan. Xaviera had a thing for the kind of Italian licorice which is produced in chewing-gum form. We both adored walking through the Galleria, and one day we saw a fight there between two men. I don't know how the police got there so quickly, but they did, converging from all around, and picked up the two gladiators and unceremoniously dumped them out in the street. We went to the theater one night and saw an Italian version of an American musical which I knew almost by heart, and so I had a good time, and we went to an Italian comedy where I didn't understand a word of what was going on, but still had a great time because I dug the Italian acting. We ate, generally at night, in a number of restaurants which catered to the top businessmen in this bustling, industrial city during the lunch hours, and they were all good. One night we went with Fiona, who is blonde and beautiful and who has the body to go with the rest of it, to a restaurant, La Selva, where everyone seemed to know her. When she walked in the owner and five or six patrons got up and came over to greet her, kissing her hand and greeting Xaviera in the same grand manner. Which was just the start of a grand evening. We had a fantastic meal, with Xaviera having *mosto allo spiedo,* Fiona veal Milanese, and me having sirloin *pizzaiola,* all of it divine. I was just dazzled with the ambience of the place, and the superb quality of the food, and when it came time to pay the check, the owner acted as though I had insulted him by even thinking of paying. Not only that, but he brought over a bouquet of flowers and presented them to Xaviera. Was she impressed? I can *tell* you she was impressed.

For pure kicks, however, our favorite sport in Milan was hooker-watching—that is, observing the streetwalkers making their rounds. At first I didn't believe that some of these spectacular-looking creatures were prostitutes, but here they'd be coming around the block again, each carrying a certain kind of strapless handbag under her arm. They were colorful ladies, these gals of the Milanese night, because not only were most of them pretty attractive, and *all* of them built like an Italian pizza parlor, but

233

when they weren't out there making their rounds on behalf of sexual freedom, they'd be in the neighborhood cafe, talking up a storm with friends and/or sisters of the night.

One day, as a gag, Xaviera let me walk quite a bit ahead of her through a streetwalker area, and a few girls, immediately recognizing me as an American because of my clothes, came over and very courteously asked me, in broken English, if I wanted "to be entertained." Of course I wasn't interested—in my lifetime I may have been intrigued on a few occasions, but I have never paid for a woman's favors—but one of these girls was *so* good-looking that I lingered with her for a few minutes, and then I saw Xaviera moving up to claim me as her own. When she got near enough for me to offer her my arm, she moved into my dignified embrace. At first the girl didn't understand that Xaviera and I weren't just acquaintances, but as soon as she understood the relationship she warmed up and soon Xaviera and she were jabbering away in Italian. Because they seemed such good friends, I suggested to Xaviera that since I thought this young lady was very pretty, we should invite her up to our room.

If looks could kill, I'd never have survived to write this book, but suffice to say that Xaviera took my arm, and away we walked.

CHAPTER 30.

We were on our way to Zurich, to see friends of Xaviera's. This would be the last stop on my European trip, as there were only a few days left of my vacation.

Instead of driving over the Alps, which would have been a glorious thing to do, had we the time, we put the car on a flat-bed railroad car and let the train do the work of going through the mountains, via a long tunnel. Xaviera and I had stocked up on some food supplies before driving on the train, so all our needs were taken care of. We dined on sandwiches and orange juice and after a few minutes in the tunnel, Xaviera snuggled up on my lap and I thought she wanted to go to sleep. But instead my zipper went down and my cock went up. Then my pants went down, and so did Xaviera's mouth. After a few minutes of delicious fellatio for dessert, she shifted over to her side of the car and I moved over so she could straddle me. We made love, and timed it beautifully, both of us coming a few minutes before we left the tunnel to emerge into daylight again.

Driving once again, we made only one stop—for relief of my bladder—before reaching Zurich. We checked into a hotel and quickly changed our clothes. This left us some time for a walk around the city and then an early dinner at Kronenhalle, one of Zurich's leading restaurants and a hangout for journalists, authors, and other people in the arts. This is made obvious by the ambience of the place, with its Picassos, Dalis and Matisses on the walls. And the food is first rate: we both had a *schnitzel Cordon Bleu*, which is a superb dish composed of thin strips of veal baked with prosciutto ham and a delicate cheese. So we went to bed having had sandwiches for lunch and haute cuisine for dinner—which sort of symbolized what an interesting, diverse day it had been.

The next morning was devoted to exploring Zurich and shopping.

Zurich is a dream of a city, physically. It's divided by a river, the Limmat, which is fed by Lake Zurich to the southeast, and surrounded by hills, and there are always those snow-capped mountains in the distance. There's not much nightlife in Zurich, but its cosmopolitan character—it's been described as the "finest city in Switzerland" —is evident by the handsome restaurants, shops, and stores there. And why shouldn't the town have a luxurious feel to it—out of every five or six hundred residents of Zurich, one is a millionaire!

As a farewell present I bought Xaviera a snap-on gold watch, which I believe she still owns, and I bought myself a couple of pairs of Bally shoes, at incredibly low prices compared to what they'd have cost me at home. Here each pair cost me fourteen dollars, whereas in New York the two pairs of shoes would have set me back at least seventy-five dollars each.

We finished off the day with a drink at our own hotel bar, which was small and cozy, and then dinner at the Grill Room of the Hotel Baur au Lac, one of the city's grandest hotels. The Grill Room, I was told, is the most fashionable dining spot in town, but while we had a good meal, and the people-watching was great, I must say that I'd enjoyed the previous night's meal better.

Which perhaps was an omen, because that evening Xaviera and I had our first argument since I'd arrived in Europe.

I'd gone downstairs to get cigarettes, and when I got back to the room I caught her in the middle of a phone call to a banker friend of hers, Georgio, in Geneva, telling him she'd be driving there the next day. And from there, I gathered from her end of the conversation, they'd be going to his chalet in the French Alps. It sounded just wonderful—to Xaviera.

So of course we had a hell of an argument when she hung up, my main point being why couldn't she at least wait until I'd left before making dates! I didn't expect her to become celibate on my account—after all, there were thousands of miles between us—but she could have some manners, after all. She didn't have to be a pig about it— sex would still be in style a few days hence.

She finally admitted that what she'd done was wrong, and her apology included a wonderful time in bed, which included a spectacular blow-job—a fitting send-off to what had been almost (I stress *almost*)—a perfect vacation.

So I was genuinely sad the next day when I drove out to the airport with both Xaviera's and my suitcase in the car. I was taking a plane. She was taking the car.

PART SIX

THE FRENETIC FALL OF '72

CHAPTER 31.

It was not a very good end of summer for me, so far as my relationship with Xaviera was concerned. For a week after I'd left her in Zurich, I had no way of reaching her, and I had all sorts of depressing fantasies about her and this guy from Geneva, and if it weren't for the press of catching up on my business, I might have thought about her all damn day long.

I knew, however, that she had arranged to see Fiona in Milan again, and I'd be able to get into contact with her there. However, when I did reach her by phone, there was more bad news: now she was for two weeks in the south of Italy with a rich young Italian boy. I tried to prevail upon her not to do it, but I was once more reminded that I was more than four thousand miles away and there was nothing I could do about it. The next day she called me back and said she might not go after all because the kid had gotten very drunk and sloppy the night before, and this is something else she wouldn't tolerate. Then I didn't hear from her again, and couldn't reach her at Fiona's place, so I could draw my own conclusions. I knew she would be going from bed to bed in my absence.

So I decided to have some fun myself, and not worry about what new situation Xaviera had gotten herself into. I called up a girl named Lou—not Louise—whom I dated a few times after Xaviera had left the country, and asked her out to dinner. I said I'd pick her up by cab, since my own car was in for repairs, and she reminded me that she'd once warned me, "Larry, never take a taxicab with me, because if you do something's going to happen."

"Lou, you nut—what are you talking about?" I said.

"You'll see. . . ."

I didn't pursue the matter. This was a Thursday, and the stores were open late and Lou wanted to do some shopping at Bloomingdale's before we went to dinner. She said she could get out of work early, and I was to pick her up in front of her building at 4:30. Fine, I said, I had to be in midtown around that time anyway.

At 4:34 my cab pulled up in front of Lou's office building, and there she was, looking terrific in a green pants suit which set off her long red hair very nicely. She hopped into the cab and said, a wild kind of grin on her face, "Larry, we're finally going to do it!"

Do *what*? I thought. Screw in the back of a taxicab in the middle of Third Avenue in broad daylight with traffic bumper to bumper?

Well, not exactly. But close. . . . Almost immediately Lou's hand leaped to my fly and in about a second or two, she's taken out my penis. A few tugs on it with her hand, and then she bent over and took it right into her mouth.

Normally the ride from where I'd picked up Lou to Bloomingdale's takes about five or seven minutes, depending on how you hit the lights, but now, near the height of the rush hour, it was going to take as long as twenty minutes, and I was sitting there trying to look oblivious to the hundreds of cabs and cars around us as this beautiful redhead had two-thirds of my cock in her mouth.

I didn't know where to put my eyes. If I looked out the window, I was sure that the drivers of the cars alongside us or else the passengers in other cabs had to be staring at what was going on in my cab. If I looked at the driver, I was sure he'd be watching us in his rear-view mirror. So I just closed my eyes and let nature—and Lou's mouth—take its course.

Suddenly I felt Lou jump onto my lap, more or less hugging me and as I startledly looked around, there was a police car right alongside our cab with the cop at the driver's wheel looking right at us. Oh Jesus, I thought, here we go—arrested for unnatural acts in the back seat of a taxicab! But the cop just sort of smiled and drove on when the light changed.

Lou said, "Whew" and went right back to work on me, and in another minute or so I came, and came good. She kept her mouth over my penis during the first flow, then caught the rest in a handkerchief she'd taken from her bag for just this purpose. Then she daintily wiped me off, returned the hankie to her bag and my penis to my pants. In another minute or so we'd reached Bloomingdale's, so I adjusted my pants before getting out. Lou stepped up on the sidewalk and I leaned in the front window of the cab to pay the driver. I overtipped him outrageously, and as he handed me my change, he chuckled and said to me, a definite twinkle in his eye, "Mister, if you ever want to use my cab again . . . after a show like that . . . there'll never be a charge." Then he laughed and drove off.

Grinning myself, I joined Lou on the sidewalk and asked her, "Why in a taxicab—why not later, in your apartment?"

"Because it's fun in a taxicab!" she replied, grinning at me like some female leprechaun.

"I'll get even with you later," I said.

"Please do," she smiled up at me, and she took my arm and we went into Bloomingdale's.

Things like that little adventure certainly helped improve my mood—the rest of the evening was a success, too—and early the next week something equally unexpected happened. I was sitting in my office and one of my assistants answered the phone, and then told me, "It's for you—someone who knows Xaviera."

I picked up the phone and asked who it was. The caller identified herself as Franny, and said she was from New Rochelle, New York. I asked her how she'd gotten my phone number, and she replied that Xaviera had sent it to her in a letter. What could I do for her? I asked. She had a personal problem, and she wanted to get together with me, Franny answered.

Oh, oh, bad news. Right after Xaviera left the United
241

States, a number of young girls called me with problems they wanted me to help them solve, and while I tried to help a few of them out, I wasn't running any psychological counseling service, and I'm sure some of them needed the kind of professional help I could hardly supply. I told Franny that I was really too busy these days, having just returned from a long vacation, and I wouldn't be able to meet with her. She started to protest my decision, so I gently put the phone down. That same day I happened to speak to Xaviera, who was now back in the Netherlands, and mentioned this call from a Franny, and she said she'd received several letters from someone by that name, all forwarded by her publisher, and had finally dashed off a note telling the letter writer to get in touch with me.

The next day, when Franny called the office again, I was a bit more solicitous toward her, but I still was too busy to see her. She called twice more that week, and each time I was polite to her, but turned down any meeting. Then, to my amazement, she traced me that weekend to Las Vegas, and I had to admire her resourcefulness if not her persistence. "Look Franny," I said, after getting over my initial annoyance at her call, "this is beginning to cost you a fortune. Now what's your problem, and how can I help you?"

"I can't discuss it over the phone," she said. "It has to be in person."

"How old are you, Franny?"

"I was just twenty-five."

"Well, don't you think you're old enough to tell me why it's so important for us to meet?"

"Yes, you're right, but I can't. . . . Won't you spare a few minutes to see me?"

"Okay, Franny, I'll meet you at Grand Central, by the information booth, around 5:30 on Tuesday. I'll be carrying a copy of Xaviera's book under my arm. Also, I have all white hair, so that should help you recognize me. Okay?" She sounded very cheered up, and we left it at that.

When Tuesday came I had more or less forgotten about our appointment, but Franny called in the morning to confirm it. So I said yes, I would be meeting her there at the appointed time. Now, I have to confess, I was beginning to be just a little intrigued. She had a very sweet voice over the phone, and maybe she'd bring a pretty face along with her problems.

I showed up at the agreed-upon time, but no Franny. She hadn't bothered to describe herself, so I couldn't even begin to look for her. At about quarter to six, I was getting fed up with this silly situation, and was about to leave when someone put an anxious hand on my arm. "Hello," Franny said, "I'm sorry—the train was late."

I looked down at a nondescript-looking young woman wearing a white trench-coat despite the warm weather outside. She certainly wasn't pretty, but she wasn't homely or anything—she had good, strong features, but had done nothing to take advantage of them. She mostly looked—well, plain. Her hair was a pretty color, but if you asked me what style she was wearing it in, I'd have to answer that she seemed to be doing her best to look like a tomboy, although she'd said she was twenty-five. Given that trench coat, and the loose dress she was wearing, I couldn't tell anything about her figure. On the whole, it didn't look very promising.

I asked Franny if she'd like to go for a drink, and she said she didn't drink. "Well, *I* do," I replied, "so let's go out to the car and find a nice quiet bar where we can talk."

"The last train I can take is 1:20," she said, all in a rush.

"I'll see that you don't miss it."

We went to a nice bar on Third Avenue called Caliban—brick walls, high ceilings—and I specifically asked for a quiet corner. Then while I had a drink and Franny a cup of coffee, she finally let loose with a torrent of information about herself. She was a college graduate who had worked in advertising in New York for two years, but hadn't liked it. She now taught tennis to kids at a private school, and she was enjoying this. She came from a good home, and was now living with her parents again. She had some close friends, but no real male companions.

I hoped she didn't expect me to become a male companion for her, but I didn't want to hurt her feelings—

she seemed much younger than twenty-five, and was actually kind of charming in her innocence—so I pressed again to have her tell me what I could do for her. She looked around nervously, then said she didn't feel at ease discussing it here. As we left to have a bite to eat, I felt sure she had some sexual hangups she wanted me to help her with, and if so, I had no intention in getting involved with her. When I dated, I wanted it to be strictly with grown-up ladies.

We went to a coffee shop on Lexington Avenue which is always quiet at this hour, and Franny continued to talk about herself to the point where I felt I could write a complete resume for her. But I still didn't know what her mysterious problem was. "Look, Franny," I finally said in some frustration, "when do we come to the point of all this? You're a sweet young woman, and all that, but you just aren't being honest with me. Do you have trouble having an orgasm, or something like that? I'd be happy to give you some advice, but you've got to let me know what's going on."

To my surprise, Franny didn't blanch or anything. "Oh, no," she said very seriously, "it just isn't that simple." I tried to get her to open up even more, but she still felt that this was too public a place to discuss her problem. Okay, I'd devoted this much of the evening to unraveling the mystery, so I might as well take another little ride somewhere. "Do you want to talk in the car, or in my apartment?" I asked her. Without hesitation, she answered, "Your apartment—there's no one there, is there?"

Having reassured her that we'd have complete privacy, I drove the few blocks to my apartment and we went upstairs. I took Franny's coat, noticing for the first time that she had good strong legs, and told her to make herself comfortable. I went into the kitchen to make us coffee, and when I came back Franny was leafing through a copy of Xaviera's first book which had been one of several on the coffee table.

"I gather you've read it?" I said, pouring us both coffee.

"I think I know it by heart," she answered me. "My favorite part is where a psychiatrist sends a guy to Xaviera to lose his virginity—"

"Franny," I said, interrupting her, "you don't mean—that's not why—you don't expect me to—?"

"You got it," she said, looking directly at me. "I've had many dates where I let a boy play around with me, but when he actually starts to touch me down there, I turn to ice. Pure ice. I'm just frightened out of my wits. I'll never meet anyone I can love at this rate . . . I'll get married and not be able to do it. . . ."

"Look, Franny, you probably should see—"

She continued as if she hadn't heard me. "I wrote Xaviera because I felt she might know some guy who'd enjoy helping me lose my virginity. She didn't answer any of my early letters—and when she finally did, she gave me your name. . . ."

I didn't believe my ears. Good old Xaviera. She's done a lot of crazy things to me in our years together, but this had to be the topper.

To begin with, I wasn't turned on by Franny. I felt sorry for her, but I didn't *want* to sleep with her, *especially* if she was a virgin. Besides, the whole thing sounded so clinical and cold-blooded. And so what if I helped her lose her cherry—that wasn't suddenly going to transform her into a mature sexual being.

All the while I was sitting there thinking these thoughts, and wondering how to get Franny out of here without hurting her feelings, she was sitting there, on the couch across from me, sipping her coffee, and never taking her eyes off me. She looked so serious it was almost painful. She wasn't kidding about how important this was to her. Going to a therapist wasn't the answer—hell, *he* wasn't going to lay her.

"Yes?" she finally said, sounding more like a woman than she had all night.

"Look, Franny, if we go through this, you've got to have complete confidence in me. You're not going to leave here tonight a different person, and you *are* going to leave here a virgin. It's not going to be wham-bam-thank-you-ma'am. You'll need some lessons before you're ready to stop being a virgin." I was talking a lot because I was fairly sure this would discourage her, but no, she

245

looked at me steadily and said, "Tell me what you want me to do, and I'll do it."

"Well, first go into the bedroom and get undressed. Then take a shower. Then wait on the bed for me." I sounded like a drill sergeant in the Marines, but without a moment's hesitation she got up and went into the bedroom. Jesus, I thought, what do I do now?

I was sitting there, fully clothed, when her voice came out from the bedroom. "Larry . . . I guess I'm ready." Well, time to face the music, I told myself as I stripped down to my shorts and went into the bedroom.

Franny was lying on the bed, above the sheets, completely naked, with her head turned away from me, toward the window. One hand was on her face, the other covering her crotch, but in her nudity she seemed a very sensual person, and men could have no reason to complain about her full breasts, with very large nipples, and her strong, athletic body. And she'd let her hair fall loose on the pillow, which was very attractive. Hmmm, maybe this wasn't such a bad idea, after all.

"Franny," I said, "turn around and look at me." Nothing. "Franny, turn around—it's not Hamlet's father's ghost speaking, I'm really in the room with you."

This time her head revolved toward me, and after a minute she started to giggle. "What's so hilarious?" I more or less snapped at her.

"You—in your shorts," she said, now really cracking up. She had a nice laugh, and it proved infectious because I was soon laughing too, and without realizing it, it was she who'd broken the ice—for both of us.

I stepped out of my shorts and lay down on the bed next to her. Moving closer to her, I began to kiss her and got some response, at the same time fondling her breasts and feeling the nipples stiffening under my touch. And if I wasn't sure about *her,* I knew that *I* was responding to what we were doing. I had a fine erection, and I wanted Franny to get familiar with it. "Franny," I whispered into her ear, punctuating each word with a little flick of my tongue, "sit up and see what you've already done for *me.*" She sat up, as I'd asked, but looked toward the window again. "Franny, *look* at it—it won't turn you into stone."

She turned her head and sat there cross-legged while I moved over a bit on the bed so that we were touching once again, the side of my body next to her shins. She kept looking down intently at my hardened penis, and I began to wonder if her gaze might turn it to silly putty, so I said softly, "Now, Franny, it's time for you to kiss it."

She looked at me, startled, but then I put my hand softly on her shoulder and said, "Go ahead . . . kiss it. Please give my penis a kiss."

Well, she kissed my penis, all right. Like someone on a rubber band, she quickly lowered her head, brushed her lips against the very tip of my penis, and then just as quickly straightened up again. It was so funny that I had to restrain myself from laughing, but I managed to say, "There, that wasn't so bad, was it? Try it again —practice makes perfect." Same thing again. Down, a quick peck, then zap, back up again. I tried to explain to her that there was no point in putting your lips on a man's penis if the contact was going to last less than one-tenth of a second, but it was obvious that she didn't like the idea of keeping her mouth down there.

We talked some about it, and I tried to explain that she wasn't going to become contaminated by making oral love to a man, and she said she understood this, but didn't think she could do it. I guess I was getting a little tired of the situation because at this point I told Franny that she obviously didn't have any confidence in what I was trying to teach her, and probably it would be better if she got dressed and I took her to the train. I was about to get off the bed myself when she said, in a kind of stubborn voice, "No, wait a minute. I'll do it." So I rolled back toward her, waiting to see how we'd make out this time, and Franny began to lower her head very slowly, her tongue protruding about half an inch out of her mouth. Then she closed her eyes, as if doing something distasteful, and lunged for my penis. She ended up kissing the bed sheet, and this time I really had all I could do to keep from laughing.

"Franny," I said after she'd recovered from her em-

247

barrassment, "let's take it from the top. Reach out your hand and grasp my penis." This she managed without missing anything. Then I instructed her to keep her hand there and to guide her lips down to the same place. She did this very slowly, and finally I could feel her tongue come to rest at the tip of my penis. I put my hand gently behind her head, and told her to keep her tongue—and if possible, her lips—right where they were for a few minutes. This should have been at least somewhat stimulating to me, but the situation had been so much more entertaining than erotic that I was having trouble sustaining an erection. It was time to call an end to lesson one. I didn't get any argument from Franny on that score—she seemed glad that the lesson was completed.

Strangely enough, though, she put her panties back on and then just sat there on the bed. "Aren't you planning on wearing clothes back to New Rochelle?" I asked her kiddingly, and she gave me a soft smile and said that this was the first time she'd been able to sit talking with a man while nude to the waist.

I took both her hands, pulled her up off the bed, and handed her her brassiere. "Time to go home," I said, giving her a friendly whack on the behind. "So get dressed quick like a bunny."

"What's the rush? My train's not until 1:20."

"I need my beauty rest," I said, as a joke, so even though we stopped for coffee, she was able to catch the 10:20 back to New Rochelle.

Two days later I received a phone call from Franny asking if our date was still on. She'd planned to take a 6:30 train, but found she could catch the 4:30 express if I wanted her to do so. I did—to my surprise, I was actually horny thinking about her, and looking forward to lesson two.

I met Franny at Grand Central and this time she wasn't wearing the trench coat—my suspicion was that she very often wore it to hide her figure and for no other reason. She was wearing her hair long, and the dress she had was pulled in at the waist by a wide belt, which accented her good body. No baggy dress this time, which

248

meant that she wanted me—and other men—to notice her and be attracted to her. I know *I* was—I actually had half a hard-on as I was taking her out to the car.

"Are you hungry?" I asked her, because if she didn't require food just then, there was another kind of sustenance I had in store for her. "No, not particularly," she said. "Right to the apartment?" I asked her. She nodded, looking happy about the whole thing.

When we got to my apartment I told Franny to make herself comfortable and I would run out and get some sandwiches and soda for us, in case she changed her mind and felt hungry. I did get the sandwiches and soda, but I also picked up a tube of Vaseline and a bottle of body lotion. Plus a package of lubricated Trojans. If nothing else, I felt prepared.

When I got upstairs I really expected Franny to be dressed in a man's shirt, or my bathrobe, or in her bra and panties, but no, she was just the way I'd left her, and watching the news on television. So I decided that maybe my mind was way, way ahead of where I wanted her body to be, and I poured us a couple of 7-Ups and sat down to see what would transpire, besides Walter Cronkite.

To my surprise, Franny put down her drink, got up and came over to my chair, and sat down on the arm. Then she began kissing me. I pulled her down on my lap and let the kisses grow longer as my hands roamed all over her body. We were both fully dressed, but I put Franny's hand on my erection and she not only kept it there, she kept giving it little squeezes as she told me about a brand-new situation which had been bothering her.

Franny had a close friend, Claudia, who, she said, was very pretty and very liberated when it came to sex. As Franny put it, "Claudia will fuck a tree if she thinks it's good-looking." So when Claudia heard about the little experiment I had cooked up for Franny, she wanted to come along. But Franny had vetoed that idea. Was she being stupid and selfish, Franny wanted to know. Because she wanted me all to herself?

My response was to lead her over to the couch and curl up there with her, kissing her and slowly undressing her

249

and as each part of her body became revealed to me, kissing her there. Then, since I was still fully clothed myself. I lay back to see what *she* would do.

"Uh, shouldn't we go into the bedroom?" she asked, her head cuddled beneath my chin. "No," I said, "the couch is very comfortable." So then, rather clumsily, to be truthful, she started to undress me, everything except my shorts. I reminded her that I was still wearing them, and with a small laugh she got up and took them off as well. Of course there was junior, standing tall, but Franny made no comment about my state of readiness, and crawled back into my arms.

I spent the next few minutes munching on her breasts, which were really firm and wonderful, and moving my hands into every nook and cranny of her body, and she began to grind against me. However, when her hand began to travel down my body, across my shoulders and chest and stomach, it came to a firm halt just above my groin, on my lower abdomen. "Why'd you stop?" I said into her ear. "Just move it down a little bit further." But that hand didn't stir from where it'd stopped, and I resisted the temptation to take it and place it on my cock—which is what I think she expected me to do. For that matter, I could have moved my body up slightly so that her hand and my penis would get together, but I wasn't doing that, either. Either she was going to hold my cock, or she wasn't. Well, she wasn't. . . .

We just lay like that for about fifteen minutes, her hand about two inches from my penis, and my hands lightly caressing her body. Time for a different tack. I took Franny's hand and pulled her up off the couch, leading her toward the bedroom. On the way I picked up the bag of items I'd bought in the drug store and, arm in arm, we went into the bedroom. "Please get on the bed, Franny," I said, "because I've got some things to explain to you." So while she lay there, on her side, I stood over her, my hard-on pointing toward her, giving her a short lecture which would have been funny if it weren't sincerely meant as instruction. Come to think of it, it *was* pretty funny after all.

Like a small boy with a rehearsed speech, I removed

250

the three items from the paper bag and began to explain in detail the purpose of each of them. The body lotion, I said, would be for rubbing into my genital area, perhaps not tonight, but definitely at some future date. The Vaseline was to ease my sexual penetration that might occur this evening, or at some occasion in the immediate future. And the prophylactics, since she didn't take the Pill or wear a diaphragm, were the most important item of all: they were to prevent her from getting pregnant tonight or at some occasion in the days to come. "Got it?" I said when I was done.

"Larry," she said, "I *know* all that."

"You do, huh?"

"Well, except for the stuff about the lotion—what'd you say that was for?"

"That's to use, when you really feel at ease with a man, on his entire genital area so that he continues to smell good after sex. It also feels very good when it's applied —care to try doing it?"

"Uh, not tonight, thanks."

Well, *okay*, I told myself, that *is* for advanced students, and putting the things on the night table, I hopped on the bed and moved into her arms. Amazing—this time Franny immediately began to stroke and touch my body all over with her hands, and then, pushing me back on the pillow, she started to kiss me in the same places, beginning with my mouth, then my neck and chest, and then straight down—no detours—to my penis. I couldn't conceive of her having gotten in any penis practice since the first lesson two days earlier, but here she was, handling my penis like an old friend.

Was this the same girl? What a transformation! Franny had taken her hands and placed them under my balls, and was moving her mouth over everything in sight, using not only her tongue but her lips as well. Then, keeping one hand under my balls and placing the other around the base of my penis, she took it into her mouth and really began sucking on it. I was so surprised that I wasn't really enjoying it—I kept expecting her to bite me by accident or at least to leave teeth marks on it, but she seemed to know what she was doing. Granted that it was a kind of

251

jerky rhythm, but it was certainly getting to me, and suddenly I knew I had an orgasm on the way and there was no stopping it, so I firmly, but as gently as I could manage in a hurry, pushed her head away and rolled over to my side of the bed, promptly coming all over the sheet there.

Franny was startled. "Did I do something wrong?" she asked, sounding worried.

I told her no. I don't think she'd realized that I had come, and had just barely avoided coming in her mouth, so I rolled over and pulled her to me and began kissing her all over. My mouth must have been exploring her body for ten minutes or so, and I had Franny in a high state of passion, that was for sure, and I also had a brand-new throbbing hard-on. Was it time? Only one way to find out. . . .

Having Franny lie on her back, I asked her to spread her legs apart some and then I began gently eating her, using my finger in her as well, and twice I brought her to orgasm that way. However, she didn't seem to be experiencing the normal kind of female orgasm—thirty of forty seconds of spasms—but instead something terribly brief, just a few seconds of shivers and throbbing. Still, I wasn't about to start discussing the nature of female sexuality with her just at that moment. Her cunt was now quite lubricated—I was able to push my finger in and out quite freely—and so I reached over for the Vaseline and put a little on the head of my penis.

Franny now looked a little more than a little worried about the next step, so I explained to her that I was just going to run my penis along her outer vaginal lips and then, if things were going well, attempt some slight penetration. "I don't want to get pregnant," she said, almost whimpering, and I reassured her, explaining that I wouldn't let me myself even get close to an orgasm. If I did, I'd withdraw and put on a rubber.

She then very cautionsly opened her legs and I put my penis next on the outside of her vagina, moving it slowly back and forth with my hand. Then I removed my hand and was able to get a little bit inside through slow motions of my body. I was perhaps inside her an inch or so when she began to complain of pain, and pushed me away.

I could feel the tension mounting in her body, so I continued to kiss and caress her, playing with her breasts and stroking her hip and thigh, and gradually I was able to bring her body entirely on top of mine, her legs on either side of my thighs, and her vagina just in front of my erection. This was a position in which she could control the degree of penetration, I explained to Franny, and did she want to try it this way? No, she didn't. It would hurt.

Ouch. *I* was beginning to hurt, and I wanted to get inside this girl with her sexy body, and virginity be damned. But I wasn't going to rape her, so we settled for some more penis-to-outer-labia manipulation.

"Let's try another way," I suggested, and I turned her around on her side so we were cuddled sort of doggie-style, and I began to titillate her clitoris. When she seemed very excited by this, I moved my penis to the entrance of her vagina and exerted a small degree of pressure forward, in order to get just the head inside her, and she immediately tensed up again. I withdrew completely, and lay there as calmly as I could manage, cuddling her ass and legs and rubbing and fondling her breasts from behind. This seemed to alleviate the tension and I began to work on her clitoris once again, and she became excited once again, and I then gave a lunge with my penis toward her vagina from the rear.

Whoops, wrong move. She gave out a small scream, and I was sure that I'd broken through her hymen and she was no longer a virgin. No, I'd penetrated her anus by mistake—my turn to miss the target—and would I please get my cock away from there in a hurry!

I felt silghtly mortified by what I'd done, but the devirginization of Franny was rapidly becoming a charade and I couldn't help but find the whole thing hysterically funny. Finally she did too, and we both relaxed and fell asleep in each other's arms.

When we awoke about an hour later I told her to follow me to the bathroom, and I'm sure she thought we were going to try some exotic position on the sink or toilet seat, but all I had in mind was to take a bath together, and get really relaxed. Then, who knows?

Franny was slightly amazed that two people could take a comfortable bath together, and we each washed each other's backs and fronts, though I think I easily got the better of the deal here as I rubbed soap all over her full breasts. Then I stood up and did my own middle and legs —I knew if she soaped up my cock it'd want something more than soaping, so rather than risk another fiasco, I washed myself in that area—and got out of the tub so she could finish washing her lower regions. Then we helped dry each other off, kidding around a bit but not starting anything really sexual. Then out into the living room, both of us completely naked.

Franny, not knowing what I intended next, looked at me sort of uneasily, or so I thought, and I went over to her and kissed her lightly on the lips, not allowing my body to touch hers, and said, "Franny, it's time to get dressed. . . . I'm a little hungry, so let's have some dinner [we'd never touched the sandwiches] and then I'll take you to the station." She looked slightly bewildered by what I'd just said, so I reminded her, "Look, I told you that this would take time. . . ." What I didn't say was that I hadn't expected it to be this difficult, or take this much time.

We had dinner—two of the biggest steaks in the house —at Manny Wolfe's, and then I drove Franny to Grand Central, just a few blocks away. Before she got out of the car, she came over and snuggled in my arms, murmuring, "If I come in next Tuesday, I hope we'll be able to go all the way. Then the next time, if Claudia wants to come along, maybe I'll let her . . . but I'm *not* going to bring her along so long as I'm still a virgin."

Go figure Franny. The second she's no longer a virgin, she's willing to try a three-way scene. "Good night, nut," I said, and she responded, "You don't think it's such a good idea?"

"No, no, it's a fine idea—and while you're at it, why not bring along your entire senior class in college—at least all the ones who aren't virgins." She grinned at me impishly, blew me a kiss, then got out and headed for the train.

254

CHAPTER 32.

However, Franny had given me an idea. Perhaps another person, another female, would make Franny feel more at ease—particularly if the female were someone very experienced sexually. It sounded a little crazy, so I called Lou and asked her what she thought of the idea. Her response, after first asking me if I'd left my senses, was to invite Franny and me over to discuss it the next time Franny was in town.

So when Franny arrived in town at 6:30 the following Tuesday, I told her we'd be seeing a friend of mine later in the evening and that we had only an hour or so to have some fun. "Let's go straight to the apartment."

Without any preliminaries, Franny marched into the bathroom and took a shower. Then she came out, nude.

I still had all my clothes on because I hadn't expected her out of the shower so fast, but the long bulge in my pants was one answer to how she looked, and she saw it and grabbed hold of it. I was getting hornier by the second, and so I said, "Race you into the bedroom," and I have to admit that the tip of her left breast went past the bedroom door first, so I conceded the race to her. In exchange, she helped me out of my clothes in the most sensuous manner.

We were both ready to make love, I was sure of that, so I took some Vaseline on my finger and lubricated her vagina while I kissed and played with her breasts. She was nice 'n' wet down below, so I decided to put my penis in to see if we would be able to avoid any pain or discomfort this time, and in it went partially, and then in some more, and then, damnit, I felt the fury of an orgasm on its way and I had to pull out in a hurry so I wouldn't come inside her. I hadn't worn a rubber because I simply didn't expect it to go in so easily, and there'd been no way to hold back.

But, more important, had she felt anything—had I finally managed to penetrate her almost all the way? She didn't know. I didn't know. There was no blood. Maybe she had no hymen, after all, and her state of virginity was strictly a psychological problem? She didn't know.

We lay back on the bed and decided not to sweat it. If it hadn't been this time, it'd surely be the next. After about twenty minutes I was ready for the next time, but I'd told Lou we'd be over at a certain time, and since she was doing us a favor, I didn't want to be too late.

On the way over to Lou's I explained to Franny that Lou was a good friend of mine, but just a dating friend, and that she could feel completely relaxed with her. And oddly enough, despite their vast differences in personality and experience, Lou and Franny seemed to take to each other almost immediately. Lou made herself and me a gin and tonic, and gave Franny a tall milk, and we discussed the possibility of a threesome making things easier for Franny. I was a little surprised at how quickly we got into the subject, because Lou is strictly a man-loving lady, but the idea of this twenty-five-year-old woman wanting to lose her virginity through a complete and rewarding sexual experience—after all, she could have gone to a physician if it were just a matter of removing her hymen —seemed to touch her. If Xaviera had been in the country, the whole thing would have been simple—and I could see Franny's eyes light up at the mention of Xaviera—but maybe, Lou said, if Franny and I didn't achieve success the next time out, we'd try a threesome with her. Franny didn't say no, and she didn't say yes, so we just dropped the subject and all went out to dinner.

While driving to the train station to drop Franny off, she leaned over and whispering in my ear, asked if I would stop and buy a vibrator for her. That might help widen her vaginal passage, she said. For some reason, I vetoed the idea. Somehow, given the circumstances of the past two weeks, it just didn't appeal to me.

256

After Franny left the car to catch her train, I looked at Lou and Lou looked at me, and I drove back to her apartment as fast as traffic would let me, and we made love for the rest of the evening—no Trojans to worry about, either—and I'd be a liar if I didn't say that being with Franny that evening had turned on both of us. For different reasons—Lou had responded in her own way to Franny's innocence—but both of us were now on the case.

It was Thursday and the weather was terrible—raining cats, dogs and several other creatures—and while driving up from downtown I wished I'd cancelled the date. It was a bitch to park near Grand Central and I was lamenting the evening even more. However, when I walked across the broad expanse of Grand Central and saw Franny waving at me from where she was standing by the information booth, I was really glad to see her. Each time she arrived she looked more attractive to me, and there was certainly nothing demure any longer about the way she dressed. This evening she had worn hip-huggers and a low-cut cotton jersey which gave a broad hint of cleavage.

We got into the car and almost immediately she started to talk nonstop, and I finally had to tell her, in a mock-loud voice, to shut up. It suddenly got very quiet in the car. Then, in a stage whisper, I asked her what she'd like to eat. "You," she said brightly. I told her that would —er—*come* later, and with the weather so bad, we should get dinner out of the way. "Fine with me," she said, and then she surprised me by asking if Lou was going to join us for dinner. I said no, she wasn't, and Franny said why didn't I call Lou up and suggest it? I pulled the car over and told her that we'd be joining Lou later on in the evening. "Great," she responded, "I'll pretend she's Xaviera." This kind of annoyed me. "If Lou's there, you won't have to pretend she's anyone but Lou," I said. Then I thought, what the hell, and drove to the nearest sidewalk phone booth and called Lou and asked her if she wanted to join the two of us for dinner. "Great," she said, suggesting a small Italian restaurant called Gloria's—which we both knew and liked—on East Twenty-sixth Street. I was be-

257

ginning to wonder if Franny and Lou had planned this entire evening, apart from the miserable weather.

Dinner was actually very pleasant, the three of us dining at a very leisurely pace—as though we wanted to delay the rest of the evening as long as possible—and then, since it had stopped raining, we walked back to Lou's apartment, which was just two blocks away. Franny and Lou chatted away like two sorority sisters all the way back.

When we arrived there I noticed how clean and neat the apartment looked—and Lou had never been famous as a housekeeper—and more and more I began to wonder if this whole evening had been engineered by the two women, and I was just the instrument designed to bring them together. Well, if *that* were the case, I'd make sure my instrument got used by me—as well as me being used by others.

As it turned out, my galloping paranoia was way off base. Since Lou's apartment is called a studio apartment but is actually just one gigantic room, with a small walk-in kitchen, I didn't think we could get this portion of the evening underway with the three of us in the same room, so I sent Franny into the shower and then suggested to Lou that she "go check the mail for fifteen minutes" while I got Franny and me into the sack, and she readily agreed.

Then I stripped and hopped into the shower myself, joining Franny for a soaping-up festival that left me cleansed of any suspicions about the evening and ready to begin where we'd left off the last time. We dried off and then went out into the living room—happily Lou was still absent, so there'd be time to establish the proper sexual rapport between us—and together we opened up Lou's very large convertible sofa. More or less falling onto the broad sofa bed together, we began kissing—Franny loves to kiss, and so do I—and fondling each other, when all of a sudden I felt a cooling hand very knowingly caressing the entire left side of my body and I knew Lou was back. Since I like to have my eyes closed when making love, in order to concentrate on sensations, I hadn't seen her, but Franny, the little devil, *had* seen Lou come in and quietly, but very sexily, undress, and this had added to

258

her overall excitement. And watching Franny and me had certainly gotten Lou excited.

Okay, there I was, with a horny, voluptuous female on each side of me—I could write an entire page on the delicious contrasts between Franny's breasts and Lou's long, pointed breasts, but that would stop the story—and just for the hell of it I pulled the two women together on top of me. Forget it. At least they suddenly seemed to forget *I* was there!

The two of them began kissing and then devouring each other's breasts and playing with each other's vaginas, and I just let it happen because it was some turn-on, believe you me. Then I moved behind Franny, intending to enter her from the rear—a Trojan properly installed on my penis this time –and when Lou saw my cock rising between Franny's legs, she put it in precisely the right spot and together we pushed Franny between us. And in it went, all the way home. No question about it this time. Franny was no longer any kind of virgin, technical or otherwise.

At first Franny seemed stunned. She hadn't realized what had happened. I felt her hand probe her vagina, which, she had to understand, was filled with a cock right up to the hilt. She started to laugh—for just a second I was fearful that she'd gone into some kind of shock—and then the tears of joy filled her eyes and she began wildly kissing both Lou and me, and I continued doing just what I was doing, and when she had an orgasm this time, it was a wild, howling, deliriously happy orgasm. In fact we both came together. Success knows no bounds.

Mission complete. It had been a great trip. Out into the universe and back again, all members of the flight safe and happy. No strain, no pain, and no regrets.

Afterward we all toasted the end of Franny's virginity. With French champagne, no less, which Lou had thoughtfully supplied. It was her first drink, ever, Franny said, and she liked it.

I've seen Franny a few times since then, and we've remained friends. We would always share something very close and dear, but we'd never be lovers again. For it was time for her to find her own for-real lover.

259

CHAPTER 33.

Xaviera was now living in England for a few months and there was going to be a big press party, sponsored by *Penthouse*, to herald both her debut as a *Penthouse* columnist and the hardcover publication of *The Happy Hooker*. She wanted me to come over, and I wanted to be there, but it was a busy time in the office for me and I didn't know if I should spare the time for what would be, at best, a long weekend. And, if I knew my friend Xaviera—and who knew her better?—a frenetic, hectic four or five days. Then, too, despite my official contractual status as Xaviera's business manager, the invitation was strictly a personal one—I'd be paying my own way, and it would be an expensive little holiday. Would it be worth it?

I went. And it was worth it. I can't say that I was bored —not for a minute. Other things, yes, but never *bored*.

The two days-plus we spent in London were every bit as hectic as I'd imagined. When we weren't at a press event, we were at a private party, when we weren't going out to dinner, we were having a drink at one of London's great old pubs—maybe if Xaviera lived in London long enough, she could have gotten at least one pub to stock fresh orange juice, but hell, the English are just beginning to discover that ice and drinks go well together. If we weren't meeting new people, we were saying hello to old friends. If we weren't gambling late at night, we were doing something else late at night. We were so busy that I didn't even have time for jet lag.

Stop the whirl, I kept saying to myself, I want to get off.

Then onto an Air France jet to Paris, for a quiet two days.

Quiet, hell, the only thing missing was the Penthouse Club.

On the fourth day away from quiet, placid New York, after a particularly luxurious lunch at Maxim's, I decided to retreat back to the hotel for a nap, while Xaviera was going to spend the afternoon shopping. She could buy the Eiffel Tower for all I cared. I needed a little sleep.

When she got back she woke me up, all excited. The cause of this excitement? Had she actually bought the Eiffel Tower?

"Larry," she said, "we're going to a *partouze* tonight!"

"We are . . . ?" I said, enthusiastic as hell. "Good." Then: "What's a *partouze*?"

"You'll find out," she said, dashing into the shower. Yep, I found out.

A *partouze*, for those few hundred of you who somehow have never been to one, is a private house where you go to swing. You can only go as a couple. The female in each couple must present her passport before being allowed admittance—that way, horny guys couldn't pick up a streetwalker just to gain entry. Made sense.

Since two's company, and four's double your pleasure, I'd called up an American newspaper friend, Max, who worked for one of the wire services in Paris, and asked him if he wanted to join us for a *partouze*. At least he knew what a *partouze* was. "Sure thing," he said, "but I'll need a female companion."

"Don't worry," I said. "We have a beautiful date for you. Name's Cecile, and she lives outside of Paris. But she's meeting us at the hotel, so you meet us there too. Okay?"

"Sure thing," said Max. Being a newspaperman, he didn't waste words.

As we'd promised, Cecile was really something to behold—a tall, willowy, auburn-haired beauty with magni-

261

ficent hazel eyes. We introduced him to her, and Max beamed with pleasure when we were having a drink before leaving the hotel to go to dinner. I got him aside and asked if he was pleased with his date. "Sure thing," he answered.

Actually, I knew Max was more than a little pleased with being Cecile's date—and all that that implied for the evening—because not only was she a fabulous beauty, but she seemed to know everyone in Paris and around the Continent, too, for that matter. No homebody, this gal. I'd been given her name by a friend in New York, as someone to definitely look up when I got to Paris, so Max was lucky as hell we'd been able to get her for him.

We decided to have a light dinner at a restaurant Max picked, which was near the *partouze*. At dinner Cecile and I found we had a lot to talk about, and someone watching us might have thought that I was Cecile's date, instead of Max's, because we were having so much fun together. Then we walked over to where the *partouze* was being held, with Cecile and I still kidding around a lot.

At the *partouze* itself, once you'd gained admittance, the rules were simple: (1) You paid an entrance fee, around ten dollars a head, as I recall; (2) You had a drink, if you cared for one, and that cost extra; (3) You checked your valuables; (4) You went upstairs and got out of your clothes; (5) You combed your hair, and (6) You screwed. Anyone. And everyone, too, if you could manage it.

Actually the place reminded me a little of the Continental Baths in New York. They both smelled like a gymnasium. And while I only got to hear about the "Orgy Room" at the Baths, there was no doubt about what the rooms here were for—they were all orgy rooms. Just double beds, and almost no other furniture.

At a casual estimate, I'd say that there were between forty and fifty couples on the premises. It was hard to tell because so many of them were on top of each other. But when I did get a good look at people's faces, most were fairly young people—between twenty and forty—and generally attractive as well.

We toured the place for a while, then decided to do like the natives were doing. It wasn't exactly easy to find

262

an empty room with a double bed in that place, but we finally did and we all got on it and started to horse around. To be very frank, while I knew I'd have a great time with Xaviera, I was also looking forward to balling Cecile, because not only was she a beauty, but her body was something extraordinary—her clothes didn't reveal what fine, high breasts she had, and her long, slim waist gracefully flared into shapely hips, and those long legs, why, they could haunt a man with less willpower and self-control than I have.

So while we hadn't paired off into couples as yet, my attentions were mostly being directed toward getting to know Cecile a lot better, and she seemed pretty responsive to starting off the evening that way, too.

But suddenly we had a tigress in our midst. I felt that Xaviera was jealous of Cecile, and that she was just going to show us that she could make love to Cecile better than I could. She moved between Cecile's legs and began eating her, and I can't deny that Xaviera was getting to her —Cecile began to scream and moan—so Max and I had to be content with just watching the show. We lay there on the bed as Xaviera was driving Cecile out of her mind, and so intently was I watching the two women that I wasn't conscious of anyone else in the room. Suddenly I looked up and there were about ten sets of eyes staring down at us, each of them shining with lust. I could feel my erection begin to wither, and rapidly began to wish I were somewhere else.

These people were like sexual vultures. They'd been attracted by the screaming and moaning, and sensing fresh blood in their midst, they were descending upon us, their hands and fingers grabbing and probing not only the two women, but Max and me as well.

I didn't like it at all, especially the feel of a masculine hand on my body, and I got off the bed and over to the side of the room. Max did too, but it was hard to avoid the groping clutches of these animals.

Xaviera, on the other hand, seemed to be in her glory. Girls were putting their pussies over her face, and the more, the merrier. Then she was astride someone's cock, and then she was kneeling down, blowing some guy while

263

another guy was behind her, fucking her from the rear.

I wandered out of there for a while, and each time I returned, Xaviera looked as though she'd come another five times. Her passionate cries resounded through the room.

In the midst of all this I tried to get something going with Cecile. and even though she was blowing me in the great French manner, it was to no avail. This just wasn't my scene. If only we could have found a quiet corner!

Finally even Xaviera had her fill of all this sex *a la carte*, and we took off.

Downstairs we got Cecile a cab—she was off to Rome the next morning- -and Max, Xaviera, and I had a bite to eat and a nightcap at a small bistro nearby. When I got the check, Xaviera leaned over and said to me, "Larry, get rid of Max and let's go home. I'm horny as hell . . . I couldn't come once in that crowd."

One hour, one bath, and one session of *soixante-neuf* later, two tired people fell asleep in each other's arms.

I left Paris the next morning and Xaviera returned to Holland, and now at least I know what a *partouze* is.

CHAPTER 34.

I went back to Europe several more times after the Paris-London-Paris trip. I guess I was trying to keep the relationship going. and while it wasn't hard to keep track of Xaviera when she was in Manhattan, it was next to impossible from across the Atlantic.

One week she was involved with this guy who'd been designated by a British magazine as one of the nation's "Most Eligible Bachelors." Another time she was flying off to Copenhagen to keep an assignation that had nothing to do with romance. Whatever the circumstances, she was causing me to act like a romantic fool—who cared too much for his own good.

Meanwhile, I was having very serious problems, of a legal nature, in New York. Because I'd gotten involved with Ted Ratnoff, known as "Abe the Bugger" in Xaviera's first book, in trying to get evidence to help indict a corrupt judge—who very cleverly escaped that indictment by retiring—I was accused of trying to bribe a judge. I have a notorized legal document from Ratnoff attesting to the work I was doing on behalf of that part of the state judicial system which oversees the activities of members of the bench themselves. I got that document on the advice of my lawyer, before agreeing to work with Ratnoff, but now he is out of the country and unavailable to me. In fact, the U. S. government is still trying to extradite him from England, with little success. There is a forty-count open indictment waiting for him.

Since it is a rather entangled legal web we're discussing here, I had better tell you how I came to be involved with Ratnoff in the first place. One legal mess led to this even larger one.

I have a flying buddy, a very close friend, who is an insurance broker. We have worked closely on claims on hundreds of occasions. Therefore, when I got a call from his secretary saying that an envelope had arrived in the office marked "Hold for Larry," I thought nothing of it. I told her I'd come by later in the day to pick up the check. That afternoon I stopped by his office, said hello, signed for the check, and went back to my office. I didn't immediately recognize the name on the check, but with hundreds of insurance claims being processed through my office during the course of a month, no one name has any particular significance to me unless I personally know the parties involved. The check was for a six-figure sum, which was very good news to me since I work on a commission basis.

265

I had some other business to conduct, and when I got back to my office there were two very tough-looking gentlemen waiting for me. They wanted a private conference with me, about the check I'd picked up earlier in the day, so I told them to go into my office. Meanwhile I handed my secretary the check and whispered to her to photocopy it, then put it back in the envelope.

"You have a check that belongs to us," they told me in a very unfriendly way. I said I'd have to check my files, which I did, and whether or not the check actually belonged to them, I knew it didn't belong with me. I wanted to call my friend's office, but they clearly weren't in the mood to hang around any longer. With menace in his voice, one of the guys informed me to hand over the check in a hurry, and so I told my secretary to bring in the check and give it to them. They left, I might add, without saying good-bye.

I immediately called my friend and informed him of what had happened, and I suggested that the next procedure would be to stop payment on the check until the matter got cleared up. So imagine my surprise when the next afternoon two plainclothesmen showed up, asking for the check. I told them I no longer had it, and then explained what had happened the previous day. I had signed for the check, I pointed out, which I certainly wouldn't have done if I'd known the check was stolen or in any way improper. I had nothing to hide, and since they were being very courteous to me, I told them everything I knew—which proved to be a mistake. (I should have talked to my attorney first, just to avoid statements which could be twisted into something self-incriminating.) At one point one of the cops suggested that I might need police protection from my two visitors, but I only laughed at this. Actually they weren't so far from wrong.

The two policemen said they had to make some calls, and I said, "Sure, please use my phone." Then I was informed—to my complete shock—that they'd have to arrest me because the insurance company was pressing charges: receiving stolen property.

I didn't believe my ears at first, but about half an hour later I found myself in the station house answering question after question—which I answered, when I knew the answers. Then I was locked up in a cell while they looked for my criminal record—which of course they never found because it didn't exist. Meanwhile I was standing in that incredibly filthy cell—smelling of urine and vomit and worse—because the two benches already had two sleeping customers on them.

Five hours after I'd been arrested, five hours which seemed like a small lifetime of horrors, I was released in my own custody.

I thought the nightmare was over. In reality it was just beginning.

My case kept getting postponed, which was causing havoc with my business life, not to speak of my emotional health, and when Teddy came into Xaviera's life—via Robin Moore—and performed a small miracle in helping my friend, the police sergeant, I wasn't reluctant to discuss with him the absurd difficulties I was having with the judicial system. He said he could get the damn case thrown out of court if I helped him with his little project. And like the sincere schnook I've been on too many occasions, although none so significant as this particular occasion, I agreed to do so, providing I got a legal document from Teddy substantiating the nature of my activities—a document which is still in my lawyer's possession.

Well, those of you who have read *The Happy Hooker* know how complicated my life became at that point—actually I could go on at book length telling stories the public has never known about this, but because none of the parties involved has had his day in court, I can't speak out at this time—but the shit really hit the fan, to use an apt phrase, when Patrolman William Phillips used not only Teddy's name, but also mine and Xaviera's, during the first day of the Knapp Commission Hearings. Armstrong, who was directing the investigation for the commission, could have torn off Phillips' head for mentioning real names connected with the ongoing investigations, and henceforth it was Mr. X or Mr. L or whatever. But the New York *Post* had picked up my name, and here I was—being branded not only a briber but a pimp as well. The latter label really hurt, since I'd never taken a nickel from Xaviera and, indeed, had spent many thousands of dollars on her.

My lawyer immediately contacted Mr. Armstrong and asked for a hearing with him as soon as humanly possible. But Armstrong was unavailable to us for the next few days because of commitments to television appearances, and we agreed to see Julius Impellezeri, an assistant director of the Knapp Commission. My lawyer accompanying me, I reviewed the entire situation with Mr. Impellezeri, showing him Teddy's sworn statement and explaining why I'd done what I'd done. He seemed genuinely impressed with my sincerity, and said he'd discuss the matter with Armstrong and Mr. Knapp himself. The key thing, he agreed, was how to clear my reputation without stirring up too much noise about Teddy, since his work was so central to their investigations.

Unfortunately, Mr. Ratnoff's own reputation was about to go under, since it turned out that he had a criminal record—which didn't make his word to me very useful to me, after all.

I wanted to institute an immediate suit against the Knapp Commission, but both Assistant District Attorney Kenneth Conboy and my own attorney warned me that I'd accomplish nothing in this manner, since the commission had been guaranteed immunity, in its charter, against any lawsuits.

I kept hoping that Teddy would be extradited, but it was explained to me by someone in the district attorney's office that this was highly unlikely because Teddy had been connected with too many people in high office for the government to want him back here. If Teddy's mouth ever really began flapping, there'd be seen quite a can of worms inside. So much for justice for all before the law.

Finally, on March 22, 1973—almost four years after the original charging, and three years after I'd submitted myself to a lie-detector test which established that I had no way lied about that check—I stood before Judge Irving Lange in criminal court once again. My stolen-check case had had so many postponements that I now felt like a commuter between my office and the courtroom. This time, Judge Lange told me to approach the bench.

I looked around. My lawyer had not appeared yet.

I walked up in front of the bench.

"Not there," the judge said in a kindly voice. "Please stand behind the defense table."

Moving behind the table, I said, "Your Honor, my attorney has not appeared yet." *Please, Your Honor,* I was thinking at that instant, *please don't postpone the case until tomorrow again—I have two important business appointments tomorrow.*

The judge, perhaps recognizing the great look of frustration on my face, said: "It will not be necessary to postpone your case until tomorrow. Your indictment has been dismissed on motion of the district attorney. You do not have to appear tomorrow."

My legs turned to water just then, but the judge and I had seen each other so often that I felt I knew him, and I would have kissed him if he'd been any nearer, so great was the load he'd just taken off my shoulders.

So my case had finally been thrown out of court—and without any help from Teddy Ratnoff. In this instance, the only help I got—and damn slow help at that—was from Justice.

My mood that day in March was one of complete elation, but my mood—in reliving those thirty-six postponements —gets pretty grim when I am reminded of not only all the chicanery Teddy Ratnoff was involved in, but how I got involved with Ratnoff in the first place.

I have to thank Mr. Robin Moore for that, and so long as I am speaking of people's reputations, I would like to warn him that his own has been diminished by his new book, *The Making of The Happy Hooker.* Not only was the book cancelled by at least two publishers, Robin was so low on material that he offered me twenty-five thousand dollars against fifteen percent of his book if I would help him with his manuscript. It was an astounding offer, but for a variety of reasons, I declined. So what he ended up doing, in order to get the semblance of a manuscript, was to dredge through the material cut out of *The Happy Hooker* and use that. If Robin wishes to dispute this in court, I'll be only too happy to see him there—as I have the original manuscript.

In any case, I do plan to see Robin in court because his

269

book contains statements about me which are untrue, and which I do not plan to ignore. I'd like a little justice on my side for a change.

The original cover of *The Making of The Happy Hooker* had Xaviera's photograph on the cover, and it was being used without her permission. I stopped that. Now I plan to do something about the insides of the book. It's called *nonfiction*. But it isn't.

For instance, and I will cite something which has nothing to do with me—for the obvious legal reasons—on page 25 of his book, Robin, describing his first meeting with Xaviera, writes:

"What an hour that was! First she explained the sado-masochist scene and when I was stripped naked she took a thin riding crop and slowly, deliberately, beat me across the chest and stomach with it. Each stroke was delivered with more force. I'm no freak but I got some perverse enjoyment out of seeing how much pain I could endure. I had seen a great deal of torture administered in Vietnam and now I let her inflict pain on me. Xaviera stopped before I uttered a sound.

" 'You can take a lot of pain, baby,' she said admiringly."

Now this makes Robin look like one helluva researcher, except it *never* happened. Xaviera swears it never happened, and she isn't reticent about such matters.

So why that little scene, Robin? Is it the "in" thing these days to say you've been whipped?

PART SEVEN

GOOD-BYES, AND
NEW HELLOS . . . TO MYSELF:
A NEW START

CHAPTER 35.

I have been fighting with my editor about this chapter. He says that I've gathered enough material to be used here to create another book instead of just a chapter. He says I should be brief—and to the point. He cites the paper shortage. He reminds me of the energy crisis. We mustn't keep the printers working overtime, he says.

I don't know. Maybe he's right. About the paper shortage and energy crisis, that is. But I'm going to try it his way. Then, if I don't like it his way, I'll try it my way. Or else write another book. That'll show him. . . .

When Xaviera came to Canada in late '72, I was delighted. With her just an hour's flight away in Toronto, I felt sure we could restore a lot of what we'd had before—when I could watch after (and over) her. And for a few months, that's the way it was. We had great times in Canada, and also on long weekends in Acapulco. And if Xaviera hadn't come to Canada, I would have missed out on meeting a lot of wonderful people whom I now hold as life-long friends.

But Xaviera, whom I've called a tigress more than once in this book, is also a leopard who can't change her spots. In Canada she still continued to display great errors in business judgment. For example, I had to save her from lending her name to a book about massage parlors. She was supposed to introduce the book, but when I saw the contract, it granted the publisher the right to use photographs of her on the cover and in promotional material for the book. It also granted the publisher the right to use biographical material about her in promoting the book. You didn't have to be a lawyer to see how this contract was designed to rip off her name and celebrity to sell this book.

However, when I told the slick-looking young man who'd brought me the contract to sign—I had power of attorney for her in that regard—that I thought her literary attorney would wish to review the contract as well, he obviously didn't care for the idea. He made a lot of veiled threats which said, in summary: Don't make waves if you know what's good for you. I invited him to leave my office by the nearest exit, and that concluded that little business deal, so far as Xaviera was concerned. The book may have appeared, I really don't know, but it sure as hell didn't appear with an "Introduction by Xaviera Hollander" on the cover. And if it did appear, no one had cause to confuse it with her own new blockbuster of a book, *Xaviera!* So that's one small thing this "square businessman" was able to do for her.

How many crooks have I kept away from her front door?

But it's Xaviera's personal life that I finally began to find myself unable to forgive. I knew she was continuing her penchant for getting involved with good-looking young guys —on lecture tours, any number of attractive young kids would come along and say they were virgins, and would she help them as she's helped others?—but these incidents, while of course they had to bother me, proved no threat to our relationship. I was no stranger to Xaviera's impromptu performances with men, after all. . . .

For example, once I took her flying with my friends, Mike and Stanley. Mike and Stanley and Xaviera were in one plane, and I was in the other. She took Mike in back of the plane—it was Stanley's plane, and he was doing the flying—and gave him a blow-job. So I lost a friend—namely, Mike, for even allowing this to happen behind my back —and Xaviera gained a few black and blue marks for about a week.

Another time, in London, a friend of mine named Jack flew there with me to spend a nice weekend. While standing

273

on the sidewalk in front of his hotel, as we were getting the bags from the cab to the hotel desk, Xaviera gave him a soul kiss, and Jack got so embarrassed that he bit her tongue. Then he charged into the hotel, grabbed his bags, and headed back to the airport to take the next plane back to New York. I think he spent something like two or three hours in England, altogether. Sure, Jack overreacted, but what business did Xaviera have flirting with one of my good friends that way!

No, I was never really surprised by Xaviera's various little flings. Apparently she has to do this to keep reasserting her femininity, but when she proclaims that she has gotten serious with someone, and he is the new Great Love of Her Life, if I'm to understand it and walk away from it with some respect for her and the guy, there has to be cause for that respect. I have to believe in—no other word will do—the integrity of a relationship, and Xaviera's current thing with a gentleman (sic!) who shall here be known as Paul leaves me in utter disgust for her taste and in despair for her future. Because if Paul, who runs a small shop in Toronto, really loves Xaviera, he has strange ways of showing it.

For example, how could Paul—who professes to love and cherish Xaviera—permit himself to disappear into the woodwork on consecutive weekends when I stayed with Xaviera! True, I've learned that Xaviera first sought him out—he reminded her of Carl, the man she'd come to America to marry—but for a period of six months he was seeing Xaviera behind my back and the only way I learned of it was through friends in Canada who called me and warned me that they were seeing each other constantly— during the week days. When I questioned Xaviera about it, which, being a jealous son of a bitch, I had to do, she poo-pooed the whole thing. Paul and she had an occasional date, that was all. Some "occasional date" that turned out to be.

Well then, too, did Paul respect and try to enhance Xaviera's new career as an author and lecturer? Did he make sure she made her appointments? Hound her to work and meet her deadlines? Protect her from all the characters who are always trying to move into her life with a new deal which would profit them, to her disadvantage? The hell he did!

274

It's always been my feeling, and there's certainly no fun in saying this, that Xaviera has never really gotten over her love for Carl. When she first met him, she didn't know— had no way of knowing—that he was still married. When she came to America to live with him, she had no way of knowing what a neurotic, self-indulgent SOB he was, how he could watch football on TV the weekend round instead of being a companion to her.

But she hung in with him, because she loved him. She wrote poetry to him, because she loved him. She tried her best to make his mother overcome her objections to her, because she loved him. I've seen that poetry and read those letters, and while they may have pained me and given me real cause for jealousy, I had to respect the depth of her feelings, the integrity of her love for him.

Several times when we were in Acapulco, Xaviera said, seemingly in a casual manner, "How close we are to Caracas?" And I knew I couldn't stop her if she wanted to hop on a plane and jet to Caracas to see Carl again. But she never did go. Xaviera has her pride, too—God, how many times I wished she had even more pride and self-esteem! —and unless Carl invited her, she wasn't about to take that trip.

When *Xaviera!* was published she sent Carl an autographed copy, and the inscription as much said "Look! I came to America an immigrant secretary and now I am a best-selling author!" but no reply ever came.

In the past, I've somehow always been able to rationalize Xaviera's "deep" affairs with other men. With Jacques, the TV reporter, there was the obvious glamour of his profession. Then, too, he'd befriended her in a time of trouble and he reminded her of her father, whom she loved dearly. So I didn't completely blame Xaviera.

Jacques, on the other hand, was a liar and a cheat. He used Xaviera to promote his career, then ran out on her when she could have used him most. He lied to my face when I confronted him with the possibility that his interest in her was something more than professional, looking at me squarely in the eye as he shook my hand and said he liked me and that his only concern here was television news. What wasn't shown on the "11 O'clock Report" was his sneaking back to see her after we'd been together. How gullible *I* was with Jacques! We went out to dinner a number of times, the three of us, and he always let me pay. Then he used the receipts for his expense account! Jacques is a big spender—with other people's emotional expense accounts as well.

With David it was another story. He was a great-looking kid and Xaviera was quietly socking it to Polly, whose young man David had been, by taking him away from her. Those are female games, and I have never pretended to understand them. But what Xaviera didn't bother to figure out, or want to figure out until she couldn't ignore the truth any longer, was that David was a male hustler.

There.

I hope I was brief enough.

And, much more important, to the point. . . .

CHAPTER 36.

I decided to declare it a new year, and a new beginning. I'm not referring to January 1, 1973, but to my emerging consciousness that the Xaviera years were behind—not ahead—of me.

So I've had to look for a new identity. Being Xaviera's boyfriend, part-time, full-time, interim or otherwise, would no longer do.

Doing this book has been one route, I hope, to attaining part of that new identity. Since you've stuck with me this far, I hope the book has provided you with pleasure, entertainment, and insights. That was my goal, not *War and Peace* as though written by J. D. Salinger.

And I've been sexually liberated. Not that I was sexually repressed before, but I've been liberated from my thing . . . with Xaviera.

It didn't happen overnight, to be sure, but I gradually began to give up using, however subconsciously, my relationship with Xaviera to make me more interesting to women. I certainly didn't carry her books around anymore, as a little status symbol to draw attention to myself. No, the only thing I wanted to gain attention was *me*. Take me or leave me, but this is who I am, and what I am, and judge me by that, and not by so-called glamorous associations.

During the early part of 1973 I was sexually more active than I'd ever been without Xaviera—there was a lovely weekend in Acapulco where I went to bed with two beautiful young women all by myself, no Xaviera to get things started—and I dated like crazy, not so that I'd forget things, but to find new things to remember, and eventually I succeeded. But before I talk about that, I'd like to share with you one crazy wonderful night which symbolized something important to my emotional growth: Xaviera had taught me to swing, but not how to swing without her. She'd always been the stimulus for my swinging, and the impediment to my having more of a good time whenever she was around. So swinging was kind of a test for me, and if I never swing again—hmmm, good title for a song—this was an important one for me. *I did it my way*, as Frank Sinatra said in song.

Ironically enough, it was the presence of Leo—whom I'd met and become friendly with in St. Tropez—which inspired this merry li'l evening. The last time Leo had been in town he seemed rather subdued and even sad, and I wondered if it had something to do with Marika. However, he didn't offer any information in that regard, and I didn't pry. We had a good dinner together—none of his famous spaghetti, alas—and when I suggested some socializing to complete the evening, Leo settled for a nightcap and early to bed.

However, the next time he was in town he was in peak

Leo form, and when another Dutch friend via Xaviera—Piet—called to say there was going to be a party with many swingers present at a loft on East Sixteenth Street, I asked if I could bring Leo along. They didn't know each other, which would make even more fun. Fine. Piet then asked if we had dates. I said no, but we could get them without much trouble.

"No, never mind," said Piet. "Just bring your friend to the party and find your dates there."

As it happened, we got to the party before Piet did. It was being held in an old office building—large and dark and dingy--but the large freight elevator took us up to a giant photographer's loft, truly a spectacular "apartment," if you could call it that, half a city block long and ceilings three stories high. Given our nice 'n' light mood of the evening, we didn't care that Piet wasn't there yet, and we made ourselves a drink and mixed in as though it were our own party, and all these good-looking people our invited guests. This was terrific fun. but you didn't have to take anyone seriously. especially if they were the types who say, "*Who* are you—and *what* do you do?" The answer, obviously enough, is: "*I* go to large swinging parties—what do *you* do?"

Eventually Piet showed up, with two gorgeous creatures in tow. One was Marthe. a budding pornographic movie star—blond. busty, and full of pizazz—and the other was Bonita. a quieter gal who was dark and pretty and had a dancer's body which was a very nice coincidence since she happened to be a dancer. I must say I was immediately attracted to Marthe, and I good-naturedly asked Piet if she was his girl.

"Larry." he responded, suddenly much more lucid than he'd seemed when he came rollicking into the loft, "when you go to a swing. nobody is anybody's girl. You are there to have fun. and the worst thing a swinger can bring along with him is emotional attachments. Any girl you'll ever see me with, except my wife. it will be a pleasure to turn over to you—if she cares to go with you."

Leo was off somewhere else in the room, for which I was a little bit sorry because we might have gotten into a lovely little debate about swinging, but Piet deflected any serious thoughts I might be entertaining by saying, "Oh, fantastic, there are lots and lots of delicious ladies here—I'm sure there are a few who will be happy with me." Just then, Leo did come by, escorting a ridiculously pretty redhead named Jacquie. "You know what," he said, trying very hard to be solemn, "this is not a swing, this is merely a party for swingers, merely a social gathering." You'd think he was presiding over the Nuremberg War Trials the way he uttered those words.

We all headed for the bar to consider the dire implications of Leo's utterance—I was having a fine time, but was Leo?—and there we fell into conversation with Mary Lou and Mark, a couple of perfect physical specimens. Mark was handsome and didn't have an extra ounce of weight on his lean six feet of masculinity, and Mary Lou had just the right amount of weight in all the right places. I don't think she was a farmer's daughter, but she'd certainly grown an award-winning set of melons! I know, it's a bad gag, but you had to be there to appreciate the bountiful gifts of nature. I was instantly envious of Mark for being able to be so close to nature right in the heart of the city. Yet suddenly Mary Lou was rushing off toward the doorway, shouting in her wake, "Excuse me, excuse me, I didn't know if she'd show up or not!"

Trying to follow her as she dashed through the crowd toward the door, we saw the object of her haste: She was the tallest woman in the place, now that she was in the place, and an absolute giant of a woman. If she'd been five-three or so, her statistics would have been 37-24-36, but I didn't dare project what they would be, keeping those proportions on a woman her size. She had raven-black hair, dark eyes to match, and a face which was rivaled only by the superb underpinning which lifted her above most of the women—and a hell of a lot of the men— in the room.

"Debbie!" Mary Lou exclaimed as she brought her over and we all said "Hello!" in unison. Mary Lou then proceeded to explain that Debbie had just arrived from Chicago and that she, Mary Lou, had invited her to the party.

"You know something, Leo," I commented to my friend, "this is beginning to be more than match for St. Tropez."

"I know, I *know,* but what are we going to do about it?"

"What do you mean?" I said, content at that moment to sit back and enjoy the sights.

"Larry, I told you," he said, "this is a fucking social gathering instead of a social gathering for fucking. These are all swingers, but it's talk—not action—they're gathered here for."

"So?" If he had any bright ideas, he wasn't exactly communicating them.

" 'So'!" he said after me. " 'So'! 'So'! *So* we should gobble them up and take them over to your place for a *real* swing. That's 'so'!"

"Leo," I reminded him, "there are about sixty people here already. My apartment is large, but fifty people would make it seem like a subway car."

"Leave it to me," Leo said, giving me a sly wink. "You go over and get the place ready, and I'll provide the bodies. You game?"

At first I thought he was recalling the swing in St. Tropez, when I'd lived up to my reputation with Xaviera—and Xaviera only. But after regarding the mischievous look in his eye for a moment, I said, "Give me twenty minutes to straighten the place up, provide booze if there's any need, and then bring on the troops!" He gave me the V-for-victory signal, and away I went.

But not before making a decision about having at least one companion for the long, hard ride home—at least ten blocks—and I looked around for Miss Right. She could have been any one of the nearest eighteen women, given my mood, but the spectacular Debbie was close by and I grabbed her hand and said, "Your place or mine? You lose—my place." She grinned and waved good-bye to Mary Lou as we hurried out.

On the way over to my apartment I remembered that the place was very neat, the liquor cabinet was very well stocked, there was food in the refrigerator, and plenty of ice, so there was no need to stop off en route, so Debbie and I just relaxed and got acquainted. She was eighteen going on nineteen, studying to be a painter, and wasn't New York groovy! At the moment, I couldn't have agreed more.

When we got upstairs I checked to see that I'd been

280

right in my estimations of the food and drink and ice supplies, and all was in readiness. Now I had to think about whether I could get something going with my teenage giantess before the others arrived. How suave did I have to be? What little games did I have to play?

I sat down beside her on the couch, the same couch where such agonizing lessons with Franny were held, and put my arm around her lovely shoulders. which, as it happened, were nearly as broad as mine. She smiled—not up, but across—at me, and I said, very suavely, "Would you like a drink?"

She reached down, unzipped my pants, and took out my penis. "I'll have a little tug on this, if you don't mind. I don't drink hard liquor."

Well, having substituted a hard-on for hard liquor, she proceeded to fondle my penis with her mouth in a wise way, way, *way* beyond her years. Migawd, what do they teach 'em in art school these days!

Then when she had all the evidence that I was sufficiently aroused she got up and made sure I stayed that way. Dancing in front of me in swaying beautifully rhythmic motions she did a kind of striptease which was limited only by the fact that she was wearing shoes, a dress, and nothing else. She didn't need anything else. At last, my childhood dream come true—Tarzan had come to swing with me!

I must say that I didn't behave like a good swinger at all —I didn't wait for the other kids. I simply brought Debbie back to the couch and encouraged her to go back to home base—in this case, the root of my sex, which she did in astonishingly proficient style. I mean, it isn't every day that you see a giant beautiful woman take your cock in her mouth until there's nothing left to see but her mouth next to your balls. She didn't seem to mind what she was doing, or gag, or do anything but work on the penis I'd last seen entering her mouth. One of her hands was playing with my balls, and the other was stroking the outside of my thigh, and I was being very selfish, enjoying all this too much to pay reciprocal attention to her—besides, I couldn't move! —and, oh dear, being a bad swinger, I'm afraid I came.

"Uh, listen, I'll catch you later," I said, sounding like a Miami Beach vacationer who found he didn't have two quarters to tip the bellboy. "Dig *you* later," she said, getting up and going into the kitchen for some soda pop.

I went into the bathroom to shower and then put on my bathrobe, which I guess was kind of silly, but the doorbell had just rung and I'm not accustomed to answering the door in my skin.

In poured Leo and a magnificent entourage of people. Piet was one of the tour guides, along with Leo, and on the tour were Marthe, Bonita, Jacquie, Mark, and Mary Lou. Atta way to go, Leo, the women outnumbered the men . . . as if it mattered.

I didn't know how to get the damn thing going, and the sight of all these luscious women was recycling my gonads, so I relied on an old Xaviera proverb—Cleanliness is next to Godliness (or words to that effect)—and told everyone to take a shower. I really meant it as a joke, to make everyone—me, mostly—feel relaxed, but, surprisingly, they all started taking off their clothes and slowly heading toward the two bathrooms in my fortunately rather spacious apartment. What was amazing about this spontaneous swing, I later learned, was the minority of experienced swingers in the group. Marthe was an understudy in porn films, and she specialized in sucking guys hard when they fell down on the job—which was all the time. Piet, Leo of course, and Bonita were also familiar with swinging.

As for the others, it was the first time, and maybe that's why it turned out to be such a remarkable evening. And me, I felt like I was in charge, the Cecil B. DeMille of swingdom!

The logistics of the bathing, as it happened, weren't all that simple. The women had no problems but the men were all awkward about touching one another, and so they took turns taking showers. As a result, the women were ready for inspection first, and what a joyous task. I'd already had some visual contact with Debbie, yet because of her take-over tactics, I really hadn't had a chance to study her body. Wow, what a bush! It was a jungle, and a grown man could

282

get lost in there, I betcha. As for Mary Lou, she may not have been a swinger, but she certainly had romance, or Mark, in her life—her pubic hair was heart-shaped, and I wasn't about to credit nature for that. Bonita had very little pubic hair, and the darkest nipples I've ever seen. Marthe, the oral accompanist for porn films, had probably the most beautiful figure of all, not excepting Debbie's statuesque, mind-blowing body. Marthe's waist was so small that it could be encompassed by two hands, and above it were two breasts, large and gravity-defying, and below . . . well, below was everything you wanted to see in sex but were afraid to expect. As for Jacquie, she was the shyest, and somehow her covering of her pert breasts, and their oversized nipples, and delicate-looking groin, was as much of a turn-on as anything else in this lineup of beauty.

By the time the men had tumbled out of the shower I'd lowered the lights and stacked some good mood music on the stereo. Fine. But everyone was standing around, looking kind of shy and embarrassed in their nudity, so I, without really thinking about it, played both host and director.

Taking Marthe gently by the arm, I said, "I think Debbie would like to get to know you better." I guessed that Marthe was experienced with women as well as men—hell, porn films are democratic as hell, sexually speaking—and left Marthe in a chair with Debbie, the two of them delighting in each other's bodies. To my surprise, Debbie was the aggressor, spreading Marthe's legs prior to going down on her. But Marthe took the cue promptly enough, and the two of them headed for the nearest bed. A good start.

Whoops, Bonita had Piet's cock in her mouth and was starting to suck it very slowly. And Piet was fondling Mary Lou's breasts.

But . . . *nobody* else was doing anything. Well, fuck it, they'd have to proceed on their own. I was being turned on by Debbie and Marthe in the bedroom, and decided to really get things going there.

I walked over to Debbie and pushed her up on the bed a little. While Marthe was still eating her, I raised Marthe's behind up in the air. I then did what Xaviera used to love me to do to her. I entered her doggie style. Fine, we were now in the groove.

283

After working on Marthe for five or ten minutes, I walked over to Mary Lou, who was sitting there having her breasts sucked by Mark, and put my cock in her mouth. After a few seconds I pushed her back on the bed, out of Mark's grasp, and mounted her. I started to fuck her with very even and rounded strokes until suddenly, I felt something very good happening to my balls. Looking over my shoulder, I saw that Marthe was skillfully playing with my balls. Then, really surprised, I felt the cheeks of my behind spread apart. First a tongue and then a finger pushed into my ass. Marthe, again! What they don't learn on the set of a porn film these days, I hesitate to imagine.

Time to check around. In my extra bedroom I found Piet and Jacquie making it. Turning around, I went into my own bedroom and relaxed for a moment. As I lay on my back I thought, let's see, who's going to "rape" me and how? Marthe, based on recent experience, got my vote.

Guess what? I'd guessed right! Marthe appeared in the doorway and then darted over to the bed. In a matter of seconds she had started to blow me in a way absolutely new to me—she took my legs and put my thighs over her shoulders, put a pillow under the middle of my back and raised up my behind. Then, starting from where she'd left off at my rectum, she started to lick and nibble her way up to my prick. When her mouth reached my prick, she pushed it only a few inches in, but her tongue did unbelievable things to the tip. Great! Don't stop! But in a few minutes she dropped my legs and mounted my prick, and I didn't complain. She started to move steadily up and down until she noticed Debbie sitting there doing nothing.

Stopping in mid-fuck, she got off me and took Debbie and laid her above my head at a right angle to the two of us. Then, getting back on me again, she crouched over and put her mouth on Debbie's cunt. She was eating away at Debbie's cunt for about four or five minutes, and suddenly I was getting slaps on the face because Debbie's long arms were flailing around. I didn't know what to do so I just held on to one of her arms. She must have thought that meant I wanted her to come over to me, so, turning a little on her side, she arched her body so that her lips were next

284

to mine and we began to kiss. I could feel through our kisses when Debbie was coming. If I didn't have strong hair, I think I would have been bàld.

After a proper interval, I got up and went to the bathroom to wash myself a bit. There I found Mary Lou and Mark, looking very unhappy. Mary Lou was sitting on the toilet, crying. She was telling Mark that he had been a little too hot after a couple of girls and that he didn't love her anymore, and a whole bunch of other hogwash along those lines. This once again brought home the statement I had heard earlier in the evening from Piet. To be a good swinger, you shouldn't hold any emotional attachment to anyone at the gathering.

The matter must have been straightened out, somehow, because a few minutes later Leo came charging through the room, with Mary Lou wrapped around his middle, her arms around his neck, his hands bouncing her body up and down on his cock. "Excellent party, Larry!" he shouted, grinning at me. "I'm having a smashing time."

"Good show yourself!" I yelled after him as he galloped into the bedroom.

Things went on for at least a few more hours after that, but truth to tell, I'd had my fill. It had been a swell time, and at one point, checking around to see that everyone was content, I noticed Jacquie looking a little forlorn. I asked her what had happened, and she suddenly wept, "Nothing —nothing has happened! Everyone is so busy running from body to body I haven't had a decent orgasm all night."

What could I do? Besides, I hadn't had normal intercourse all night.

Jacquie and I went over to the couch, which opened up, and crawled under the covers. We held each other, kissed very tenderly and then slowly loved each other until we came together, not an orgasm for all seasons, but very nice indeed.

As I fell into a deep sleep, I heard a few people leaving the apartment, thanking me for a great time, and it was easy to sleep a great many hours knowing that I'd thrown a pretty good little party. When I woke the apartment was empty—except for Jacquie in the shower—but I felt a little bit full of myself, for a pleasant change.

Spring was right around the corner. It was really going to be a great year. . . .

EPILOGUE

" . . . *Repent what's past; avoid what is to come.* . . ."

—*Hamlet,* Act III, Sc. 4
Line 149

Doing this book has given me a lot of cause for thought about the Xaviera years, and I see no reason for repentance for those years. I had over three years of fun, living twenty-four hours a day, enjoying a relationship with a girl, experiencing moments when I wanted to eat her up, and moments when I wanted to kill her. Because I truly cared for her, and because I cared what happened to her—while others didn't—she caused me no end of grief. But, as I said in my foreword to this book, the good times far outnumbered the bad. And when the ratio began to change—more bad times than good—it was time to start building a new life.

I do not see Xaviera, except on business matters, anymore. I sincerely wish her a good future, though I don't see how it can happen unless she starts showing better judgment in her personal behavior. You may read a tinge of jealousy in that statement, but the facts of her life loom a lot larger than any personal value judgments on my part.

Sex is great, sex is wonderful—it's even good for you, folks—but I have no need for swings these days. Again, this is not any kind of moral judgment. For the past eight months I have been keeping steady company, as they used to say, with a remarkable, talented, altogether delightful woman. She has class and character, and a sense of humor that makes your brain cells bang together just to keep up with her. We have been having great fun together. I hope we have a future together. She is a lady.

In the meantime, I'm of course very excited about the publication of this book, and I hope it will afford me an opportunity to turn the things I've learned during the years with Xaviera into a constructive education for others. Because I've suffered the pangs as well as the joys of sex, I think I could help a lot of males especially, and perhaps women on the far side of thirty, with their problems. This doesn't mean I won't help young women with advice if I can do so, but because I've lived a couple of years, I know I can particularly help people who've gone through the torture of loving someone and not knowing how to translate that love into passion. I'm sure I can relate—truly communicate—through lectures or a magazine column or else letters to these people. I plan to answer each and every letter I receive (care of my publisher, address on Page 4) in an effort to aid people in their personal quests.

My publisher doesn't expect more than this one book from me, but who knows—*I* certainly hope this isn't my last "literary" effort. As it happens, there are two book projects on which I'm currently hard at work—the first one, the "saucy" one, which I would like to call *Better Than The Happy Hooker*. The other is a serious biography, on which I would almost surely need a collaborator, of one of the country's leading businessmen—a gentleman who is deservedly a legend in his field.

So, if nothing else, the future holds new kinds of adventure for me. "The Silver Fox" has not stopped running.

"Moving water freezes last," it is said, and I ain't about to "freeze" in my tracks. In fact, I feel my life is just warming up. So stay with me and my further adventures, as I will be with you.

Larry,
"The Silver Fox"
New York City
February 25, 1974

P.S. If you would like to write me, or to join the Silver Fox Fan Club, write for particulars in care of the publisher (address: page 4).